# FLORENCE + THE MACHINE

### An Almighty Sound

# FLORENCE + THE MACHINE

*An Almighty Sound*

ZOË HOWE

**OMNIBUS PRESS**

London / New York / Paris / Sydney / Copenhagen / Berlin / Madrid / Tokyo

Cover designed by Fresh Lemon
Picture research Jacqui Black

ISBN: 978.1.78038.513.6
Order No: OP54681

**Exclusive Distributors**
Music Sales Limited,
14/15 Berners Street,
London, W1T 3LJ.

Music Sales Corporation,
257 Park Avenue South,
New York, NY 10010, USA.

Macmillan Distribution Services,
56 Parkwest Drive
Derrimut, Vic 3030,
Australia.

Every effort has been made to trace the copyright holders of the photographs in this book but one or
two were unreachable. We would be grateful if the photographers concerned would contact us.

Typeset by Phoenix Photosetting, Chatham, Kent
Printed in the EU

A catalogue record for this book is available from the British Library.

Visit Omnibus Press on the web at www.omnibuspress.com

*Dedicated to The Florence + The Machine Army
and 'Flows' the world over.*

# PROLOGUE

Once upon a time, in a land far, far away (depending on how far away from South London you live) there was a thoughtful, dark-haired little girl called Florence, who dreamed of being a princess. A princess with a difference, but a princess nonetheless. She could even do a mean Lady Diana impersonation on request, so you couldn't say she hadn't done her research.

Florence was slight, pale and shy – mostly – but she had a powerful voice with a life of its own. She sang every day to her school friends, whether they liked it or not. Sometimes they would tell her to shut up. She probably couldn't hear them.

Florence was a dreamer, she scribbled poems and lyrics into library books as the inspiration struck, dyed her hair pre-Raphaelite red, read Grimms' fairy tales, played in the woods and made up fantastical games, losing herself in her florid imagination, the same imagination that would produce the demons and terrors that would regularly wake her up at night. The only way to transcend them would be singing, and that would never change.

And she'd attain her dream – little did she know that her future held thrilling secrets and golden promises the like of which she could never have anticipated. Admittedly, the only way in England to become a real princess at the time of writing is to try to get hitched to Prince Harry, but Florence did something arguably rather better than that, becoming as she would a high priestess of the festival stage, a conquering queen of pop music, an undisputed style goddess. Yes, one day the little girl who warbled in the corridors of her school in front of a smattering of oft-unimpressed classmates ("It just came out of my mouth," she later protests, "and there were good acoustics") would share that voice with thousands of people in arenas, stadiums, fields. They would sing her words back to her, words that would articulate how they felt, and they would sway as one to her music, like a multicoloured and somewhat inebriated field of corn.

All she needed now to complete the picture was a handsome prince. Even a Buttons… But her new life, spent scattering sparkling sounds and wistful words hither and thither, demanded sacrifices she'd never contemplated. The loneliness of the hotel room far from home, Florence would later find, would be the most hollow kind of solitude, and she felt it intensely. But these intense feelings, the terrors and the creeping dread at the dead of night that had plagued her since childhood, would simply lead to more words that would touch the hearts of millions who could relate to her gloom (albeit for different reasons; if there were millions of hugely successful pop princesses it would probably take away the gloss) and would be uplifted and exhilarated in turn by the transcendence of her songs. The Kate Bush of the digital generation, the gloriously witchy Stevie Nicks of the 21st century, these descriptions of the heroine of this book would never appear in any of Grimms' fairy tales. But they appear in her own fairy tale, which is just as curious and romantic, just as dark and, if you love Florence, which, if you're reading this now, I'm hoping you do, every bit as engaging. (And don't worry, I won't actually continue writing it as a fairy tale; that could get irritating.)

So with a handful of glitter, a swirl of chiffon, a glass-shattering holler and several strange cocktails mixed with a silvery tear or two, let's stage-dive into the story of Florence + The Machine and celebrate the fiery damsel who rocked the world.

# CHAPTER ONE

*"When I was a kid I really didn't like my name, I wanted something really jazzy like Sarah or Beth…"*

Yes, Florence Leontine Mary Welch's name isn't 'jazzy' enough apparently, and the more traditional names 'Sarah' and 'Beth' are deemed infinitely more exciting. When Florence – known as Leontine to her sister Grace – said she 'wanted something really jazzy', there must have been at least a few people expecting her to continue this sentence with 'like Crazylegs Gillespie' or 'Snakehips Muldoon'. Now *those* are jazzy names. But still, to each his or her own. And as always, life always seems more tempting on the other side of the fence. But it was on this side of the fence, the Welch side, that was, by most people's standards, if not 'jazzy', then bohemian, curious, cultured, comfortably chaotic, enviably interesting.

Florence, named after a great-aunt rather than the Italian city, was born to high-flying parents: Evelyn, a New York academic and later professor of Renaissance Studies, a woman so bright that her younger daughter, Grace, would boast to schoolfriends that her mother had 'read the dictionary back to front', and Nick, a frustrated performer himself with a mighty record collection who brought 'a rock 'n' roll element to the family mix', having lived in a West End squat and hung out with Joe Strummer's pre-Clash band the 101ers. Nick, of course, is now better known as the advertising executive who'd, no doubt among other things, invented the 'can you feel the bubbles melt?' slogan for Aero chocolate, but the influence of his record collection (the Ramones, the Incredible String Band, Fleetwood Mac) on Florence during her childhood cannot be underestimated. He now manages an 'alternative' campsite near well-to-do Tunbridge Wells. Strummer would have been proud.

The hifalutin family connections don't stop there: Florence's uncle is the satirist Craig Brown, while her paternal grandfather was former *Daily Telegraph* deputy editor and *Daily Mail* parliamentary sketch-writer Colin Welch. Those are some smart, go-getting genes right there. Colin would also contribute some wild-card records to what would become Florence's own record collection, not least the soundtrack to *The Rocky Horror Picture Show*. It had, as you might imagine, something of an effect on Florence.

"I think one of my first crushes when I was about 10 was Richard O'Brien, in suspenders," she said. "I don't know what that says about me. My ideal man would be like a photo-fit of Buddy Holly, Jarvis Cocker, Richard O'Brien and David Bowie. That would be one weird-looking man." Indeed it would. Especially if you incorporated the suspenders into that picture.

But *The Rocky Horror Picture Show* was also an early influence in a different way: from repeatedly warbling along to the tracks, Florence maintains she taught herself to sing. Not that hearing Florence belt out a few tunes around the house was a particularly rare thing before *Rocky Horror* came into her life. As a toddler she adored watching musicals and would sing all of the songs in the bathtub "with a red flannel on my head"! And why not?

But back to her parents, it's clear that Evelyn was always the realist, "so clever it's mental", according to Florence, while Nick would be a perennial dreamer. As a result, Florence was left, as only she could put it, "dreaming in reality". Between Nick and Evelyn, you had all the ingredients for a charismatic child who would be at home in front of an audience, not just because of Nick's rock 'n' roll sensibilities but thanks to Evelyn, who, while not a performer, could cast a spell over a hall packed with students with her passionate, mesmerising lectures about art history.

"When she gets on stage to give a lecture she becomes this heightened version of herself. She can suddenly hold the whole room rapt," Florence would muse. "I think that's where it comes from. I aspire to something like that, but with music." Watching her mother give lectures in later years would have a huge effect on Florence, and this and the subsequent 'educational' family trips to the gothic churches of Italy planted a love of Renaissance art, and the immortal themes within it – sex, death, love, violence – firmly in her heart. (Her favourite painting was of St Agatha: "this saint who had her breasts cut off and she's holding them on a plate".) So the passions of her mother would be passed down to Florence. She saw her father as glamorous and exciting, and always wanted to impress him, but, in Florence's words, "It's my mum who had the really rock 'n' roll life, and she's really down to earth and academic."

Evelyn left New York as a young woman, pre-children, finding England more of an appropriate fit. Saying that, she'd also been connected to Andy Warhol's Factory clique and was a regular, alongside her clearly incredibly groovy father and brother, at the iconic seventies New York disco Studio 54, beloved by stars including Michael Jackson, Bianca Jagger, Liza Minnelli, Cher, Salvador Dali and Debbie Harry to name but a few. Florence and her siblings would grow up listening to stories told by her godmother about how, when Evelyn and Nick were first married and staying in New York City with Evelyn's family, they would be called by name to the front of the queue by none other than Warhol himself, who was, Florence has revealed "in love with my uncle, but in his weird, platonic, 'I just wanna draw you' way. The lifestyle was too much of a whirlwind for my mum and she left America."

"My mum doesn't really talk about it," says Florence. "I don't think she cares that much. She was always more interested in the Renaissance than she was about Studio 54."

Born in Rotterdam, Holland, on August 28, 1986, baby Florence would arrive home for the first time – home being Camberwell, South London (the place that inspired the name 'Camberwell carrot' as a sobriquet for 'enormous spliff') – in the height of a sticky English summer. To put it into some kind of cultural context, her birth came just days after the 1986 Notting Hill Carnival, and not long after Chris De Burgh's quivery-vocalled 'Lady In Red' stormed the UK charts, so one could argue that this fateful year which birthed both Florence and this soft-rock hit was simultaneously a good and bad year for British music.

Nick was keen to instil his musical tastes into his new daughter; even in her early months he attempted to get her to sleep by eschewing Brahms' *Lullaby* and trying some of his records out on her instead: "Florence, always a difficult sleeper, was often encouraged to nod off by being wheeled around the sitting room in a pushchair to the accompaniment of loud music," he chortled. "Her earliest subliminal influences include the Smiths, whom she found highly soporific, and Syd Barrett, less so." Whatever works, Nick, whatever works.

Four years later, Florence's sister, Grace, would arrive, and the pair became inseparable companions, as they still are. The two imaginative little girls both loved to indulge in flights of fancy, romantic nostalgia (inspired by what they were reading or which reruns were on daytime TV) and creativity, making dollhouses out of cereal boxes and pretending to be the characters in *Little House On The Prairie*, which involved an impromptu remodelling of their bedroom. However the novelty didn't last long...

"We made our bunk beds into the house and the whole rest of our room into the prairie," Florence reminisced. "There was a towel river and fields of corn made from books. It was really boring actually because the only game we could play was: go out, plough, come home, cook, fish in the towel river..."

When they weren't playing 'let's pretend' at home, Florence would be dabbling in magic and accessing her inner witch (all girls have got one), slicking on purple lipstick and dyeing her hair black (she'd already dyed it red when she was 10 – nothing to do with the pre-Raphaelites, rather because she was "obsessed with Rogue from the X Men"). Her witchy preoccupations led her to secretly make candlelit shrines in her bedroom and try to bewitch boys from afar. "I tried to cast spells to make the boy in the next class fall in love with me. I don't think he did."

Or, if she was dragged out on a shopping trip, she'd be doing her other favourite thing: dancing in supermarkets. It was an activity that Florence took to with great aplomb, although her sister needed a little more encouragement, to say the least.

"[The supermarket is] such a strange place because no one will look at you," Florence said. "Everything has such order and everyone is so focused on what they're doing that no one ever pays attention to you spinning and dancing around."

Grace Welch: "I remember her dragging me and running down the aisles. My dad had to get them to call out, 'Would Grace and Florence Welch please come to the front of the store?' That's one of my earliest memories of being really humiliated."

London life seemed to suit the growing Welch family – brother JJ would arrive a few years later – and the Europhile matriarch of this colourful brood was in her element in London. However, Nick had been rather more thrilled by the glamour and glittering nightlife of New York. When they were first married, he was excited by the prospect of living in America and, according to Florence, when he discovered Evelyn's enviable connections he thought, "OK, this is going to be fun…"

However, despite staying in the ramshackle and often distinctly unglittering London of Thatcher's eighties, there would be plenty of opportunities to escape to the sandy haven of Long Island, where Evelyn's parents lived, and enjoy a rather more family-friendly version of what New York City had to offer…. even if most of Florence's early memories of being on Long Island were rather, well, grey… And there was a ghost house, naturally. This is a book about Florence; if there wasn't a ghost house within the first few pages you'd surely be wondering what was going on…

"I remember these grey beaches with this spiky seaweed that hurt your feet and stretches of grey coast with this huge abandoned grey house in the distance," Florence recalled. "It was a massive mansion, one of those big wooden ones. But it was a ghost house. We had a house on the beach miles down, but you could see, well, this big grey house with shutters. It was incredible. And that sensation of the pain from walking on spiky seaweed..."

Florence might well have had an American passport as well as a British one, but at her core she was as English as a cream tea: porcelain-skinned and green-eyed, softly spoken, elemental and emotional with an unquenchable spark of fire in her heart. Admittedly these words don't always spring to mind when English people are being described these days – drunk, boorish and lairy tend to be more widespread – but if you were looking for the quintessential English rose, you only had to look at the young Florence, as in touch with nature as a folk-song heroine, as fascinated by the curious romanticism of junk-shop Victoriana as she was the vivid melancholia of the pre-Raphaelites. And yes, when she got a little older, occasionally drunk too. And of course, always singing, whether drunk or not. Yes, the singing, believe it or not, could be a bone of contention. "It annoyed my family so much because it was constant," Florence would later confess, and her father, Nick, cheerfully admits that many was the time he begged his daughter to "put a sock in it". Well, don't blame her. Apparently it's all God's fault...

Florence was never particularly religious, although she has always been fascinated by the high drama and "smoke and gold" of Catholicism (she was deeply disappointed when she was told by her father that she was actually C of E). Either way, the first music that truly inspired her at a young age would be the hymns that she sang at school, first at the historic, expensive Thomas' London Day School in Battersea in South West London, and later at the exclusive Alleyn's – school motto 'God's Gift' – in leafy, middle-class Dulwich, a South London suburb. Posh? Relatively speaking, yes, although naturally Florence denies this hotly, insisting, "It's not like I have tea with the Queen."

Hard as it may be to imagine now, with her endlessly long limbs, slender physique and style-icon status, Florence has described herself as a "short, chubby" kid at school and not at all 'cool'. What's more, the logistical side of school life could often be tricky, particularly as Florence is dyspraxic, which meant coordination and organisation could be a challenge, leading to her feeling self-conscious and 'different' to everybody else: "My mum describes it as not thinking in the most linear way. I'm not very logical. I always go for the most extreme option. I take things and turn them into something that perhaps they aren't."

So she particularly looked forward to the daily escape that hymn-singing in assembly could bring. These spiritual songs, full of dark warnings or transcendent messages that would often be lost in the mixed-up din of school-age voices, sparked Florence's curiosity, and the communal choral-singing experience would be one she would later repeat in her own music. From the first time she opened her hymn book to sing, flanked by her jostling school-mates, little Florence, who was normally so quiet, would throw her body and soul into it, losing herself in the music.

"Singing takes over your whole body and your brain," she said. "It's like coming back from a weird place every time you stop. I remember singing hymns at school and people in front of me turning around and looking at me funny; I must have been singing loudly." We can only hope she wasn't inspired to attempt one of her now trademark crowd surfs. Anyway, hymns. You were saying?

"It's nice to mix the mundane and the magical, the irrelevant with the huge themes. Sex, love, death, marriage, guilt – mix that with seeing a huge sky or going for a walk or turning the page of a book. Living is dealing with the everyday and the notion that you're going to die."

Big themes indeed, and themes that would stay in her heart, informing her creative decisions and inspiring her art, music and lyrics in years to come. School plays would also give Florence an outlet for her raw, powerful young voice. During her early years at Thomas' Day School she was in her element on stage in the Great Hall, which had been converted into a theatre. No damp Portakabins or giving your best Virgin Mary portrayal amid the PE apparatus here. What's more these performances gave her something to channel her musical energies into, because by the age of seven she already had what she described as "musical Tourette's"…

# CHAPTER TWO

*"My whole primary-school life was just a chorus of 'Shut up! She's singing again!' Teachers telling me off… But it would just come out of my mouth."*

At least Florence was safe from criticism when she was giving her all onstage, either in the choir or in a play. Her paternal grandmother in particular would be rapt by her performances, dabbing away her tears as she watched her beloved first grandchild shine onstage. Not that it would be particularly unusual for a grandmother to be proud, of course, but Florence already had a voice that cut straight to the quick in an astonishing, preternatural way, and she loved to encourage her grandchild with frequent trips to musicals – and yearly pilgrimages to see *Oliver!* at Christmas time. "There was never any chance of going to see a different one," laughs Florence. "It was always *Oliver!*.

"My English grandmother was very interested in me performing and singing. She would always make me sing at Christmasses. I actually sang at her funeral and at my other grandmother's funeral."

Florence's father, Nick, was also stunned by his daughter's school performances, and he can pinpoint the very moment he realised that what he was feeling was more than just paternal pride – he was discovering his little girl was seriously gifted. "It happened during a performance of *Bugsy Malone*. Florence was 10 or 11 and she was playing the part of Blousey Brown," he remembered.

"Parents are usually interested only in their own offspring, but when Florence sang, the whole audience was engaged. I remember thinking: 'Cripes, she's got a voice – this is serious.' It wasn't just her perfect pitch, she had the essence of phrasing and timing which makes a good singer great."

Her eye-opening musical triumph led Nick to persuade her to sing, in his words, a "rather obscure and difficult" Gilbert & Sullivan song at the memorial service for his father, Colin Welch, at the journalists' church, St Bride's, off London's Fleet Street in 1997.

"The great and good of Fleet Street were there," remembers Nick. "Florence sang brilliantly in front of scores of weeping crumblies."

Florence had become the go-to singer for her grandparents' funerals, which would occur painfully close together (her maternal grandmother, an art historian like Evelyn, would later take her own life when Florence was just 14). It's little wonder, then, that Florence claims her fascination with death, doom and rebirth comes from these early, formative experiences of ageing, deterioration and demise, all experiences that were occurring as Florence, conversely, was blossoming into a young woman, growing, flourishing, very much alive, even if she did nearly drown herself several times. Don't worry, she doesn't have an Ophelia complex, even though she has referenced the pre-Raphaelite image of Hamlet's tragically unhinged girlfriend in a subsequent music video. This, on the other hand, was merely because of her frequent attempts to breathe under water like a mermaid. Obviously. But, as she sadly discovered, no gills, no dice.

"I thought I could breathe underwater when I was a kid. Maybe it was a dream I had but I was convinced that it had happened once. So, every time I went to the local swimming pool, I would always nearly drown myself trying to make it happen again.

"I wanted to be a mermaid: when you're in the water everything's graceful. My local swimming pool was the Latchmere, that's where I learned to swim, the pool that the Maccabees wrote about. I spent so much time at the bottom trying to breathe underwater. I was always going down to the ocean and making offerings to the sea, rocks and things." Later, of course, she would get to be a mermaid in a safe environment, when Karl Lagerfeld invited her to sing at a sea-themed Chanel runway show in 2011. She would even have her very own giant clam shell to emerge from. But all that was to come, little did she know. All she was thinking about at this point was getting through school – or dodging it altogether.

Once Florence was installed at the visually imposing, wood-panelled Alleyn's school (alongside fellow colleagues including Jack Peñate) her talents would continue to flourish, thanks to the focus the school gave to the arts, art and music in particular. It costs thousands of pounds per term to attend Alleyn's, but while Florence was something of a dreamer during class, and often an absentee (she admitted she would bunk off and, hold on to your hats, sneak off to the library), it is fair to say she got her money's worth when she *was* present and engaged: singing, painting and reading in the mostly supportive atmosphere that the school provided, even if she did sometimes get told off when she appeared to be less than riveted during lessons.

"I'm a bit scatty, unfocused – these are things that have been told to me, mainly at school: I'm undriven, don't concentrate, I have a bad memory… but the one thing I always remember is songs. That's why I love making music." She was in the right place for that, even if she didn't always turn up to make the most of it, preferring to climb over the walls and escape to the park or the surrounding fields to climb trees or, specifically, run to the charms of the mulberry tree in her local park, a place that felt magical and safe. "I had that weird sense of excitement about being hidden and out of reach," she said. "I read a lot, and that probably has informed my lyrical style: Emily Dickinson, Raymond Carver. I read a lot of ghost stories growing up, a lot of Victorian horror. I got really obsessed with Jack The Ripper."

Childhood, to Florence, was a "terrifying" place to be – probably at least in part because of her macabre reading material – but the external "terrors" and pressures would be exactly the factors that would entice her into other worlds. She would later reflect that, being such a "scared kid", she now feels that, through her career, she's enjoying a renaissance of her childhood, the freedom, the sense of imagination but without the fear or, at least, with different fears.

"I was quite absent, mentally as well as most of the time physically. I was imaginative, a bit of a dreamer," she revealed. "I remember being completely involved in imaginary games that would last for days, weeks. It was always magic, sorcery, living in trees. Living in imaginary worlds. I don't think I've lost that. It's just now I'm doing it as a job."

But when she *was* present at school, she could still throw herself into music – Alleyn's certainly had that covered. "The music department had two floors of classrooms," remembers Ellie Emptage, a former Alleyn's student who attended the school at the same time as Florence. "It had big spaces for choirs and orchestras to rehearse and smaller one-on-one teaching rooms; you could use these on your lunch break to play around with the instruments.

"The main music teachers were Miss Connelly and Miss Gardner. Miss Connelly was very into the Beatles and in the first year you were made to audition for her choir, which was called Korale. Florence was in that. I remember she was given solos – one of the things I remember is her singing the opening part to 'The Circle Of Life' from *The Lion King*, and that she had a really big voice for her age."

The high-ceilinged, messy and heavily turps-scented art department would also be a refuge to Florence, and was no doubt the part of the school that nurtured that side of her that longed to roll up her sleeves and craft miniature people and strange, romantic and flower-strewn installations that would later inform her stage designs.

"Mr Sutton was head of art," recalls Ellie. "He would always have music on in there and wander around teaching with a cup of tea. It was always really relaxed. There was also a resource room with huge freezers where there were dead rabbits and fish you could paint." Oh so Florence.

When not flooring everyone present with her pipes and her paintings, Florence's obsessive love of retreating into imaginary worlds would, of course, lead her to the library. When Florence joined the school this once poky space was extended and re-opened by the then poet laureate

Andrew Motion, much to the delight of the more bookish students present.

It was there that Florence would escape and dream, indulging in her love of gothic Victorian murder mysteries and poring over poetry, often making up her own. When the mood took her, she'd furtively scribble nascent lyrics and musings into the pages of some of the library books there when the librarian, the stern Mrs Knowles, wasn't looking. One of the most memorable things about Mrs Knowles was that she wore huge glasses and spent much of her time blinking rapidly behind them, and evidently these glasses were powerful enough for her to spot Florence thoughtfully notating her books in the comfort of the library... "I got in real trouble for writing lyrics in school library books," Florence later chuckled. "If anyone at my old school has a look there might be some books there with lyrics in!"

Even now, Florence's lyrics are scribbled down on whatever paper happens to be at hand and, indeed, Florence's first-ever song was written in a school book when she was just 13. On the cusp of adolescence, with the swirl of emotions and angst that that can bring, Florence only had one thing on her mind when it came to song-writing. Love or, more specifically, love gone wrong. "Flowers dying rather than blossoming...

"My first songs were about imaginary break-ups. I'd never even had a boyfriend and it was all very flowery and poetic," she said. "Like: 'And the tears from the trees/Fall like raindrops/On my pain" or 'There's a rose on the table/It's the last thing you gave me/And it's DEAD!' I guess I'm still melodramatic, but now it's about real experiences."

However, when Florence did experience her first tentative kiss, it was on a trampoline, which perhaps didn't fit with her doom-laden lyrical sensibilities... Never mind 'Kiss With A Fist', the title of her first proper song, this would have been more a case of 'kiss with clashing teeth'...

For any girl, approaching your teenage years is a turning point. You are leaving childish things behind. You are becoming more self-conscious, more aware and at the same time more confused. And most importantly, you suddenly see boys (smelly, rude, slugs, snails and all that) in a completely different light. Which means you want them to notice you. Which means you have to customise your boring old school uniform into something rather racier.

Alleyn's, which recommends parents of students to purchase uniforms from the swanky Peter Jones department store in Sloane Square, insisted on dark navy knee-length skirts or trousers. Well, knee-length, schmee-length. Where there's gaffer tape, there's hope, as any self-respecting rock 'n' roll roadie knows. It probably wasn't intended for use by schoolgirls trying to look cool, however.

"We found ways of adapting our uniforms," said Florence. "I got in a lot of trouble from my stepfather for using his duct tape to tape up my school skirt. So the inside of my skirt was done up with electrical tape. Very short." Bad Flo.

But there were other changes in Florence's life at this sensitive age, and not just the usual, hormones-racing kind, but changes within the family that would shake their foundations. Evelyn and Nick were splitting up. What made this even more complicated, although ultimately quite handy, was that Evelyn's new man was in fact their neighbour. This new romance saw Evelyn and Florence move into a house just four doors away, and not only did Florence gain a stepfather, she gained three step-siblings too – and she already had one stepbrother, Nick, one year her senior, on her father's side. There was Maddie, five years younger than Florence, Sam, the oldest stepbrother (two years older), and John (one year older). So, Florence was suddenly demoted to 'middle child' status. "Talk to a shrink about that one," she quipped ruefully in later years.

It was a recipe for trouble, even though she'd always known and liked her new clan growing up. Playing happy families was a different story, not least because each family would feel that "their traditions were being stomped on by the other".

"I hated it. It was a nightmare. We didn't really fit. We'd all known each other since we were little and we'd been friends but then when we sort of became siblings, it was very difficult.

"I enjoy that we have a big family now, and at Christmas there are six of us and we irritate the piss out of each other. It sort of backfired on my parents, because we ended up getting along so well that we became not 'us versus each other' but 'us versus them'."

At the time, Florence, who had just reached puberty, was "incredibly angry. Difficult, moody, no longer a child." But she gives credit to her mother, Evelyn, who had the sense of perspective and the patience to hold out for her brood to come together into what Florence now describes as "an incredible unit".

However, none of the kids seemed to share this foresight, and this strange, multifarious new domestic arrangement left Florence feeling in need of a more stable, even more puritanical, innocent lifestyle. She would later admit that she had already sensed the tension between her parents before the split, and her unsettled, apprehensive feelings left her longing to "live in a log cabin, read the Bible and drink fresh milk". Again with the *Little House On The Prairie* fantasy. But that was not to be. Rather she would be living in a house in Camberwell crammed with teenagers, reading fashion magazines and penny dreadful-style horror stories, swooning over pictures of Jarvis Cocker and drinking cups of tea.

"When you're growing up, everything's very cut and dried, right and wrong," Florence mused. "But as you get older, you make mistakes yourself and learn to be less morally prescriptive. I'm very non-judgmental when it comes to relationships now."

All the same, the subsequent divorce of her beloved parents was hard to process, and during those difficult early years of adjusting to her new family, while her father was still just a few yards away, Florence would retreat to her bedroom and dance, read, and listen to the radio and her records. She'd already rifled through her father's vinyl collection, kept safely in a treasure chest of a trunk which was imbued with the evocative smell of the records inside, and was so strong she could dance on top of it. (She wasn't quite so taken with her mum's favourite records: "My mum only listened to Tom Jones and the Monkees...")

After all this training from Nick, it was only a matter of time until Florence started  building up a collection of her own, albeit with donations from other family members. It was shaping up to be quite an array of oddities too: amid her dad's Incredible String Band discs and her grandfather's contributions of Harry Nilsson and the *Rocky Horror Picture Show*, she also proudly included her first-ever music purchase – a cassette of the Spice Girls. "I know the whole rap! 'So here's the story from A to Z...' Posh and Ginger were my favourites!" Her tastes were catholic and she soon followed up this purchase with 'My Name Is' by Eminem.

"It was funny performing on the same stage as him at the VMAs," she would reflect later. "I wanted to find it so he could sign it for me! I was also really obsessed with Lauryn Hill, *The Miseducation Of Lauryn Hill*; me and all my friends were obsessed with it at school."

Florence also took solace in the cracked, emotional vocal style of the tragic sixties blues-rock singer Janis Joplin, who would later influence Florence's own freewheeling stage persona. "She was so unrestrained, so free, and she wasn't afraid to wail," she said. "Her connection with the audience was really important. It seems to me the suffering and intensity of her performance go hand in hand."

"I think that throughout history there has been something really intoxicating about female performers. I know from having watched and being really inspired by them. That strength and fragility in one package, which I think is wonderful, going all the way back to Ma Rainey and early blues singers."

"Billie Holiday predates a lot of other artists in my life," Florence continues. "When I was much younger – 11, 12 – I was listening to Billie Holiday records in my room on my own, with a wine glass full of orange juice, already pretending to be a sort of tortured mistress of blues, wafting around my bedroom.

"Her voice was just incredible. Her whole manner of perfoming was very restrained. So cool. Completely the antithesis of Janis Joplin, but had that same thing – the emotion she was able to create through singing."

Another female artist Florence revered was Goldfrapp singer Alison Goldfrapp. She was tall, unearthly and glitzy, and she had a voice and talent that soared. Florence loved the strange sounds she created, and was moved to imitate her as best she could. Albeit with slightly different props to those that Alison Goldfrapp tended to use...

"I remember standing on a wheelie bin trying to imitate her dance moves holding a broom – yes, this is classy!" Florence laughed. "The broom seemed like a fun prop at the time... I was very young!"

Life could often be fraught chez Welch, "like the Brady Bunch but with a lot more swearing", but music often came to the rescue, as Florence's own music eventually would for other teenagers and young people who felt lost, confused or alone. But, music aside, Florence's emerging love of fashion, and particularly vintage style, would also flourish thanks to her frequent visits to her old house where her father still lived, and where her stepmother now kept a huge and irresistible stash of antique clothes. Capes were always a big favourite with Florence, and continue to be so, as they are perfect for creating an interesting shape onstage. We're not necessarily talking floor-length à la Rick Wakeman, more waist-length little numbers. Long and wide enough to make the wearer feel airborne anyway. "I like the idea of taking off like a bird. It's this romantic idea that the music could literally lift me off the stage."

So what were some of the looks she concocted as a child? Well, there was the gothic witch, of course. There was the preppy, thoughtful look: white socks, loafers, ponytail combined with "standing really still". Then there was 'Little Old Lady': a combination of brogues and cardigans and ankle socks, a combo she still favours in her more casual moments to this day – brogues being a big favourite of Florence's (at nigh on six feet tall, it's not like she has to wear heels when off duty). Another ensemble was 'Little Lord Fauntleroy', encompassing boys' short trousers and blousy shirts.

"I was always straight into the fancy-dress box as a child – it's kind of the same now, it's that childlike element of wanting to play dress-up." Her visually stunning Cecil Beaton scrapbook, crammed with stylish, often fantastical imagery, would also inspire and inform her unique sartorial streak, as would the female artists and TV shows that she loved.

Her new family set-up also meant that, in order not to be completely passed over, Florence would quickly have to shed her formerly shy disposition and learn to speak up and "command the room". "That was part of where the style of singing came from, having to get people's attention," she said. "I learned how to control it and now what's lucky is people are already listening and I don't have to shout to get their attention."

And there was yet another benefit that would help to shape the Florence we know now: she was also being exposed to even more music thanks to her two new older brothers. This would take her to places she'd never been before (at an unusually young age) and give her a fresh musical perspective, after having absorbed and memorised her father's entire record collection... and her Spice Girls cassette, of course. She had an ulterior motive for her sudden interest in her new siblings' favourite music, however...

"My older stepbrother was a skateboarder and I fancied all of his friends and wanted to impress them," she laughed. "They got me really into No FX! The first gig I went to was the Voodoo Glow Skulls at the Astoria when I was 11. 'Charlie Brown' by the Voodoo Glow Skulls was a favourite song."

Inspired, Florence started buying more discs with her own pocket money: 'Dookie' by Green Day; Nimrod, Silver Chair and No FX! records. She plunged herself into music, and was a prime target for the pioneers of the grunge revolution: Nirvana, Hole, Deftones... and she listened avidly to alternative indie radio station XFM in the car on the way home from school, a station that would later be a staunch supporter of her own music.

Little pre-teen Flo could also be seen rocking out at the metal festival Download and the Reading Festival – and Florence's parents were far from disapproving of her new-found love of the kind of gigs that might not initially be seen as 'little-girl friendly'. In fact, her father actively encouraged it, taking her along himself (her first festival with Nick being Womad, for any Florence-themed pub-quizzers out there).

Nick enjoyed watching her discover different bands for the first time, plus it meant he could keep an eye on her. So, while other kids might relish going to theme parks, laser quest or throwing themselves into paintballing sessions, Florence was "a little punk" who was more interested in seeing as many bands as possible on a festival bill. On her 13th birthday, a momentous day, she attended her first Reading Festival wearing pink fairy wings and a padded bra.

"[Dad] was very kind. He took me to Reading Festival about three times with my little sister, Grace, in tow, I think she was about nine, on his shoulders watching Limp Bizkit and people surfing past on plywood!" It would only be a matter of time before Florence would be doing her own surfing – no plywood required. She'd always regretted not getting stuck into the crowd surfing when she first went to punk gigs in her pre-teen years, but she would certainly be making up for it in a few years' time.

What she did do was start her own punk band however, the Toxic Cockroaches, with her friend Mira. They were just a duo – Mira on drums and Florence on vocals and guitar, hindered only by the fact they had no guitar. And no songs.

Florence's father, Nick, admits that he and Evelyn, who would have been separating at the time she formed her band, "probably did not pay enough attention". Well, the band might have only lasted for "about a week" but amid the Florence fan community, the name 'Toxic Cockroaches' is legend.

"I remember writing the name on all of my school notebooks. We graffitied my friend's garage because we were going to have our band's rehearsals in there. I sprayed 'Daniel Johns Is God'. Of Silverchair. He was God."

The drums and vocals schtick would be one that, interestingly enough, Florence would take with her throughout her musical career, and it would later be the core of the Florence + The Machine sound. And this fledgling outfit, which never really progressed beyond being a concept, would encourage her further to escape school and embark on the life she really wanted to lead.

Florence had been witnessing how her voice could move people in powerful ways, and to hone this power, she asked her parents for singing lessons so that she could build her technique. This wasn't about, as she says, "jumping up and saying 'Look at me!'" This was serious, and even as a youngster, she knew she had a gift worth developing, thanks to the encouragement of her family.

"I was trying to sing like how a blues singer would, but my teacher said, 'We're going to do the arias', so that's where the gospel and the classical elements came together."

Florence was taught to sing in French and Italian, and even tried out 'operatics', but at the end of each session her tutor would let her choose a song to sing. "I'd sing things like 'I Will Always Love You' and I was also singing Nina Simone's 'My Baby Just Cares For Me', 'Spooky' by Dusty Springfield."

The mix of styles, influences, sounds and even languages is, Florence maintains, what helped her shape her unique voice. But when it came to her performing style, well, that was wrought from something rather grittier, grimier, sparklier and boozier. By her mid-teens, Florence had dived into Camberwell's underground art scene – and the parties, where Flo would sing, dance and drink, were something to behold. Clever as she was, Florence knew academia didn't do it for her. But singing with a band at a squat party full of kindred spirits felt like home.

With her friend Sophie 'Sadsack' Hart-Walsh, a comrade who remains by her side to this day, Florence was moving on. (Hart-Walsh's 'Sadsack' sobriquet, incidentally, is now tattooed on Florence's wrist – a tattoo Flo has insisted to her mother is a transfer.)

"I had one best friend at school and we entered this world of art students and these amazing crazy parties and gigs. That's what made me want to be in a band. By the end of school, I wasn't really there."

# CHAPTER THREE

*"I write about love and I write stories and I write about things I've seen on walls or picked up on pieces of paper."*

Florence's parents were somewhat easygoing with their kids, and while some would be concerned about the lack of boundaries, the freedom they gave their children certainly ensured that they would live life to the full from an early age. However, this also meant that they had access to a lifestyle that might be the kind most parents would blanch at, but the "chaotic family life" that Florence would often refer to gave her a chance to "slip under the radar" and run wild.

By 14, Florence had already started drinking and partying, losing her inhibitions and consigning adolescent awkwardness to the four winds. Shy Florence had made way for crazy, elemental Florence, and while she experimented with alcohol early, and allegedly tried ecstasy when she was 16, she insists she "never progressed to anything hard" and would generally try to stay away from drugs. But she did once run through the comfortably bourgeois streets of Camberwell without any clothes on. Another later occasion saw her waking up, still drunk, on the roof of a pub wearing a Captain America costume that was spattered with paint. Life was never dull...

"I got a lot out of my system," she admitted. "Went to wild parties, met some bizarre, amazing people and did mad things like running around naked in fields in Cornwall covered in leaves." Another party Florence recalled was a fancy dress get-together at an old hospital. Florence turned up dressed as Eleanor Rigby, a lonesome character from the Beatles' song of the same name, and complemented her outfit by carrying "a crumpled-up photocopy of my face in a jar". What else did you expect?

The teenagers inside that chaotic Camberwell house would make the most of the weekends they were home alone. Their parties became legendary, and they did their best to ensure that there was no trace of the previous night's madness when Evelyn and Florence's stepfather came home. The mammoth clean-up effort would be complete, and the grown-ups would return to find their brood sitting "innocently in front of the television".

"I remember having to wash the whole floor on my hands and knees with towels trying to be a human mop," she said. "In the morning, there'd be someone asleep in the garden, five people in each bedroom and someone asleep under the fridge and you'd have to shoo people out and begin the epic tidy up."

But it wasn't all about the house parties – you couldn't always fit everyone in for a start. Florence and her new-found friends from Camberwell's nearby art college, where she would later study herself, could party anywhere: in abandoned Texaco garages, shops, lift factories and warehouses. There would always be plenty of alcohol, plenty of like-minded would-be eccentrics, and plenty of impromptu sets by local bands whom Florence would often accompany with some spontaneous singing herself. One particularly big night saw her wigging out in a derelict warehouse in nearby Peckham. By dawn, Florence was "wrapped in a gold and green glittery curtain, being pushed around in a toy car".

It was at these parties that Florence would again get a fresh injection of musical stimulus. From being a certified grunge kid with poppy overtones, Florence would suddenly be exposed to the music of Kate Bush, David Bowie, Talking Heads, Joy Division and Northern Soul. The androgyny of Bowie, the ethereal nature of Bush, the spartan doom of Joy Division, the rhythms of Northern Soul, groups like Martha Reeves & The Vandellas…" My best friend and I would go to these parties and always be hassling the DJ to play Joy Division and Martha Reeves. Once my friend was so drunk that she went up and said, 'Oh my god, can you just put Joy Division on?' He was like, 'Erm, it's playing now."

It was a sprawling wonderland of new/old music, and Florence was in her element. But there would surely be plenty of people within that scene who would credit Florence with a similar influence, as she would have the opportunity to share her own record collection oddities once the parties died down.

"There's one [record in my collection] called 'Trains And Troubles', which is just the sound of trains humming at you," she said. "We'd get a bit drunk and then come back at 4am and turn all the lights off and sit on my bedroom floor and just listen: 'This is the sound of the b52 with engine trouble,' and this train would get closer and closer and you'd be lying on the floor, 'Arrrgh!'"

Another of her freaky favourites was the instructive *Joan Collins' Guide To Life And Health*. "You put it on and it's just Joan Collins saying things like 'Stretch marks are ugly! I liked to eat two eggs when I was pregnant every day!'"

The Camberwell underground party scene also brought Florence together with her first true love, and what a swirl of torrid emotions and feverish obsessiveness that would prompt. Matt Alchin was his name. He was the blue-eyed, messy-haired and, to Florence, completely devastating guitarist in muscular punk band the Ludes, who played frequently on the circuit. Being with Matt led to many things for Florence, not least her first-ever taste of the travelling rock 'n' roll circus.

"I would get dropped off at school straight from the tour bus. It was so heady! That combination of first love, first getting drunk … it was just like, 'There's life outside school!'"

Florence also has a scar on her right foot to mark this incendiary first love. She was so excited the first time he called her that she leapt off her bed onto the floor, getting a large splinter of floorboard stuck in her bare foot as a result.

"He turned out to be my first love, so, I mean, that worked out," remembers Florence philosophically. "But I almost lost the foot. This is the problem with being an exuberant person."

Just as life was getting even more exciting for Flo, with new love blossoming and the adoption of a rock 'n' roll lifestyle that she seemed to take to rather well, disaster struck. Yes, this was the time that the Welch clan decided to go on a family holiday, and as we know, 'family holidays' are dreaded by moon-eyed, smitten teenagers the world over.

This ill-timed vacation took Florence away from her beloved for two – count 'em – two whole weeks, a period of time which saw our romantic heroine "going completely insane, swimming to the bottom of a pool and screaming under water". Still, there was some compensation. Among the LPs where the Welches were staying was Fleetwood Mac's *Rumours*, a record – and a band – that would further define Florence's sound and image like another precious piece of the jigsaw. Fleetwood Mac's singer Stevie Nicks, with her long, flowing gowns, top hats and shawls, would set Florence's sartorial heart a-pumping while the music itself went straight to the core of how she was feeling.

"I found Fleetwood Mac at a really pivotal moment in my life," Florence explained. "[I] was 17, falling in love for the first time and being taken away on this holiday. This was before everyone could just text. It was like this 'Bonjour Tristesse' holiday, I was really sad, and the only record that was in the house was *Rumours*. I had such overwhelming emotions – it was horrible!"

Fittingly, Alchin, when not playing guitar in the Ludes, was … well, he was building coffins, actually. Or rather, one specific coffin, to feature on the front cover of the Ludes' latest record. The coffin, once complete, would temporarily contain a large red-headed Irishman – complete with huge beard – wearing a wedding dress for the purposes of the album artwork. But all Florence could think about was the fact that, while Matt was busy coffin-making, he wasn't taking her out to the cinema, like a good boyfriend should. But this affront was the catalyst for what would be Florence's first song, titled, you guessed it: 'My Boy Builds Coffins'. It was strange, folky and compellingly timeless – and it was no surprise that her initial foray into songwriting would focus on something so dark; as she told her father, Nick, "You made me sing at funerals. What do you expect?"

"The earliest song I wrote was 'My Boy Builds Coffins'. I was upset. You know, first boyfriend, 'You're not going to take me on a date! You're building a coffin, what is this?'

"That led me on this tangent of a coffin builder," she explained. "I started thinking about the fact that everyone needs a coffin. It's obviously someone's craft, but it's a bit sad because you put all this work and effort into something that's eventually just food for the dirt."

This song would be the first that Florence would record; in a tiny shed studio in nearby Crystal Palace. That colourful, throbbing little hub of creativity belonged to Isabella Summers, DJ, producer and hip-hop obsessive. Visually Isabella was as exciting and contemporary as Florence was classical and willowy – a tiny, dynamic young woman with intense, kohl-rimmed eyes and a big, tangly mane of rooty blonde hair.

Isabella, better known as Isa, had crossed paths with Florence when they were children, and for a spell as a young teenager she would babysit Florence's sister, Grace, for extra pocket money, but after a few years life pulled them in different directions. But their destinies were entwined, and, in typical cosmic Florence fashion, they were actually never far from each other at all.

"We kept running into each other at clubs a few years back," said Florence. "She'd be DJ-ing in the jungle room and I'd be whirling around somewhere, both of us dressed up in these really weird outfits. We kind of got to know each other again through art college and going to gigs."

Isabella had also been booked to remix material by the Ludes, learning to use the equipment as she went, and so Matt, and often Florence herself, would be regular fixtures at Isa's miniature studio. Isabella remembers being struck by Florence's impressive voice after hearing her sing at a party at the studio one night.

"I was like, 'Wow, she can really sing,' but I was only interested in making rap with rappers and sampling and all that geeky stuff," said Isabella. "One day I got a bit fed up with it and I was like, 'I want to hang out with a girl in the studio. I want to make a pop song.' I loved Destiny's Child, grew up with Madonna, so I was just like, 'Why not?'

"One day Florence was skipping around and I was like, 'Flo, what are you doing today? Do you want to make a song with me?' And she was like, 'Yeah!' I gave her this weird programmed beat I made. She sat down and wrote these lyrics and when she sang she was literally trembling. 'I was like, 'Ah! You superstar! Let's make an album.'

"I'm lucky that the first artist I worked with who wasn't a rapper was Flo; she has such a beautiful voice and we were learning together." And so, after finding this kindred spirit once again, Florence would frequent Isa's studio, recording her early demos there; little did she know it, she would record much, much more with Isabella in the future.

Meanwhile, with the inspirational fires blazing away, Matt and Florence had found they shared much more than romance: yes, Matt's coffin-building transgression did inspire a song, but they would also join forces creatively, bounce ideas off each other and ultimately compose together.

They were already performing on the same stage, with Florence making ever-more popular appearances during Ludes gigs, so it was only a matter of time until songs like 'Girl With One Eye' and, of course, the now legendary 'Kiss With A Fist' (then known as 'Happy Slap') were born. 'Girl With One Eye' was defiantly a Ludes song, Florence was not part of the writing process on this one, but the meaning of the lyrics, when sung by a girl, takes on a uniquely possessive intensity, and the inclusion of the song on Florence's first album, *Lungs*, was a poignant connection to her past, and to a band that was a huge influence on her.

"'Girl With One Eye' has pain and anger, I love the soul of it," said Florence. "They used to get me up to sing it with them when I was 18. A young girl singing that song has a different kind of power. It's like a warning to a girl who might be trying to take your boy. It's menacing."

Together Florence and Matt had also written 'Kiss With A Fist', a song created at a time of, it's fair to say, heightened hormonal intensity.

"I was listening to a lot of punk and rock 'n' roll, I was thinking about love in a more tempestuous way than sweetness and light, and wanted to see it like two people who love each other so much that... when you first fall in love you feel it so intensely it's like a physical thing, it's like you want to tear yourself apart or you want to tear them apart, but it doesn't actually happen, it just caused some pretty intense metaphors."

But as well as pouring her turbulent feelings for Matt into the lyrics, Florence was also observing the couples around them at the squat parties and gigs around South London. These couples were older and seemed more sophisticated and experienced and, in some cases, dangerous.

"There was this one couple who were so cool, but so visceral and intense. The guy never hit the girl, but I saw her lamp him a couple of times. It was more about the fact that their animal passion for each other was the thing that was attractive for them. It was how joyful destruction can be." This was especially intriguing to Florence, as a self-confessed 'conflict avoider'. Most of the time, at least.

"I tend to shy away from conflict, but everyone has a flipside. Mine comes out when I've had too many vodka tonics. Then I have a tendency to throw myself into harm's way. I'm ruled entirely by my emotions in life, but on stage I can channel them into each song."

This punky, lyrically near the knuckle track ('a kiss with a fist is better than none'?) was something Florence simply saw as an early song that ultimately went rather well, and it was so much part of her that there was no question that she would take it with her when she came to record an album. However, she couldn't anticipate the controversy it would spark when it came to its subsequent release... But we are getting ahead of ourselves.

With Florence becoming part of the furniture in the art-school circuit, it was a matter of time until she decided to go to art school herself. At 17, she'd been working in a bar (her least favourite drink to concoct? Pina colada – messy and time-consuming, although worth it if you're on the receiving end) and was keenly aware there was only so much more "bumming around in Camberwell" that she could do, safe and fun (and messy) as it was.

Florence adored art and knew she wanted to study illustration, and with Camberwell College of Art so close by, and already knowing so many people who had studied there, it was a no-brainer.

Another reason, albeit semi-subliminal, for wanting to stay close to home was that in her heart, she knew that music would be a strong force in her life, and that if anything was going to happen, it would be in the London that constantly inspired her with its gothic eccentricities and unique style. Florence had already built up a network of interesting people who could help her achieve her dreams, what was the point of leaving with so much already in place? It was worth noting that many of her heroes, including David Bowie and Talking Heads, were art school alumni. Since the early sixties art schools had proved to be a springboard to rock 'n' roll success. (Isabella, meanwhile, would be enrolling for Central Saint Martins.) However, on a conscious level, Florence insists that she thought she would be an artist who occasionally sings at festivals, not the other way around.

In 2004, at the age of 18, Florence enrolled for the one-year foundation course at Camberwell College of Art, a "typical scruffy art college", with a view to progress to a degree.

"We were separate from the rest of the college," says artist Debra Fear, who attended the foundation course with Florence. "A lot of the tutors had been through the sixties and the mantra was that they were all practising artists.

"People got shocked going to foundation from A-level; they thought they were going to be taught art in lessons. One of the first things they did in the first term was try to get you into a mindset, get you into a different way of thinking. It stopped you from being disillusioned after institutionalised education.

"You were free to express yourself, in a way. You're trying to work out what's required of you, and what contemporary art is, and what you want to do... it focuses you."

By the time dark-haired, skinny Florence was walking through the doors of the studios on Sumner Road, Camberwell, to begin her first term, she was culturally fired up by a whole new set of sounds and visions, particularly the intense, stripped-back music of the White

Stripes, and drew great inspiration from the morbid juxtaposition of dancing skeletons and blowsy roses of the Mexican Day Of The Dead. This combination of flowers and startling imagery no doubt sparked one of Florence's proudest art-school moments: the six-foot-wide artificial floral installation that spelled out the words 'you're a twat' — (directed at herself, she maintains, and not a fellow student or, indeed, a tutor...).

She specialised in 'environments', which stood her in good stead for the set design of her early gigs, all garlands, bird cages and oddities. "Bat For Lashes said she makes microcosms — tiny worlds in a shoe box or something," Florence mused. "But I was turning a whole room into something else, with bird cages and things, kind of like what I do on stage... Maybe in music you're making an auditory environment and maybe you change your environment around you to suit your own way."

One of Florence's finest art-school hours was, intriguingly, a cake she baked. It was iced with the doom-laden statement 'it's going to get worse'. She ate it, although it was part of the installation to do so, naturally. It wasn't just that she was a bit peckish and needed a sugar rush. But again, art is open to interpretation...

"Florence was a very nice girl, very pleasant, very art studenty. Very thin," remembers Debra Fear. "I was always amazed though because she was never in! But when she was there she just kind of got on with it.

"We all had little spaces and a table. Her table and space was part of the walk-through so everyone had to go past her table, I don't know if that was because she wasn't around at the beginning and she didn't dib the right space quickly... But she created an ambient space.

"She would string up garlands, quite feminine, flowers... And she would have a sketchbook diary, which was full of all her thoughts and sketches and it was bits and pieces. She also did a big painting, it was quite dark and very fantastical, less cutesy than some of the installations she was doing. She used to take a lot of Polaroids and they would go into the diary — that was just before they stopped manufacturing Polaroid film. She'd be taking pictures of her installation, her diary, herself... her work was quite personal."

The theme that was also emerging within Florence's work was not only the fairy-tale darkness that she loved so dearly but the use of the bold statement that stopped you in your tracks. Florence was always an admirer of artists such as Tracey Emin, David Shrigley and Ed Ruscha, although she always found plenty of inspiration from the signs, notices and warnings that were around her in everyday life. Art school always reboots how you see what others would view as mundane, and Florence was already noticing what others passed by, and processed those things in thought-provoking ways, not just in her artwork but in her music.

"One of the songs I wrote was called 'Are You Hurting The One You Love?' I just saw that printed on a bright pink sign attached to a church, and thought, 'What a fucking question!'"

And, in her opinion, *was* she hurting the ones she loved? "Yes, probably. Isn't everybody?" Yes. Probably.

Art school also afforded Florence the chance to delve back into the imaginative realms of her childhood, when she and her family made up their own fairy tales ("My mum would try to tell a story with plot and adventure, but me and my sister would be like, 'No! I would have a crown of rubies and emerald shoes! 'My dress would be made of pure gold!'" Truly prescient…), and Florence remembered what she used to create as a child on a rainy day alongside her sister, Grace, particularly those cereal-box dollhouses. She revived the idea but this time gave it an adult, Edward Gorey-esque twist. "I made some at art college for fun," she said, "except they had weird mini people in them and a man that sat in a tree with these endlessly long legs. It's hard to explain why that was." It's art. No need to explain.

Florence also recalls "drawing lots of cannibalistic stick men who'd eat each other in really violent ways." Probably best not to explain that one either.

But even though Florence was out of school and able to concentrate more on where her heart lay, her laissez-faire attitude towards attendance remained. Let's not kid ourselves that suddenly Florence was knuckling down, eschewing Camberwell's enticing nightlife and concentrating body and soul on her art. She was still all about the late nights, the sleeping-ins, the booze and the impromptu singing sessions – and the odd pub gig with Matt, who was now playing in a band called Rum Shebeen, and accompanying Florence as she sang her heart out and whacked a drum. The pair would play increasingly at Nambucca, in Holloway, North London. An old Irish pub taken over by middle-class kids with big ideas and good contacts, Nambucca was the epicentre of the North London live music scene and Florence loved an excuse to stay up all night, dance and sing and listen to music before facing the next day through her fingers… The pain of having to work the following day was part of the fun.

"My favourite mode of being is having not slept. You know when you've been at a party and the dawn rises? Everything seems to be really open. The reason why it's so special is because you know that it's going to crash."

Bruno Wizard, frontman of punk band the Homosexuals and Nambucca mainstay, saw Florence when she was "still in the bedroom stage". She might not have found a voice she was comfortable with at this point, but Florence already had a strength that blew everyone away.

Bruno remembers: "There were a lot of people at Nambucca who even now I'm realising are doing things and have top agents or are in bands or managing bands. I met someone recently and they were really familiar – I said, 'Did you used to go to Nambucca?' and he said, 'I used to *live* there!'"

"There's a joke about it being a lot of trust-fund kids but it's sort of a mixture," Bruno explains. "It's a nice healthy balance. Most of them came from good schools: even if they were getting off their tits you knew that after a while they would settle down and a lot of them would go into fashion or music PR, media and stuff like that. They weren't stupid. There was a big art-school element there too as it was close to the sculpture school at Holloway Art College.

"Nambucca was kind of blokey because of the bands that were playing there but there was a lot of female energy there too, not so much in the bands though. You had the kids of rock stars all sneaking there when they were 15 or 16. I don't remember there being many bands with a strong woman fronting it. It just happened to be like that. There was Kid Harpoon, the promoter Tom Frog, the Holloways, Kooks, the

Fratellis, Lisa Moorish, Will from Mystery Jets, Alice Dellal was always there, Peaches Geldof... It was a hectic time. I could see who would fall by the wayside, who would be a casualty and who would come through. And Nambucca meanwhile was this grand dame spawning her indie progeny!

"When I first saw Florence, I was like, 'There's definitely something going on here, there's already a buzz.' She couldn't really hear herself but it didn't matter. She had the head voice that makes everyone go 'Wow, that's astounding', but she was nervous. You can always tell when someone's nervous because the voice is the only instrument that's part of the body, so when you go out in front of people and make yourself naked, it's a big thing. If you've got a guitar you've at least got a barrier.

"It was just her singing with a little amplifier and she had this different voice, it was really dramatic and operatic when she went into the top register but there was also a bottom to her voice as well as it was coming through her chest, it was almost like two voices."

Two voices, and two lives – and this thrilling dual lifestyle Florence was leading, a lifestyle she could barely keep up with, understandably meant that Camberwell College Of Arts did not see much of Florence, and vice versa. But, when she did turn up, thanks to the good old interpretative nature of art, she could work around her hangovers in an ingenious way.

"I made a bed under my desk with curtains and a lamp and some books, and I called it a performance art piece, but actually I was just sleeping," she admitted. "I wasn't the best student at school or art student." Florence would snuggle into her corner, switch on her portable radio and draw cartoons and scribble thoughts into her diary sketchbook. "It felt really safe," she remembers. "It was like my place at the library."

"I remember the tent she made under the desk," chuckles Debra Fear. "That whole space was decorated and made like a permanent walk-in installation. It was maybe influenced by Emin. Maybe she was gigging late hence the snoozing. She had a foot in both worlds at that time."

Thanks to her sheer talent, Florence would somehow manage to progress to the BA course despite her absenteeism at the college (even though she practically lived next door). "The tutors were very good at spotting interesting people," says Debra. "They're already looking at foundation level at people who could be good 'products'. Well, Florence has turned out to be a magnificent product for them!"

However, Florence continued to burn the candle at both ends, and it soon became clear that, music-wise, she was taking off. Florence and Matt's intense, visceral appearances were making waves and getting noticed by all of the right people, and in all the right places: Nambucca, the St Moritz in Soho, Plastic People in Camden – all the haunts that attracted music scouts, like-minded souls and the movers and shakers that could take her to the next level. Nambucca, handily, had a strong association with *NME,* thanks to Tom Frog's work with its then features editor, Malik Meer, under his 'Frog Promotions' umbrella. As Bruno Wizard observed, "It was just one of those happy concurrences of energy."

But Florence was starting to find working with her boyfriend wasn't always easy. Florence is a veritable typhoon of emotions at the best of times, and difficulties had started to arise in the Welch-Alchin camp. When Alchin finally decided to move on, Florence was bereft, not least because she was on her own musically.

"I wasn't sure how I was going to be making music. I was still doing gigs, but I wasn't sure what was going to happen." Her heart was broken too, and to this day 'These Foolish Things' by Bryan Ferry, which was 'their' song, makes her think of him.

Matt's departure, however upsetting, was ultimately vital for Florence's progression as an artist, being as it was the catalyst for her to find the confidence to write a song entirely by herself – lyrics, music, drum parts, guitar parts – despite "having no idea how to play anything".

Florence might have felt like she was making it up as she went along, but she had imagination, musical instinct and determination. When she combined and focused those qualities, the song 'Between Two Lungs' was born, the title having been pilfered from an eighties pulp fiction book she'd picked up at a junk shop.

'Between Two Lungs' was all about sense of space, the pulsing drums at the beginning and the inevitable ecstatic crescendo. Florence: "I've always been interested in the lulls between notes and the atmosphere that silence creates. It's all about the build, and the final release – the euphoria that you can get from music."

The song was written about a kiss, but it can also be taken as a musical metaphor for how far she'd already come with Matt, 'the sigh that blew her forward', starting as it does with a bold beating heart and increasing in intensity, launching her into a new stratosphere that would ultimately mean the music would always take precedence over any lover.

# CHAPTER FOUR

*"If I wasn't a singer I'd probably be still at art college making bad art..."*

The year 2006 was pivotal for 19-year-old Florence. Having picked herself up and dusted herself off after parting ways with Matt Alchin, she had found herself a new boyfriend, a young man from Bedfordshire called Stuart Hammond, who she met at a bookshop. Being surrounded by even more poetry and romantic literature could only lead to one thing – a rumbling crescendo of emotions that would lead to love between Florence and Stuart and, as a result, a flurry of creativity and heart-felt songwriting.

Florence had also joined a new band, Ashok, a jazz-tinged, hip-hop indie group. In fact, if you look up Ashok on that musical graveyard that is sadly now MySpace, you can still hear some Ashok tracks featuring Florence's vocals.

Ashok recorded an album called *Plans* on the Filthy Lucre/About Records label, and the release included Florence's song 'Happy Slap' (later known as 'Kiss With A Fist'). But excited as she was, with her musical dreams seemingly flourishing into brilliant life, something wasn't right.

Florence's father, Nick: "Florence and her bandmates were 'spotted' by an old-school music manager and there was talk of a contract. 'Don't sign anything until we've had a chance to have a look at it,' we implored. 'Yeah, yeah,' said Florence – and went ahead and signed it.

"That's where it all could have gone off the rails. She was 19 and miserable, in the wrong band, life signed away... I phoned a friend who was a music lawyer. It turned out the contract was only binding on Florence as part of the band, so all she had to do was resign. After that we paid a bit more attention."

Musically, once she had flitted away from Ashok, Florence spread her wings and was working increasingly with her childhood friend Isabella Summers, freshly graduated from Central Saint Martins. The pair loved hanging out together; they were like musical playmates and were obviously on the same wavelength. The process of collaboration was, like most things in Florence's life, organic and relatively free-form but still ambitious. Florence wasted no time in recording 'Between Two Lungs' at Isabella's studio, complete with 'studio hiss', a sound that Florence treasures on the recording.

Isabella and Florence played with the notion of character, playing parts, and would soon start putting out work as the jokily named, Moloko-esque Florrible and Misrabella, creating vibrant and imaginative musical sketches, such as 'Little Donkey' and 'Filthy Fingers' – a jazzy variation of 'Girl With One Eye'. They'd also make strange, marionette-populated videos with Isabella's former art-school chum Jonathan Batten at Supine Studios in Hackney, with help from members of the artists' collective based at Supine. The videos and songs still capture the imagination for those who care to dig around on the internet and look them up. Florrible and Misrabella would become Florence Robot Isa Machine... and ultimately, Florence + The Machine. With Isabella on beats and synths and Florence's unearthly voice, it wasn't long before the quirky pair was in demand. At one point Florence would be gigging in different forms daily for six months straight. It was a gruelling but intensely creative time.

"The name Florence + The Machine started off as a private joke that got out of hand. I made music with [Isabella], who we called Isabella

Machine, to which I was Florence Robot. When I was about an hour away from the first gig, I still didn't have a name, so I thought 'OK, I'll be Florence Robot/Isa Machine', before realising that name was so long it'd drive me mad."

That first gig together was such a triumph that, after driving home in Isabella's turquoise wagon, "the strangest car ever", Florence ended the night by diving euphorically (and possibly drunkenly) into a pond. "We should have a tiny ornamental pond by the stage and re-create it, with lots of electrical sparks flying out..."

With help from Isabella, and also her sister, Grace, Florence managed to get some demos up on MySpace, then an absolutely key site for musicians to get their work heard. Florence has never truly taken to technology, and admits she preferred good old word of mouth.

"I didn't have a MySpace for a really long time. I'm a technophobe, it doesn't really work for me. I had to use my little sister's email address and I kind of stole it from her because I couldn't work out how to do it," she said in an interview at the Grammys 2010. "I'd always be sending things by carrier pigeon and using a gramophone...

"The way I really got out there was through performing live. The songs I had on my MySpace were demos that didn't even make it onto the album, I was just putting stuff up there. I wasn't an artist who had a finished piece of work and would put it up there on the internet, I was a live artist and I was constantly changing. Demos from one period would be completely different to the next, and that actually made it quite difficult trying to pin down the album. But I've always been a live artist, that's where I came from, gigging in pubs and clubs, sending out a message to my friends in a text, 'Hey, come to my show!'"

As well as assisting on the technical side, Isabella also helped Florence to expand her ideas sonically and "get everything in time", while Florence, amongst other things, ensured they both stayed focused by constructing a list of '10 Florence Commandments' and pinning them to the wall of Isabella's recording studio, alongside a felt-tip drawing of a spaceman, bearing the words 'Florence Is A Machine'.

★

And, if you wish to follow the Florence Commandments, they are as follows:

Always carry seeds
Always have a book
Support your local charity shop
Support Diet Coke (crossed out) listen to Dave and play football
Wander about a lot
Never know the exact details
Dance to all music dancehall style
Appreciate your feet
Be a country singer
Climb anything

Good luck.

The 'Appreciate your feet' commandment was particularly pertinent to Florence, especially as she wasn't always as kind to them as she should have been. "As soon as I get into party mood, I'm like, 'Shoes gone! I don't need shoes,'" she trilled, although she would invariably end up with bruised, bleeding feet at the end of the night.

'Never know the exact details' is the ultimate flake's strategy (Who knew flakes even *had* strategies?). And of course, 'Climb anything'... Florence is still following that commandment to this day, although little did she know when she scribbled it down that in a few years she would be using the lighting rig at Glastonbury as a climbing frame, much to her mother's chagrin. All that practice climbing the mulberry tree in the park must have come in handy. "I think during that set I might have had the most Dutch courage on the planet..." she laughed.

Florence, still technically an art student, was also climbing the proverbial social ladder, which was key to succeeding in London's competitive music scene. She might have played the 'flakey' role, but Florence was no fool, and, sporting a drunken smile and her favourite tuxedo – a style she favoured around this time – Florence pulled off her greatest coup in December 2006 one night at a party at the formerly notorious strip club the Raymond Revue Bar, also known as the Soho Revue Bar. This coup took place in the toilets, to be specific.

Florence had spotted Mairead Nash, one half of the DJ duo and general London scenesters the Queens Of Noize, with her friend and collaborator Tabitha Denholm. Mairead was the golden girl of the indie world and something of a muse to the alt rock glitterati, having had songs written about her by everyone from Blur guitarist and then Camden bar-propper-upper Graham Coxon ('No Good Time'), Razorlight ('Golden Touch') and the Von Bondies ('Mairead'). The Queens of Noize were seriously well-connected, DJ'ing at celebrity parties, broadcasting a radio show on BBC 6Music and hanging out with everyone from Pete Doherty to Johnny Borrell. Florence knew that Mairead put on successful club nights, knew she was someone she had to impress, and followed Nash into the ladies' toilets with one mission in mind – to sing at her with that powerful voice. The song? Etta James' 'Something's Got A Hold On Me'. Why the toilets? Why not? There's a bit of privacy – not that Mairead had much of that when she was commandeered by Flo – and, as Florence herself observed, the acoustics are always good for singing...

"It was one of those parties that got a bit weird," said Florence. "Mairead was there and we were talking about boys, and then I was like, 'Oh I can sing!' and started singing this Etta James song. She booked me to sing at her Christmas party.

"Then on the phone she asked me to sing rockabilly covers and I said, 'I'd like to sing my own songs!' I remember the silence on the phone and then: 'Can you do some covers as well?' I sang my own songs and she liked it so much she wanted to manage me. She'd never managed anybody before so we were both just chancing it but it went pretty well." That's putting it mildly.

"I was kind of fronting it," Florence explained. "I was pretending that I had a band, and I didn't really have a band. So I kind of had to get a band... You know what's funny? I think Etta James herself auditioned for her manager in a bathroom!"

The following week, at the Queens of Noize Christmas Party,

Florence turned up to rock the proceedings, with cute rockabilly family group Kitty, Daisy and Lewis alongside her on the bill. But it was Florence who grabbed attention, despite being accompanied by a house band whom she'd never met, and with whom she'd only rehearsed for an hour. Mairead knew she'd struck gold with Florence – she recalled watching her new protégée during that fateful Christmas party and remembered turning to her friend and fellow Queen of Noize Tabitha Denholm in amazement.

"She turned up with her dad, who looked like Andy Warhol," said Nash. "She belted it out, and I was thinking, 'Oh… my… God…' I had literally never heard anyone with such a powerful voice *ever*. I turned to Tabitha and said, 'I have to manage her.'"

"It's funny," remembers Florence. "No-one would take (Mairead) seriously when she started. I'd say she's great and people would say 'What? You're being managed by Queens Of Noize? Like, do you know about the Queens Of Noize?!' But we did it, and we did it in spite of people thinking, you know, that it's not going to work."

The right people were becoming magically magnetised into Florence's life – well, thanks to the fact that she was hanging around at the right places. So… not magic really; just right place, right time, plenty of front and plenty of talent. Onstage, there was no shortage of people to sing alongside, despite her initial fears of going it alone: for example, Florence would occasionally appear with her friend from Nambucca, the underground indie king Kid Harpoon, whose star was on the rise (and who would also later step up for songwriting duties on her second album, *Ceremonials*, in 2011). Also around this time, Florence became close friends with a prodigiously talented Texas-born, Essex-raised multi-instrumentalist who was trying to make it on London's live circuit, just like Florence. This bespectacled, furry-hat-sporting individual's name was Devonté Hynes – better known as Lightspeed Champion – and he quickly became a close collaborator of Florence's. In fact, even when he was in the midst of promoting his debut album, *Falling Off Lavender Bridge*, in 2007, he would be by Florence's side as often as he could, wielding his guitar and accompanying her at small London gigs.

Florence, conversely, would be in one of the earliest versions of Lightspeed Champion alongside fellow vocalist Emmy The Great. Mairead Nash adored both Florence and Dev, and in August 2007, she ensured that the pair would take pride of place on the MySpace Main Stage at the inaugural 1-2-3-4 Shoreditch Festival, which was hosted by the Queens of Noize themselves.

What Dev and Flo had was a truly symbiotic musical relationship that was sparked by a mutual love of Green Day, despite Florence's father's best efforts to steer her instead towards the Ramones. This visually startling pair – "we called ourselves Team Perfect" – would work together as often as they could, writing songs (including 'Bird Song'), recording their own versions of Green Day's *Nimrod* (the "best album ever recorded" according to Florence) on Hynes' MacBook in his kitchen, and generally chewing the fat when they weren't performing; indeed, some of Hynes' arrangements and ideas would end up on Florence's debut album, *Lungs*. The pair were so inseparable and in tune with each other, they even dressed the same: "Weird matching outfits, T-shirts, lumberjack trousers…" reminisced Florence.

The way things were going, particularly in the light of Florence's new management deal with Mairead Nash, a choice had to be made. Continue trying to live a double life and complete the BA at Camberwell College Of Art while simultaneously juggling her life as a musician, or drop out of art school. The solution was clear, as far as Florence was concerned.

"I wasn't going to be able to do both cos I wasn't going to be in Camberwell," Florence said. "I had to make the decision. But I'd lived in Camberwell my whole life. If everything goes tits up, I can still go back to art college, but with music it's a once in a lifetime moment so you have to go with it and you have to go with it with your whole heart."

The buzz around Florence was already building thanks to Mairead's network of priceless music industry connections. In October 2007, *The Guardian*'s Paul Lester hailed the as yet unsigned Florence in his 'New Band Of The Day' column when it was still just Florence and Dev playing live. He had evidently seen Florence play a number of times, noting that she was "accompanied by a different – disposable? – male guitarist at most gigs (although at the moment Devonté 'Dev' Hynes is hanging on in there, and she's looking to form a band, possibly around him). She hasn't got a record deal yet," he continued, "but she's managed by the Queens of Noize, which is probably why the light-skinned 'enchanted skeleton' with the dark subject matter, kooky stagecraft of Kate Bush, feisty growl of Janis Joplin and pastoral menace of Sandy Denny, is currently being chased all over London by men bearing chequebooks." This was just the beginning.

Nash wanted Florence to get her ideas recorded as demos, and was busily connecting Florence up with different producers and musicians in a bid to find the perfect fit. One of the initial sessions would be with the legendary record producer Stephen Street, who'd famously already worked his magic on the Smiths, Blur, the Cranberries and Kaiser Chiefs, as well as a raft of artists now considered to be Florence's contemporaries, including Mystery Jets, Babyshambles and the Maccabees.

It was at this early session that Rob Ackroyd, still very much a "bedroom guitarist", would be invited to come and hang out at the studio while Florence recorded her vocal takes on a version of 'Bird Song' with co-writer Dev Hynes and Rich Mitchell from Chapel Club on drums. "I ended up playing ukulele!" says Rob.

"Florence + The Machine is actually the first band I've played with," said Rob. "We met through mutual friends and it was fortunate timing as Florence was looking to expand her gig.

"I was working for a production company in Soho at the time and would have to smuggle my guitar into the office and escape early afternoon under the guise of attending meetings." It all worked out rather well in the end.

Rob and Florence had met before but musically, they immediately clicked: their tastes were similar, sharing as they did a love of hip-hop and American indie, although Rob drew the line at pop which "cuts through me like a knife". You can't have everything. However, for the gig he was being sized up for, the gig of a lifetime, as it turned out, he was just right.

"In terms of our own music, we are perfectly matched," Rob continues. "Florence and I are more interested in modulated electric guitar sounds as opposed to clean playing. Our instrumentation should provide a hearty, austere and forceful support for her voice, which after all is the star of the show." You're hired.

"Rob was a friend, he used to work in film and we hijacked him," remembers Florence. "And his friend was Chris who drums, and then Cherish [Kaya, originally from female group Ipso Facto], she told me that she was looking to play, and I was just, 'OH COOL! YEAH, COME AND BE IN MY BAND!' Mairead actually said to me, 'You know we can't actually afford any more members now? Just chill out! You're not the Polyphonic Spree!'"

Thankfully, Florence could be her very own Polyphonic Spree just by layering up her vocals to create that signature choral sound, even if, when the time came, the engineer who mixed the tracks "nearly had a nervous breakdown"...

Soon Mairead would effect a record deal for Florence with Moshi Moshi, the small indie label that launched Hot Chip, the Rakes and Kate Nash amongst others, and which is still involved with Florence to this day despite her since being taken on by Island Records. Everything she'd ever wanted was rushing towards her like a tidal wave − so why wasn't Florence happy?

"I was freaked out by the pressure," admitted Florence. "[Mairead] got me a record deal so I had to make an album. I'd gone from being an art student messing about with music to all this. It was everything I'd ever wanted, but all I felt was paralysing fear. Plus I'd split up from my boyfriend and I was utterly bereft and unable to cope. It seemed so wrong that I was so unhappy just as my career was taking off."

This seems to be a recurring theme for Florence, the more quickly her dreams came true, the more she would feel the need to hold herself back, plague herself with fears, allow the demons in at night. "Just as I was becoming successful I totally tried to sabotage everything." As Florence would sing in 'Dog Days Are Over': 'Happiness hit her like a train on a track.' It's a lyric that perfectly encapsulates the euphoria mingled with shock mingled with terror that Florence still admits to feeling to this day. And at this point, the Florence Express certainly showed no signs of decelerating, let alone stopping. Not with Mairead driving.

Thanks to Mairead's bubbly manner and determinedly enthusiastic promotion of Florence, her nervy new project came to the attention of BBC stalwart DJ Steve Lamacq and his show, *BBC Introducing*, which mined the UK clubs and venues for the hottest cutting-edge talent. Lamacq was entranced by Florence, the self-confessed "choir girl gone horribly wrong, desperately wrong" as she put it, and he would ensure that she and guitarist Rob (and her now trademark drum) would be sharing her songs – or rather "stories with consequences and weird morality issues" with the good people of Austin, Texas (or rather, musicians and music industry bigwigs who'd flown to Austin, Texas) to perform on the *BBC Introducing* stage at the ultimate rock showcase, South By Southwest, the following spring. March 2008, to be specific.

"One of the first gigs Florence and I played together was at South by Southwest," Rob remembers. "Prior to our trip to Texas, the extent of my travels was holidaying in the Canary Islands…"

Transatlantic travel aside, after touching down in Texas, the still-brunette Florence seemed particularly excited to learn that she'd been given a complimentary drinks pass. Needless to say, the way things were going, the idea of getting a free drink backstage wouldn't be a novelty for much longer.

Florence's performance was typically ramshackle, with one appearance ending up with Florence diving into a swimming pool by the side of the stage. Explain yourself.

"At the start, I'd promised the audience that I would dive into this pool beside the stage, so I had to keep my promise," she said. "When I came out, soaking wet, I knew I couldn't go back onstage because of all the electrical equipment, so I had to crawl under the stage to get away.'

Florence's unique show certainly impressed the Brooklyn band MGMT, who were sharing the *BBC Introducing* bill with her at SXSW. In fact, they were so taken with her that they invited her to support them on their European tour that May. Florence jumped at the chance.

"The MGMT pairing made sense," says Mike Walsh, programme director of XFM. "It would have appealed to that alternative 'big song' kind of audience. And I know she likes a night out and MGMT do as well, so I'm assuming that was also a good match!"

Just one day before she kicked things off with MGMT, Florence had been invited to support her friend Pete Doherty at the Manchester Academy, an experience that could have sent her running to the hills: while Florence and her band were playing, she realised the Pete Doherty fans in the audience were becoming more and more agitated. They did not want to see Florence + The Machine. "It was terrifying, his fans are so hardcore. They were shouting, "Who are ya? Who are ya?"

Not exactly every young pop princess' dream. Florence turned to her band members and instructed them to just go hell for leather and get through the set as quickly as possible, resulting in what Florence described as a "thrash version" of their songs.

While this was a survival technique to get them off the stage, it seemed to go down well, and even a trademark Florence stage-dive was eventually well received. When Florence later joined Pete onstage to sing a Johnny Cash song with him, the antipathy was all but forgotten. Mostly.

From Nick's, Florence's father's, point of view, the sight of thousands of angry Mancunians baying at his daughter paled into insignificance next to the piece of news this self-confessed 'rock 'n' roll dad' received that evening. At the bar after the gig, he found out that Pete Doherty had proposed to his daughter. Lovely as he found Doherty to be, perhaps ignorance would have been bliss after all...

"I shared a light ale or two with the rock 'n' roll Rimbaud and found him to be quite charming, if a trifle vague," said Nick. "I must admit though, a report that he had proposed to Florence earlier in the evening did cause a momentary attack of the vapours."

Florence: "He was seriously worried! He heard Pete had proposed and got very anxious I might say yes. He's a cool dad, but I think that was a step too far even for him." Florence assured her doting father that marrying Pete Doherty, a man best known for his widely publicised substance abuse and 'blood paintings', was not on her agenda.

So once the events of that nearly fateful night were behind them, it was time to head off with MGMT. "That first tour definitely changed me in a few ways!" she'd later laugh. She would no longer be in her comfort zone, although she wouldn't be allowed off the leash for too long: while it was a perfect opportunity for her to experience her first real tour, it was also the perfect opportunity, in her parents' eyes, for Nick to go along for the ride and keep an eye on things. Under the guise of 'providing transport', Nick Welch filled the family camper van with petrol and drove behind the MGMT tour bus around Europe. "All for a princely sum of 75 euros a gig," recalls Nick.

It wasn't about the money though, of course. Not at this stage. It was about impressing his mates. Oh, and it was the perfect next step for Florence too. "My early days as de facto tour manager are a great source of envy to my fifty-something chums who would give their eye teeth for the chance to go 'on the road' with a band," Nick said. As Florence quipped, "Dad has been really supportive because he's a bit of a free spirit and wants free tickets to gigs. We definitely didn't have to tone things down when he was around..."

Florence remembers the tour as being "one of the best times of [her] life", not least because they had so much fun, particularly having her dad in tow. The US psych-rockers meanwhile regarded their support act's eccentric camper van, complete with pots and pans a-clanking, with benevolent amusement. "We would pull up next to their massive tour bus shouting 'Coo-ee! We're here!' They must have thought we were completely insane.

"I came back all hippified, I'd been hanging out with [singer] Andrew VanWyngarden, so I was all glittery and bandanna'd. We'd stay on their bus sometimes and travel with them from Munich to Paris, it was cool."

The MGMT tour was awash with new experiences for Florence – not least a trip to Paris during which Florence apparently dived into a brief Sapphic interlude which got the blogosphere talking ("I'm only a lesbian in Paris," Florence later explained, not sounding in the least bit pretentious) but there was one experience she definitely hadn't expected – a visit from beyond the grave from her beloved grandmother, the woman who had encouraged her so enthusiastically when the rest of the family were telling her to shut her cakehole.

"She did come and visit me in a dream. We were staying in a German wood on the MGMT tour in the camper van. My dad was like, 'This will be fun' and it was pitch black and terrifying.

"It was a run of the mill dream and I was trapped in a school and everyone was throwing pool balls at me. All of a sudden my grandmother was there – she was luminous and was wearing clothes I recognised but they were all shining, gold jewellery and I went and held her ankles and then I woke. It was her telling me she knew, she understood what was happening…"

By the end of the tour, Florence had barely washed the glitter from her face and the sweat from her hair before she was back in town for the May Bank Holiday Camden Crawl, one whole weekend of music and debauchery. She crowd-surfed with the Cribs, marvelled at Kate Nash's DJ set ("She just played one album') and hailed the moment she saw singer Amy Macdonald sing a Killers cover as "one of the best moments of my life". It's fair to say some alcohol had been consumed. Musically, Florence did her bit too. "I played a life-changing DJ set, the first thing I played was the *William Tell Overture*. Amazing." What, no Joan Collins or train noises?

And so, during the summer that ensued, Florence, Nick and members of the ever-fluid Machine bombed around the UK to festivals and gigs for their then early-in-the-day sets in the Welch-mobile. Next up? Reading and Leeds. Reading Festival was, of course, close to Florence's heart, not least because it was the first festival she had ever been to; taken, presciently enough, by her father when she was barely in her teens. This time she would be singing, but her excitement at being at Reading, particularly as it fell on her birthday weekend, almost got out of hand.

"I was in the middle of the Rage Against The Machine mosh pit dressed as a clown. It was like, 'Who do you think most Rage Against

The Machine fans most want to beat up during a mosh?' I got really over-excited and crowd-surfed all the way to the front in the first song and couldn't find my way back."

The clown outfit was eschewed when it came to her performance, however. She might have been playing at 2.45pm, but Florence was determined to give her all during her performance and that meant pulling out all of the stops visually as well as sonically.

"I wore a lime-green catsuit with a curtain," she recalled. "Catsuit, curtain, ready to go!" This was translated by *The Guardian* rather more romantically as "emerald robes and a cape". It's all smoke and mirrors. Or, in this case, catsuits and curtains. She packed out the Festival Republic tent, proving that she already had a staunch following that could barely squeeze itself in to see her.

XFM's Mike Walsh, who was already a fan thanks to being sent her demos by Mairead, caught her set at Leeds. "I saw her around lunchtime, and I remember thinking she should be higher on the bill, she was one of the first bands on in the new music tent. Typical XFM, we're always ahead of the curve so we wish our artists to be bigger than they are. But she really stood out, the tent was busy for early in the day, and it reinforced the feeling of 'This is going to go!'"

*The Guardian* was also suitably impressed: "Opening songs 'Between Two Lungs' and 'My Boy Builds Coffins' demonstrate Welch has learned how to rein in her unbelievably powerful voice (to much more powerful effect). Instead of bellowing and yodelling her way into the audience's consciousness, the singer exudes confidence without being overpowering, flinging herself about in glee with the full support, and imitation, of the audience." Is there any greater compliment than having your songs sung back to you by an adoring crowd?

While we know in hindsight that mainstream success was not far away, Nick, meanwhile, was now shifting the focus of his anxiety from possible son-in-laws and the dangers of crowd-surfing to more prosaic concerns: would his beloved daughter ever make any money from music? Or would they eventually have to have that dreaded conversation about getting a 'real job'? The money issue would be a concern for longer than many people might have imagined.

Nick: "I may have to wait a while for that bungalow in Weybridge that rock stars seem to buy for their parents."

A house in Camberwell and that ever-faithful camper van would have to do for now.

# CHAPTER FIVE

*"I've got my ideal job. I like to sing, I like to dance, I like to bang drums and dress up, and someone pays me – it's incredible."*

Florence's musical journey continued once she'd returned from that wild and fabled place known as 'the road' to the cosseted, messy comfort of her scarf-draped, Victoriana-crammed bedroom back at the house in which she grew up. It was the perfect place to retreat, kick off her shoes, place her enormous headphones over her ears and open herself up to new sounds. Or at least, sounds that were new to her. One evening, as Nick passed her room, Florence bellowed out that she was "having a bloody epiphany". Sitting on her bed in a state close to ecstasy, Florence had heard Jefferson Airplane's bone-shaking acid anthem 'White Rabbit' for the first time.

Jefferson Airplane might later go through several incarnations (they became Jefferson Starship in the Seventies, went all AORish and had a huge hit with 'Nothing's Gonna Stop Us Now') but the sixties was the decade that birthed them, and the decade that saw them flourish into their most potent form – and it's no surprise that Florence would take vocal inspiration from Grace Slick's powerful, dramatic holler. Florence was probably also taken with the oft-repeated story that Grace had joked to nurses that she wanted to name her baby daughter 'god', but 'god' with a small 'g' as she wanted to keep her humble. She'd also tried to spike former president Richard Nixon's tea with 600 micrograms of LSD at a party. Rock 'n' roll mischief at its (almost) psychedelic best.

While she was still listening to plenty of hip-hop ("It's the most forward-thinking music around!"), Florence had moved her listening on from the urgent punky fare that had taken up residence on her Walkman in her mid-teens and had inspired, in turn, 'Kiss With A Fist', and she was now embracing more expansive contemporary music, including Arcade Fire's first album, *Funeral*. "It just blew my mind. That was when I was about 20, and that song 'In The Backseat' was so beautiful and heartbreaking." No surprise that when, just a few years down the line, Florence met Arcade Fire's Win Butler, she was "so star-struck I cried."

Listening to Arcade Fire, and letting them weave their spell around her as she sat alone in her room, had prompted Florence to move away from garage rock and open up her own sound into something fuller and more multi-dimensional. And of course, their sense of gloom appealed to Florence no end. Ultimately, the aim for Florence was to "sound like a mix of Björk, Radiohead and Elvis". Mission pretty much accomplished.

The clock was ticking, and while this was all good research, Florence had an album to write for her new label, Moshi Moshi, which had just released 'Kiss With A Fist', the fastest song Florence had ever written, in June 2008 as the lead single from the album, just one month after she returned from her triumphant tour with MGMT. A haunting cover of Cold War Kids' 'Hospital Beds' graced the B-side.

'Kiss With A Fist', the song she wrote with Matt Alchin back in her art-school days, was revived and produced by Pulp bassist Steve Mackey (surely a dream come true for Florence, given her adoration of the Sheffield Brit-pop band during her teens and, particularly, her crush on singer Jarvis Cocker). While this song came together in a drunken haze, the finished product would bear no traces of the general ambience of exhaustion and nausea. But while the release undoubtedly impressed, and was a spiky debut single, piercing through the fug of anodyne pop, it didn't come without its share of controversy, and Florence soon found herself having to defend the track from those who saw it as a clear glorification of domestic violence. With lines like 'A kiss with a fist is better than none', it's no surprise that this song garnered something of an angry response from some.

But Florence insisted the whole scandal was "ridiculous. That's not ever something that even crossed my mind. I don't think there are any victims in the song, it's about giving as good as you get, it's very tongue-in-cheek and playful, I wrote it when I was 16 and had never experienced it, it's an absolutely horrendous thing to happen to anybody and there is no way I would ever endorse it."

However, after the inevitable questioning she received from the tabloids, Florence did admit to that august publication *The Daily Star* to lamping an ex-boyfriend once. "It was kind of funny," she said. "It was on Valentine's Day. He came to my house in the middle of the night after we had broken up and started screaming. I probably should have just stayed inside but I was furious with him for coming to my house. And then he wouldn't leave so I punched him in the face." Fortunately Florence's then boyfriend Stuart Hammond didn't seem to be eliciting such a response.

There was plenty of work to do but, luckily for her, she could work on and record some of the main songs that would be included on the album with Isabella at her studio, before entering a more sterile atmosphere with engineers she didn't know and equipment she wasn't familiar with. The release was always going to be, as Florence put it, "a scrapbook of the past five years... it's about guilt, fear, love, death, violence, nightmares, dreams..."

Her preoccupation with death, however, would conversely inspire and comfort legions of fans who would turn to her music in their droves during darker times. One striking theme when speaking to fans for this project was the number of individuals who referred to how strongly Florence's music had affected them after the demise of a loved one. The fears, the depth of feeling that is sometimes so hard to articulate or express and the intense sense of love, Florence had all of this covered and more in her music. Not that she was professing to have all the answers, mind, far from it. She was as much expressing her vulnerability and confusion as anything else.

"Is there life after death? I'd like to think there was, maybe it's a blank nothing, which is way more frightening than any kind of paranormal idea. The fear that there's just nothing…"

Nightmares and fears had always plagued the over-imaginative Florence since childhood – she had experienced terrifying sleep paralysis, feelings that there was something monstrous hiding under her bed or in the wardrobe. She would have auditory hallucinations in which words and sounds would fade up and down, and more tangible hallucinations in which demons would pounce onto her chest and pin her down. When insomnia – or demons – would strike, sometimes the only solution would be to get up and roam around in the darkness, giving in to the night and exploring the neighbourhood while most people were asleep, and the sort of people who weren't asleep, well, you probably didn't want to bump into them.

Her nocturnal wanderings would often lead her to rummage through skips for interesting curios and old paintings, which she'd hang in her already crammed old curiosity shop of a bedroom.

"My bedroom is full of stuff I've collected," she said. "A massive old painting of a stag, a stuffed bird in a glass dome – a lot of Victoriana. I do have loads of paintings but I've nowhere to hang them so they're all stacked up in my house.

"London is kind of gothic and it's old and it's spooky and it's a bit haunted, I think, and it's ancient and bloody and violent. I think growing up in London definitely affected me." Pure night terror territory – her description of the city conjures images of gruesome penny dreadfuls bearing sketches of Jack the Ripper's latest victim, amongst other things. And if she really didn't like waking up in a cold sweat, her perpetual fascination with doom wasn't doing an awful lot to stem the flow of spooky, dark artistic influences entering her mindset. At least now she could indulge her dramatic nightmares and channel them into something creative and cathartic.

"My imagination takes me to a dark place. I had a really over-active imagination as a child, and now it's good because I can write a song about being scared of a werewolf. I'm having a second childhood where I can use it. I'm still afraid of ghosts and vampires – but I can just put them in the songs."

Her songwriting was always very different to that of her contemporaries, singers like Lily Allen, Kate Nash and Amy Winehouse. Their lyrics were very clear, obvious, prosaic. But Florence's metaphorical musical musings were part of her ultimately deeply discreet nature. "[I would] feel too exposed. They're braver than me; a fantasy world is easier to live in.

"I think it's a way of sort of tackling my own demons, maybe? If I can lay them out in my characters or in animals, it's just a way of maybe confessing. Or expressing something that I couldn't say literally."

The album that would be *Lungs* was not just inspired by the experiences that Florence had enjoyed – or endured – it was also influenced heavily by art, books, poems, slogans and images that were around her in daily life. It was like a patchwork quilt created with Florence's reference points and sensual experiences, vibrant with the things she'd seen, heard, felt, loved and feared.

"You pick up lines here and there from poems or from newspapers, church bulletins. If you're feeling open, like you can access stuff, then that's a good time to write. Sometimes if you're worried or nervous about something it can be hard to write songs."

The title for 'Dog Days Are Over', and the feeling engendered by the resulting song, was inspired by Ugo Rondinone's uplifting rainbow-like installation on London's cultural centre, the South Bank, which bore the very words 'The Dog Days Are Over' in eighties-esque bubble-writing, redolent of childhood innocence and joy. Florence used to cycle past this piece of art during the years she was at art school, and thanks to the imagery, the words and the sheer association of wheeling past it on a sunny day by the river, she was motivated to write a song about "that feeling of being free".

"There'd be that amazing moment when the sun would be setting, I'd be listening to music – which is very dangerous on a bicycle! – and the music would reach a climax and I'd see that sign and it was that feeling, that rush you get, I wanted to create a song that encapsulated that, that feeling of release, freedom, riding a bike with your eyes closed!"

"I've also got this book of Ed Ruscha paintings called *They Called Her Styrene*," Florence explains. "All of his paintings are these hot phrases like, 'Went out for cigarettes, never came back.' Random phrases hold so much weight. If you string them together, you can create a picture and this emotion you never even knew they initially had. Even though they have no correlation to each other, you string them together in a song and it creates this beautiful poetry and this whole new meaning. It's like a riddle, but it's for yourself."

The album would have a very clear trajectory, particularly considering the songs included were written between the ages of 17 and 22, from adolescence to early womanhood. She had the sketches and ideas in place, she now had to get on with it and bring those ideas together and breathe *Lungs* into life. Having the right people around her was key.

"Isa couldn't play piano but I was doing loads of music with her," remembers Florence. "I wrote 'Cosmic Love', 'Dog Days' and 'Lungs' with her, and I was like, 'Come and be in the band! It doesn't matter that you can't play piano, you'll learn!' Enthusiasm over skill." And skills, of course, can be learned. Unlike enthusiasm, ingenuity and imagination.

"Making music was more like improvising," said Florence. "So it was such a rush when I found something that worked. It was all about the feeling, and I think that comes across in the music. You can hear this absolute joy at being able to make sound. And building things out of my own ideas of what a song should be like was exciting. It was like building and experiments, y'know? With rhythms and chords. That's why everything's like 'bang, bang, stop, start.' It's because I have no skill, I just have enthusiasm."

With Florence's songwriting, there's often an almost tribal use of rhythm, and this would be a theme that would recur in her music which, at this stage, was being cooked up by herself and Isabella, bashing away on the piano, whacking a tin tray (this sound was the prototype for the drumbeat for 'Dog Days Are Over'), hitting the walls (à la 'Drumming Song') or playing around with celestial harp sounds on her Roland keyboard. A useful element of Florence's close relationship with Isabella

'Isa Machine' Summers was that, after they'd partied themselves out together, they'd often end up in the studio in the early hours of the morning, forcing themselves to write. That's dedication.

"'Cosmic Love' was a joke title, but it stuck," says Florence. "The most hungover I've ever been when writing a song. I went to her studio after having been to a party, and I was lying on the floor wanting to vomit. We were working really hard on a song and just trying to make this shit piano part work, and all of a sudden I hit on one note, and I'd got it. We wrote the whole song in 10 minutes.

"We initially did it with a Yamaha and some shitty effects. I was trying to create a weird sort of piano opus. The first line, 'A Falling Star...' it all just fell out of my mouth. I've never written a song so quickly, apart from maybe 'Kiss With A Fist'.

"I think probably 'Cosmic Love' is my favourite song," she later reflected. "I think that one feels like it just happened so naturally. I wasn't even thinking about it. I mean it didn't even exist before that half an hour; none of it existed. Not on the piano, or going round in my head. It just suddenly appeared and it was perfect. Well, I thought it was perfect. At first I thought it was a bit too romantic even; but it's not that romantic, it's quite dark."

Florence admitted she had to leave off "a ton" of tracks that didn't fit with the concept of the album, but another early song, alongside 'Kiss With A Fist', to make the cut was 'Between Two Lungs', the emotional paean to the ethereal anticipation of a kiss. It was initially made "just for a laugh", but it ultimately inspired the album's title.

"It opened up the whole sound of the album," said Florence. "A release so to speak, and singing's all about your lungs anyway and breath control – your lungs are your instrument." *Lungs* is certainly a snappier title than *Fuck The Cake, Take The Ice Cream And I Think I Just Punched The Waiter*, one of the titles Florence jokingly came up with before settling on something a little more appropriate.

"'Between Two Lungs' is where I think I found my sound," she explained. "But also, often I'll play a gig where I'm just drumming and singing, because I love to play drums and sing, [and] I think that takes it down to the bare elements of music. With music the drums are the heartbeat, and then the voice is the lungs, so that's your two core elements. The lungs are just me, I think. And the rest of the body is the Machine."

Experimenting was very much the order of the day, and thanks to Isa having the space and equipment at what was then her main base at Antenna Studios, near the twinkling light of the Crystal Palace transmitter in South London, they were free to try things and see where they went. "We started using synths and arpeggiating things," said Isabella. "*Lungs* was really organic, [we were] writing parts that suited Flo's voice and that we could imagine real instruments playing; so, writing violin parts, an organ part, and re-recording it."

Isabella's studio was tiny but impressive, a multicoloured treasure chest – with a skull and crossbones flag – so crammed with notes and pictures that it looked like the walls had been decoupaged. As we know, the 10 Florence commandments still adorn the wall, as do some of the lyrics of 'Dog Days Are Over' felt-tipped onto a board.

"It'd taken a long time to find the sound I wanted," Florence mused. "I spent a long time working with guitarists. But I knew I didn't want a whole album of 'Kiss With A Fist'. I never wanted to make a guitar album. But I didn't want anyone to pigeonhole me, and when I started people were like, 'Oh, she's indie rock.' I was just like, 'No, no way.' I wanted to make something that would make people feel an emotion.

"I wanted to make it into something that was a wave of sound that would envelop, something that was soaring, slightly church-like and then doom-like. I guess I wanted to make something with an overwhelming sound. There's strings, there's timpani, we use an elevator shaft, pens, me banging my hands on the walls and wailing into synthesizers, loads of backing vocals, loads of drums; I'm obsessed with drums."

When working with different drummers on the tracks, Florence knew what she wanted, but would find that it was hard to communicate how she wanted them to play on her tracks – basically, more like her, a non-drummer bashing away on the drums.

"It's kind of hard because you tell a really skilled drummer: 'I want you to play the drums worse. Play it more like I play it!' I think they understand it. They understand the passion…"

It wasn't all work, work, work. Once the musicians had gone home and Florence and Isabella were on their own, it turned into a rock 'n' roll-style girl's night in. Isabella even introduced Florence to the eighties fantasy movie *Labyrinth*, featuring David Bowie as a Goblin King, Jennifer Connelly as an adventurous young girl who whines "it's not fair!" quite a bit and a bevy of grotesque muppets. Perfect escapism.

Florence: "Isa said, 'Oh my god, you haven't seen *Labyrinth*? You ARE *Labyrinth*! How have you not seen it?' I watched it with her and yes, it's amazing..."

Isabella remembers: "When we were working on 'Dog Days', and we were being messed around by boys, we would come in here and lock the doors and turn the sound system up and listen to Madonna." Isabella always knew how to cheer Florence up and make her laugh at the best of times, but the almost shamanic whipping-up of female energy that infused the Shed studio during the making of this song must have had an effect on the resulting release of 'Dog Days', which would become Florence's euphoric second single.

And it was with this boundless, euphoric energy, and an army of equally energetic friends (crucially ones with skills, time and rudimentary equipment), that the video to 'Dog Days Are Over' was created. The promo was shot with a single camera and directed by Mairead's fellow Queen of Noize Tabitha Denholm and mutual friend Tom Beard. Denholm had also been charged with the duty of creating the album artwork for *Lungs* and the Florence + The Machine logo, and she did so with typical panache. The cover of *Lungs* is already a classic image, biological and yet romantic, featuring a close-up of Florence's head and torso. Florence herself looks delicate and ethereal, but inside her transparent blouse is a pair of red, solid lungs.

Florence knew how important it was to get the visual side just right. "With the songs you're trying to create an auditory landscape in someone's head, so with the video it's important that you capture that. Especially with 'Dog Days', my first video. I wasn't sure what was going on, so I was like, 'Right, we're really going to figure out what we're going to do here', it was much more involved. I just did it with my friends, it felt much more real to me, that's the way we did videos."

And so, with a crack team, a carrier bag of provisions (healthy, middle-class ones like hummus and carrots – no Monster Munch and Fanta here), armfuls of multicoloured bunting and Florence in her trusty tuxedo from her art-school days, team Flo set out to Sydenham Hill in south London to make a promo. Who could have known that within four years the video would have been viewed by 3.5 million people on YouTube alone.

"I think my only specifications were that I didn't want to look pretty," explained Florence. "And I wanted there to be exploding people.", Exploding people. Not much to ask. Do continue.

"We kind of had a free-for-all stylistically, going from ethereal goddess with blue Bhangra back-up dancers, through to kabuki sex monks with a psychedelic choir and tribal drummers, and a feral smoke child complete with riot explosion. I think we managed to get away with it without all being committed..."

There was something pagan and celebratory about the video, almost *Midsummer Night's Dream*-like: Florence awakens barefoot in a woodland glade among an array of colourfully attired, heavily made-up characters playing percussion, who view her curiously and eventually take her over as the scene explodes into a wild glittering party among the trees. There were plenty of bird cages around too – a Florence trademark since pre-art school and an image that can be seen as part of her stage sets to this day, often containing images of the lady herself. It's fair to say that if you went down to the woods that day, you'd have been sure of a big surprise. Teddy bears were probably the only things that *weren't* included in this vibrant jamboree of a video.

"We needed to give the video a hyper-real saturated look," said Aubrey Woodiwiss, who later graded the promo for when it was released with the single that November. "We did this by exaggerating the colours in the video. For consistency we stuck to a palette with a similar look and feel to the album artwork."

Putting the promo together for 'Dog Days' was a lot of fun, particularly given Florence's highly developed visual sense. Getting creative was also an all too vital distraction because, as Isabella observed, 'boys' were proving a bit of an issue. One boy in particular in fact: Stuart

Hammond, Florence's beloved. Florence had been "dumped", as she put it, and her world had been plunged into turmoil as she struggled to cope emotionally. She would spend hours wandering London or peering over Waterloo Bridge into the broiling Thames below, listening to the plaintive strains of Bon Iver on her Walkman, tears pouring down her face. "The walking weep", as she put it.

"The Bon Iver record, I think that was my 'woe is me' record," she recalls. "That record still holds a lot of memories of tortured walks through central London hugging this Walkman! I think 'Creature Fear' is the song that would break me, I would always be walking over Waterloo Bridge when it would break, just floods of tears under the open sky."

She was, she admitted, in a "seriously bad way, raw", but again, Florence would find that the sense of loss – although it would be temporary – would inspire her anew. Florence took solace in her days and nights at Isabella's studio, but the material they would generate from this painful time would be career-defining, inspirational and would reach out to her growing legions of fans in ways she could never have imagined, as she was, inadvertently, articulating heartbreak for others as well as herself.

It wasn't just the strain of romantic loss that was getting to Florence. It was the expectations that everyone now had of her. And those expectations were growing day by day. Flattering, yes. Pressurising? Scarily so.

"I'd gone from being this art student messing about with music to this girl with a record deal, magazine front covers and all this hype," said Florence. "In many ways, it was everything I ever wanted, but when it happened all I felt was total, paralysing fear. I couldn't cope with the idea of making the album. I just wanted to sabotage the whole thing, not do it and just disappear. It seemed so wrong that when I was so unhappy in my personal life, my career was suddenly taking off. Something inside me wanted to ruin everything."

# CHAPTER SIX

*"I can't hide my feelings; it's there in my music. That's why I think people can relate to me."*

Florence's understandably concerned family decided to whisk her out of town, convinced that a break from her familiar London surroundings, and everything that reminded her of Stuart, would do her the world of good, but Florence spent much of their holiday together in tears, lying in bed, despairing, and unable to think about moving forward. Only music could reliably lift her up and out of the mire.

"My parents just allowed me to go through it but I didn't know what I wanted," Florence explains. "I came back to London and I had an appointment in the studio, so I thought I'd better go. I started singing and all the bad feelings started to fall away. I got through heartbreak and so many other things with the album, which is why it's so emotional."

So thanks to her family, Isabella and the process of making the album that it conversely seemed so impossible to make under the circumstances, Florence slowly started to heal. Mairead's support and warmth were also instrumental in keeping her on the right track. Thanks to her innate understanding of Florence's 'self-destructive streak', she could ensure that Florence wasn't going to simply jack everything in – something the singer was tempted to do on more than one occasion, just as everything started to fall into place professionally.

"We really understand and help each other," said Florence. "She keeps me from the pitfalls of this industry. She looks after me, and I think it's a project for her as well. She's my facilitator, but she's also my advisor. She's been through this industry, and she's really wise to it."

It wouldn't be easy, but Florence's recent break-up, and the ever-mounting external stresses she was having to cope with, would inject her music with a tension and depth that would enrich it beyond measure. Florence had always loved to embrace the darkness, and now it seemed that somehow, the darkness was embracing her back. Fortunately, working with Isabella meant that things couldn't get *too* heavy. When they weren't singing out their frustrations along with Madonna on Isabella's stereo, they were perusing the all too conveniently positioned bazaar next to Isabella's studio. No wonder they got most of their work done after dark.

"The antiques store right next door is perfect for me," Florence enthused. "We've got this big picture of Snow White, and a china dog, and we buy all these dresses and hang them up and then we make music with teacups…"

Isabella also worked in a space affectionately known as the 'shloft' – named so because it's like a cross between a shed and a loft, and it was here that 'Cosmic Love' was written. Florence loved it, and as time went by, after experiencing less ramshackle studio environments, she valued the colourful junk-shop comfort of the 'shloft' all the more, not least because of the strong emotional connection with her early days working with Isabella.

"The walls get hit, we use anything we can to make music," explained Isabella. There were drums under scarves, a bucket of percussion, an expensive microphone, a keyboard that just sounds "like dogs growling"… There was also a tiny cupboard insulated with duvets which acted as a vocal booth. Necessity is the mother of invention, and it's no surprise that this female Heath Robinson and her techniques appealed to Florence. It's just as well she didn't suffer from claustrophobia.

And of course Isabella had her beloved Roland Juno Di. Her favourite sounds? "Bright brass, the harp setting... the harp chords at the beginning of 'Dog Days' all came from that – that was all me on the keyboard. It's such a beautiful noise, now I use it on everything. [Harpist] Tom Monger will often replay what I've written, but I always use the harp setting to begin with."

Recording at Antenna certainly seemed to bring Florence luck. As is often the way in the music business, things happen by accident and sometimes the greatest developments are born of chance meetings. Two of these happened within quick succession of each other, all in the studio complex. First, after recording 'Dog Days' with that bright, sweet simulated harp sound that Isabella loved so much, Florence was gazing out of the window when she saw a man walk by carrying what looked like "a telephone box wrapped in a blanket". Curiouser and curiouser...

Isabella rushed out, stopped him and asked what it was. He told her it was a harp. She asked him in and he proved his strength on the strings – no gavottes or minuets here, thank you very much. This was a harpist who'd been playing all of his life and developing his own style, which included using barrel-loads of electronic effects. How could Florence and Isabella resist?

It wasn't long before Florence asked Suffolk lad Monger to join the group, a move which, in turn, would eventually help to vicariously subvert people's preconceptions about this usually pastoral, angelic and strictly classical instrument by showcasing his vigorous, exuberant playing. Tom had studied at the prestigious Trinity College in London, but his objectives were at odds with theirs, and they soon fell out. He'd grown up playing in school rock bands and wanted to take this to the next level. He wasn't your average harpist.

"I just wanted to play in a band! They didn't quite know how to deal with me, I suppose," he reflects. "I was stubborn and they were stubborn! When I had to choose between audition training and a gig with the band I chose the latter. They nearly threw me out of the conservatory because they don't understand a gig to me can be as important as an audition to a classical harpist."

Tom also suffered misunderstanding on the jazz scene: apparently one jazz club in London simply laughed when he asked for a gig. Jazz harp? They had never heard of such a thing, and certainly weren't taking any chances on it. Not that he's likely to be worrying about that now... Some years earlier, in 2005, his own band, the electronic collective Lunamoth, caught the attention of Björk, no less, who was impressed by his version of her song 'Army Of Me'. The track ended up on a compilation of remixes, selected by the lady herself.

Bumping into Isabella in the car park of Antenna Studios would ultimately lead to another dream coming true for Tom, even if he might not have realised it at the time. Here is Tom's memory of that fateful meeting with Isa.

"We got chatting and she said she was a producer working with this vocalist. 'It would be really great if you could put some harp stuff down.' She sent me all these tracks – pre-Florence + The Machine, really. If I remember rightly, they were still working together as Florrible and Misrabella.

"She used to email me songs and I'd record the harp part in my flat, and then email it back to Isa. She'd mix it together. We did this for a couple of years. Some of the songs she sent me ended up on the album: songs like 'Dog Days Are Over' and 'I'm Not Calling You A Liar.' I know for a fact that some of my harp part on 'Dog Days' was recorded in my flat."

Harps, effects... Florence's sound had already come a long way from the early gigs, at least one of which featured Flo accompanying herself only with a metal dustbin lid.

Tom came from a musical, unconventional family: his grandfather was a jazz guitarist who made harps, and his mother, Eileen, also played, releasing an album called *The Lilting Banshee* in the eighties – the title alone must have sent Florence into raptures when she found that out.

"My father worked at the Museum of East Anglian Life and our family grew up in the grounds. We were sort of renting a house in the grounds. We were very lucky, because we didn't have any immediate neighbours – which meant I could make as much noise as I wanted without disturbing anybody else.

"There is still this kind of stigma or stereotype to the harp being a romantic instrument played by ladies in long dresses and very regal settings," said Tom. "That doesn't have to be the case."

Tom was more than happy to join the merry throng in Isabella's Shed, not least because it was nicer than most of the studios he'd recorded in, despite its size. "It's one of the less claustrophobic rehearsal studios," he said. "At least it has windows, which most don't seem to."

The second chance meeting would be when Florence proved she had left any traces of her childhood shyness well behind her once and for all. On hearing that James Ford, Simian Mobile Disco member and über producer of the Klaxons and Arctic Monkeys, was rehearsing next door, she grabbed a demo CD, knocked on his door and thrust it into his hand. The result? He told her to go away and stop bothering him. Of course he didn't. He took one listen and decided he wanted to work with her.

Ford would produce the early *Lungs* tracks which had been written by Welch and Summers: 'Between Two Lungs', 'Dog Days' and 'I'm Not Calling You A Liar', while also sharing a writing credit on the track 'Drumming Song', a track with quite a different feel to 'Between Two Lungs'.

"I wanted to write something that was indoors," said Florence. "So much of it has been about the bucolic English countryside, so I think I wanted to do something a bit grander, a bit tougher.

"'Drumming Song' is about that electricity between you and a boy, and it's completely unspoken," Florence breathlessly explained. "When they're standing in front of you and you can't breathe, can't think, can't do anything properly. Again, it's really gothic imagery – fairy tales and Edgar Allan Poe stories. I'd read a lot of gothic horror when I was a kid. Also Sylvia Plath. I've always been a literary miserablist…"

The song is replete with religious overtones: bells, churches, heaven and hell, but it's also interwoven with an element of something more pagan and earthy, not only in terms of the almost shamanic sound, but in the verbal description of that throbbing, speeding pulse that fills the head to a deafening degree whenever the object of desire is near: "There's a drumming noise inside my head/that throws me to the ground/I swear that you should hear it/It makes such an almighty sound."

Pure Florence drama, and an example of her "incorrigible maximalism" (her words) in practice, perhaps – it isn't unusual to read through Florence's lyrics and see references to being 'thrown to the ground' or 'screaming' – but it's an almost perfect summing up of that heady rush of first love. "I love any music that makes me feel like I want to jump in the air, fall on the floor, scream, throw myself out of a window..." No half measures in Florence-land. Potentially dangerous though.

Before 2008 was through, Mairead Nash, who had been determinedly pushing Florence demos in front of everyone who was anyone, had managed to affect a deal with Island Records' Ben Mortimer, the executive who, while working with Virgin Records, discovered the singer Jamie T.

"Mairead knows the score with the business," says a former colleague of the Florence + The Machine team. "She knows what it's like to be a young artist in the music business and I'm sure Florence has benefited hugely from that.

"Mairead's company Luv Luv Luv Management, now Luv Luv Luv Records, have signed several artists in the wake of Florence, and I don't think Island will be getting their hands on many of those. That's what's happening now in the industry generally, if you've signed someone like Florence and you've got the political or financial clout to have a go at breaking some other artists, why would you sign up to a major these days? There's not a lot that a major can do for you that you can't do yourself if you've got a bit of cash and you know your way around."

Island had, like most people in the music industry, fallen in love with the whole Florence + The Machine package. The time was right for a more romantic, more elliptical pop heroine, all Kate Bush sensibilities and enigmatic lyrics as opposed to shoot-from-the-hip Lily Allen musings.

XFM programme controller Mike Walsh and DJ John Kennedy had also been sent demos of Florence, as well as the first single, 'Kiss With A Fist', on Moshi Moshi – and, after falling for her music, they watched her trajectory with interest.

"John told me that he had this single by a girl called Florence who was friends with Johnny Borrell and managed by his friend Mairead," remembers Walsh. "All the elements looked good before I'd even heard the record. He played 'Kiss With A Fist' on his Xposure show – he's really a total new music guy, he's really our John Peel in many ways – and he got very excited by Florence + The Machine and that spurred me on.

"I remember the A&R chase. I had friends at Parlophone and Virgin who were desperate to sign her. As you would imagine with an artist of such obvious quality, the heat in the A&R community was high. It seemed to happen quite quickly. I remember seeing her perform twice within the space of a few months when she'd done the deal with Island, and we kind of knew it was going to get the big major label push. That felt great for us because we wanted her to have the biggest platform – Moshi are great and what's good about the Florence deal is that they're still involved, which always made it feel ethical. It wasn't like the indie label that had found her had just got pushed aside when the major took over. I remember thinking, right, she's got the big label money behind her, let's see what she's got.

"I saw her at Iceland Airwaves festival, and she played this big beautiful hall in Reykjavik, the art museum – there was lots of buzz and chatter about it. I met her dad who is a wonderful, charming and eccentric man, and saw what was just a jaw-dropping performance.

"I remember thinking, from a songs point of view, that the best songs in the set were her two covers: 'You Got The Love' by the Source and Candi Staton, and 'Hospital Beds' by Cold War Kids. That was before I was really aware of the songs that were then going to make up *Lungs* and be this incredible classic album. I remember thinking even then that if she gets a good recording of 'You Got The Love', then that's an absolute global smash. It's an evergreen song that just needed a sharp update, and boy, did she give it a sharp update."

As with many elements of Florence's life, the decision to re-imagine this "song about life", as Candi Staton put it, a song which now seems to define Florence's incendiary live performances, was initially a mere whim.

"I decided to do it in my friend's kitchen," she explained in an interview with Irish website RTE, looking very like Princess Diana, all Bambi eyes peering shyly up under her lashes. "That song has always been me and my best friends' anthem, we've had so many amazing moments together.

"We were playing the dance tent at a festival, and we're not a dance band, so we thought we'd try that. It sounded really good in rehearsal and when we played it live the reaction was unbelievable! I love the original so much, it amazes me that people have taken this version to heart. You can't argue with the power of that song, it's such a good song and I cannot take credit for it, the song speaks for itself!"

What Florence can take credit for is the feeling her performance of that song engendered in the audience at this still relatively early stage in her professional career. "The overall feeling was that you were enraptured by her," remembers Mike Walsh. "You were sucked into her world for 20 minutes or half an hour, as with all great artists, and nothing else really mattered. It's that kind of luminescent charisma that is the genuine X factor! Forget the crap Simon Cowell TV show, what actually separates normal people from stars is this kind of intangible, hard to describe something, and she had that something.

"I remember thinking, 'Great, this is it, this is going to be an exciting time.' You knew you were looking at something that had the potential to be enormous, which was very exciting for us as an alternative music radio station – we're ambitious for our artists, we want them to be global superstars! That performance told me we were off to the races."

Who could have predicted that, by November 2009, Ed Miliband, the leader of the Labour party, would have selected this glittering cover version to amble off stage to after a speech at a Labour party conference, while the Conservative leader David Cameron chose, oddly enough, to take to the podium to the rousing sound of 'Dog Days Are Over'. So at least there's one thing the two party leaders can agree on: the rousing power of Florence + The Machine.

Inevitably, though, the media buzz around Florence was spiked with the usual cynicism that unfortunately tends to accompany the launch of a female artist.

"We saw it with Lana Del Rey," says Walsh. "You have this odd, slightly misogynistic backlash to any strong female success in music. Everyone has to ask the question, 'Is it real, does she write her own songs? What's the back story? Is she a rich kid? Is she the result of a producer-led lab?' Oh piss off! Like Lana Del Rey, she's a star, she writes, she does co-writes too, who gives a shit? If the end result is as good as that, I don't care who co-wrote it. She's obviously had input, and led the creative side of it.

"Certain DJs at other stations were saying, 'Sounds a bit more like the Machine than Florence.' Surely it doesn't matter what goes into the recipe as long as the cake's amazing! She definitely didn't get hit as hard as Lana regarding the online hate. It's awful. But there was that typically male indie cynicism towards a strong successful woman. Thankfully she survived it and did very well!"

But as Florence's ever-loving dad would observe, seeing her inevitable success unfold in 2008 was strange, fantastic and worrying all at once. Not least because of how his eccentric daughter's doom-tinged lyrics reflected on him...

"I occasionally feel a twinge of unease about this whole extraordinary thing, and I remember the first time I felt it," said Nick. "Florence was playing a gig in an inexplicably fashionable joint in Hoxton, Hackney. As I watched Florence putting her heart and soul into the performance, I glanced round at the audience... there were the A&R men. They weren't here to enjoy themselves, they were taking care of business, and the business was my daughter. It was a sobering thought.

"It was at this gig that one of the A&R men who knew I was Florence's father turned to me with a quizzical expression as she launched into another of her perverse, gothic tales of death, dismemberment, and bloody revenge. 'I know what you're thinking,' I shouted, 'but I can assure you she had a perfectly normal upbringing...'"

Joking aside, Nick knew very well that his daughter would need his support more than ever in the coming months. Florence was becoming a big star. Quickly. And while this was hardly an overnight success, as these things often appear to be, it was not easy to prepare mentally for the excitement – and expectations – that were to come.

# CHAPTER SEVEN

*"Florence looks set to skip barefoot through 2009 as a sort of surreal-folk PJ Harvey with lungs the size of the bellowing sails on an 18th-century ship."*

The Guardian

While 2008 was exciting, or in Florence's words: "fun followed by fear, followed by fun, followed by fall over, followed by more fun", it was merely the set-up for an incredible year to follow. In December 2008, just days after the release of her second single, 'Dog Days', it had been announced that Florence would not only be performing on the Shockwaves *NME* Awards Tour the following January and February – a valuable showcase for any new artist – she would also be the next winner of the Brit Awards' Critics' Choice honour, just like Adele before her. Florence had only released two tracks and already she was being hailed as the queen of Britain's emerging musical talent. No pressure. The award, which can only be given to an artist who has not yet released their debut album, was only in its second year.

Brits chairman Ged Doherty said: "The aim of introducing this award last year was to help boost the career of a new British artist by giving them a platform to reach a wider audience. Adele clearly fulfilled all our hopes and ambitions for this award. I hope Florence + The Machine goes on to enjoy similar success."

And Florence's take? Shock. Not least because she didn't know she was even up for the award. This was deliberate, as her management didn't want her to freak out. But when Mairead called her to tell her the happy news, she... well, freaked out. But in a good way, at least. "I screamed and fell on the floor," she gushed excitedly.

"Blimey, a Brit Award, wowtheworldsgoneweird [sic]. Thank you so much to the critics," she wrote, in a nod to those who chose her as the recipient for the award. She then verbally gave fans a sneak preview as to the sound of *Lungs*: "It's sort of sounding like a choir, a harp, some metal chains and a piano all put through a car crusher, then hit with wooden planks really hard. I will see you at the awards. I'll be the one trying to get off with Katy Perry and passed out next to Leona Lewis."

She didn't do either of those things, as far as we know, but such promises were enough to keep the world watching, as was her quip that she was considering turning up on the red carpet in her pyjamas. "I'll be the one in the teddy bear shirt and pants combo on the red carpet." Fortunately, she elected not to follow this through.

This naturalness and often self-deprecating sense of fun around a business that so often takes itself rather too seriously was no doubt a huge part of what made young people in particular love her. Teenage girls are bombarded by fake imagery they are supposed to aspire to emulate, but here was a refreshingly authentic role model – both visually and musically. Fans respected this.

"She has shown that modern music doesn't just have to be over-Autotuned with bland, meaningless words," said Zoë Swann, a member of the fan club The Florence + The Machine Army. "The sheer depth of emotion captured in her lyrics and her powerful voice are qualities that the majority of 'musicians' sorely lack today. She has also shown that you don't have to be what society thinks of as 'normal' to be successful in whatever creative thing you are doing."

In between rehearsals, writing, getting rid of hangovers and no doubt "screaming and falling over" a bit more (not to mention giving taxi drivers heart attacks by shrieking whenever her songs came on the radio and demanding them to turn it over), it was soon time to wow the assembled music industry bigwigs and her contemporaries with a performance at the Brit Awards Nomination Launch Party on January 20, alongside fellow pop stars Gabriella Cilmi and Scouting For Girls. The Brits Launch would be the first gig for which Florence would buy a dress, specifically a mint-green lace thirties gown that she felt was like armour protecting her during this high-pressure event.

The ceremony was just a few weeks away, but first Florence had an *NME* Awards tour to open, and a big slice of the rock 'n' roll lifestyle to enjoy. Busy? Just a bit. It's no wonder Florence would soon have to retreat into solitude from time to time just to catch her breath.

"[The tour] is amazing but it's something I'm not really used to," she said. "I always just wanted to make music and art and perform, all this other stuff is like, 'OK, cool, if I can do this too!'"

"The *NME* tour was interesting," remembers XFM's Mike Walsh. "I think she was first on the bill which is now a legendary slot: Coldplay were first on the *NME* tour, a couple of years later so were Franz Ferdinand, Kaiser Chiefs, then Florence. Every couple of years a future million-selling artist opened the *NME* tour. Which is interesting. It was certainly significant as a profile-raising tour."

The Shockwaves *NME* Awards tour began in Liverpool on January 29, featuring, as well as Florence + The Machine, Friendly Fires, White Lies and Scottish indie kings (and queen) Glasvegas, who were headlining, and a wild time was assured. Glasvegas frontman and Joe Strummer lookalike James Allan promised they'd be loading up on the champagne and teased reporters by asking them to imagine what it might be like having hedonistic hair-metal rockers Mötley Crüe on the *NME* tour.

Florence immediately impressed critics with her big voice, unique costumes and devil-may-care stage-diving, and the then *NME* editor Conor McNicholas hailed the tour line-up as "deeply talented artists who produce music of real quality. All four acts boast the strongest and most distinctive new songwriters in Britain at the moment and the sheer quality of artists on the tour has meant it is being hailed as the strongest for years."

Florence was incredibly excited if the backstage videos on *NME* TV are anything to go by: she and Isabella give each other piggybacks, primp each other, dance to Beyoncé, scream (of course) and push each other over like children at a party after too much fizzy pop. Florence would help trim Isabella's fringe and they happily played with clothes and make-up as if they were two little girls messing about at their mother's dressing table.

"My skin is holding up pretty well considering," said Florence. "I moisturise a lot but sometimes I do sleep in my make-up. Isa is really into lots of black eye make-up and wherever she sleeps you know where she's been, there are black tear marks everywhere, it's like some little emo girl has slept over and cried herself to sleep."

Florence brought plenty of props: she loved dressing her stage – although, as she has since proudly stated: "Now I have people who do that for me!" Boxes and bags full of goodies came on the tour with them, ready to embellish every surface and create a truly Florence-like atmosphere. There was bunting displaying pictures of bird cages and also free birds (which, alongside customised school exercise books, you could buy – or versions of, at least – at the Flotique merchandise stall after the gig), lampshades and garlands reminiscent of Florence's art-school installations.

"[The flowers] remind me of funerals, there's something morbid about them," Florence would ponder, as she decked the drum kit with yet more blooms. Arguably she was also re-creating her bedroom: Victoriana-tinged, gothic, crammed with paraphernalia and curiosities. Only this 'bedroom' had an invisible fourth wall with thousands of people staring through it.

"There's a Chinese dressing gown, a shawl, a chintzy lamp that we take around with a picture of the Virgin Mary…" she said. "At art college I was obsessed with making my environment like home. I think you should surround yourself with beautiful things, and have beautiful things to look at. I'm really obsessed with the way things look, and the positioning of stuff, like even on the stage and around me, I think you should always create an environment where you feel like, it's beautiful and romantic."

As for costumes, Florence just decided to bring everything she could and decide on outfits as the mood took her – but the bigger, and sparklier, the better was the general rule. She refused to plan anything, but one thing was for sure, it was going to be theatrical and it was going to be 'weird'. The first night saw Florence, with her face covered in glimmering gold leaf, attired in a spectacular but ultimately rather unwise wardrobe choice which was so heavy it caused her to sink into the crowd after a stage-dive. Florence romantically described this as her 'lady of the lake' moment. As well she might. She might have been a mere slip of a thing, but gravity was not on her side on this occasion.

"My friends come with me, it's always more fun when you go on tour with friends because it becomes a bit more like a road trip. One of my friends, her life revolves around dressing up, and she always brings this dressing-up chest with her," she said. "There was this amazing gold metal dress that went down to my feet."

And what did she do in this dress, which weighed a ton? "I stage-dived on the first night of the *NME* tour in the chain-mail dress," she guffawed to *Virgin*. What else?

"It was really heavy, and some guy cheekily tried to get a snog in and grabbed me, I was fending off a snog attack and trying to get back on top of the crowd."

Apparently she had gone into that stage-dive wearing lots of bracelets, all of which had disappeared by the time she'd reached the stage again. That's showbiz. But the feeling of being pushed back up by the audience was something that Florence was swiftly becoming addicted to. "You feel that everyone is in it together," said Florence.

"I'm a stage-dive specialist! When I was younger I used to go to punk gigs when I was 12, and I was always too scared to crowd-surf, so I feel like I'm having a renaissance, doing stuff I should have done."

Tips for those wishing to stage-dive? "You have to time it right. You can stand on the ledge where the crowd barrier is then fall forward, that's more like crowd-surfing, but sometimes you have to do a leap of faith, so there's the edge of the stage and then there's the crowd a bit further away – you've actually got to jump. Once I did a face downward stage-dive when I went head first into the crowd and they had to pull my feet out, it was more like a stage sink!"

The perpetually black-clad Glasvegas, who topped the *NME* bill, were described by Florence as "really nice, really tall..." She was a fan of their music, and enjoyed their company on tour, not least because, thanks to Glasvegas having a female drummer in Caroline McKay, it made the road experience that little bit less blokey and intimidating.

"It was our first proper experience of being on tour with a crew and everything," she later explained. "We really fucked ourselves, threw ourselves in head first, not much sleep, far too much vodka... but it was incredible and really nice to hang out with other bands and see the way other bands operate on tour."

It had been a good learning experience, but it took a while to recover – not that Florence would have much time to do that. On February 12, it was time to greet the world and appear at the *NME* Awards Show at Brixton Academy, a venue not far from Florence's old stamping ground of Camberwell.

She was on home turf for once, although the circumstances were, for her, unprecedented: she would gather her old friends from her early gigging days and sing with her childhood hero Jarvis Cocker – a heartthrob for her ever since she first heard Pulp in the nineties. She would also see her friend Pete Doherty pick up an award for Best Solo Artist, and she would smooch her contemporary Little Boots (Victoria Hesketh). A publicity stunt? A passive aggressive statement of dominance to a 'pop rival'? Not a bit of it, Florence insisted. She was just spreading the love... and alcohol may have been involved. But there has never been any outward evidence of Florence bitching about other female artists, so there is every reason to believe she was trying to show the world a bit of sisterly solidarity, albeit uninvited.

"I just did it to show that there's no love lost between young British female artists," she said. "I love them, and I love grabbing them and kissing them." Steady on. Sadly, a shocked Hesketh would insist that she had not consented to any lip-lockage. But it was all about the greater good.

"I was trying to make a statement," Florence continued. "We all love each other and we are all in this together. I'll kiss Elly [Jackson, La Roux] if that's what it takes." Amazingly, Florence managed to control herself when onstage with her old crush Jarvis Cocker.

"I sang 'Underwear' with him. I'm surprised I managed to stay standing. It was this collaborations gig we did for the *NME*. I got Patrick Wolf to come and play with me and Kid Harpoon and Jack Penate. On a whim I thought, 'Let's ask Jarvis Cocker.' I never thought he would do it but he said yes!"

Florence's power was evidently growing… and her nervousness was increasing. The Brit Awards ceremony was just six days later, but, excited as she was, Florence was also suffering bouts of listlessness.

"I regressed into being a total moody teenager [after the tour], refusing to talk to anyone and just going 'I'm sooooo tired'. And being really afraid of what was about to happen." Might that 'moody teenagerism' have had anything to do with missing a certain person? Rumours swirled during the tour that Florence and Glasvegas' toothsome singer James Allan enjoyed a bit of a liaison while on the road, but you know what they say: what goes on tour, stays on tour. We might never really know the truth.

What we do know is that they certainly got on, with Allan going so far as to say he found Florence of the tuxedo top and sparkly hot pants, "so special, such a good laugh". They also displayed tremendous onstage chemistry when they'd duetted together during the show, singing Elvis Presley's brooding 'Suspicious Minds', during which Florence even managed to persuade James to remove his sunglasses, which are otherwise seemingly surgically attached to his face.

"James chose that song," said Florence. "I think he's got a real Elvis thing. And for a song like that you need a bit of eye contact." Indeed. They sang the song in a way so meaningful that it set the audience's tongues a-wagging, and then Florence hopped on James' back and they piggybacked off. So whether her grumpy attitude and lack of enthusiasm for the future were anything to do with being estranged from her new chum, we don't know. But what we do know is that she had to pull herself together for the Brits.

During a round of press interviews around this time, the BBC, noting that her star was on the ascendant, thought it would be prudent to ask whether, at this stage, Florence really was ready to be a pop star – it seemed inevitable that it was going to happen, but was it what Florence wanted? "Um… yeah, why not?" she answered with a nervous chuckle. "Might as well."

# CHAPTER EIGHT

*"The Critic's Choice thing was pretty big. I got that before I released any albums, it was terrifying! Like, 'Yeah, I hope I make a good album too!'"*

While Florence was as ready as she'd ever be for the Brits, she couldn't help but feel a little unsettled. Like Adele before her, she hadn't even released her first album yet, and although that was the point of the Critic's Choice award – to push an artist who was emerging and had not yet put out their debut LP – Florence didn't feel ready to be shoved into the mainstream international spotlight just yet.

"I was still working out what sound I wanted," she later recalled. "Still figuring out how to hold myself in the public eye."

However, she hid her fears well and strode out onto the red carpet before the relentless snapping of the paparazzi and the shrieking pop fans, bangles and cuffs a-jangling, black nail polish and a full face of war-paint. Florence might have been dressing for attention and success, but the truth was that she felt gangly, awkward and bemused, and of course, thrilled, by the whole phenomenon. She was as excited to meet Peter Andre as she was Lady Gaga, she wasn't just interested in hanging out with the 'cool' set. All of this was, of course, just a preview of the fame and accolades that were to come.

"I disgraced myself," she blushed. "I was completely shocked. I stood up and walked to the stage, and there was Kylie Minogue. I said, 'Oh fuck, it's Kylie,' live on TV. I felt a total idiot. I also felt like a freak standing next to her. I'm nearly 6ft, big and gangly, she's about 5ft, tiny and perfect. It was all a bit crazy.

"I got the award, couldn't look at anyone, just reeled off a load of names. I felt so humbled, I hadn't even finished the album, and I felt like I should say thank you to everyone who'd supported me. I didn't feel like it was for me, it was for everyone who'd championed me. And then I cried and walked off as quickly as I could.

"I felt so out of my depth, like I didn't belong. Take That were coming down in a spaceship, Girls Aloud were doing a burlesque show and there was me, shaking… I went backstage and just burst into tears afterwards."

But it's moments like these, when a 'star' suddenly shows their vulnerability in a situation like this, when ordinarily complete poise is the order of the day, that are all the more endearing to fans.

One fan, Oskar Kirk Hansen, a member of fan club the Florence + The Machine Army, admits the Critic's Choice acceptance 'speech' is his all-time favourite Flo moment. "The first thing she said after being handed the award? 'Fuck! Er, fuck!' She was a new artist who was suddenly receiving an award from Kylie Minogue in front of thousands of people, and it must have been an overpowering moment for her. But she wasn't afraid to say what she thought. And that's why I love her."

There's nothing like family, of course, to level things out and keep one's feet on terra firma once the glamour and excitement of the Brit Awards ceremony had died down and normal service had resumed. Florence thought it would be amusing to put her Brit in the toilet (not *in* the toilet, obviously – that really would be self-deprecating) but her amusement soon faded when she realised that her family had found a practical use for it: its long, slim shape made for a nifty toilet-roll holder.

"Thanks guys!" laughed Florence. "So I moved it into the kitchen. I came in the other day and saw my little brother had his friends round in the kitchen, they'd just finished their exams, and they were all in there running around with it making pretend acceptance speeches.

"I was like, 'Hey, what are you doing?' My little brother JJ had been taking them on a tour of my room...I was like, is this some kind of racket?"

Florence's family had different ways of dealing with how her skyrocketing success was affecting them. "JJ thinks it's all pretty cool," Nick Welch wrote of his son in a piece he authored for *The Daily Mail*. JJ was 15, and Florence's life gave him instant street cred, not to mention possible access to famous people. Admittedly, at this point, JJ was more interested in how his connection to pop star Florence could help him talk to girls.

It wasn't quite so simple for the rest of the family. Grace was studying at Sussex University during these incredible early years, so she at least had some space from what Nick described as the "all-embracing tsunami that Florence's life has become".

"The fact that Florence has become public property can invade one's life and conversation," Nick admitted. "We do have evenings within her extended family where all mention of the 'daffy diva', as I call her sometimes, is forbidden."

It must still be hard for anything that is going on within the family of any pop star not to be eclipsed by the more obvious 'big story' that will run and run, and despite the obvious pride the Welches must feel, they are right to do their best not to let it throw the balance of their family life. But back to the, er, 'daffy diva' with us... There's a debut album to finish, after all.

Unlike the other Brit Award categories, the Critic's Choice honour, whether kept in the WC or otherwise, was not just a reward for work well done so far, but an expectation of great things to come, and there was still plenty of work to do on the album, which was due to be released that summer. There were yet more ideas to realise and the right producer needed to be brought into the picture to shape the work Florence and Isabella had been developing.

Despite her frequent attacks of the fear, Florence has always been a great example of someone who knows how to go with the flow, who is often in the right place at the right time and doesn't plan too much – and it was thanks to this ultimately rather relaxed approach that she discovered someone who would play a vital role in her career going forward. Just a few weeks before the tour, Florence had been invited to attend a recording session by Jamie T, who was putting together his 2009 album *Kings And Queens*, and, while she was in the studio, she stepped up to provide some backing vocals for one of the tracks. Jamie and Florence had crossed paths many times over the years, so it was significant and exciting that these two ragamuffins from the London pub circuit were now doing so well.

"One of my first-ever gigs was an open mic just after he played," Florence recalls. "I was drunk and walked up and sang and clapped my hands, and that was it. I didn't really have any words planned. I used to go see Jamie play when it was just him and a guitar, and he came and saw me play when it was just me and a guitar. He is really nice."

The resulting Jamie T song which Florence contributed to may have ended up on the proverbial cutting room floor, but Florence would get something far more lasting out of this impromptu collaboration: an introduction to the producer Paul Epworth.

"A lot of the songs were demoed and then taken to James Ford and Paul," explained Florence. "We wanted something really – boom – epic." They went to the right place for that.

Paul Epworth was something of a production wunderkind. He'd worked with Doors collaborator Bruce Botnick and the legendary Beatles producer George Martin. Crucially, Epworth was obsessed with getting the right drum sound, something Florence had in common. "[Botnick] taught me about making drum sounds that were exciting," said Epworth. "I never forgot it, the tricks he taught me I still use today.

"Many years ago [Bruce Botnick] taught me something the old Stax drummers used to do, which was to detune the snare really low and then stick a wallet on it," Epworth reminisced. "I think part of it was that because you couldn't have the kick drum very loud on those cuts, the main part of the rhythm was the snare drum, so the snare drum had to be big and heavy and push the groove. I remember him saying to me that the guy who had the heaviest snare drum was the guy who had the heaviest wallet because he was doing the most gigs! So there was a little bit of one-upmanship there."

Epworth had previously worked his magic on music by artists such as the Arctic Monkeys and Bloc Party, and he remembers Florence impressing him from the off. He also witnessed how powerfully music took her over, often to the detriment of the track. At the Jamie T session Epworth had to repeatedly ask her to stop stamping her feet while she was singing, as it was coming out on the recording and resulting in them having to record take after take. In his words, "She was clopping around like a horse."

'Cosmic Love' was the first *Lungs* track Paul Epworth and Florence worked on together. "When it came to Paul, he was trying to create a big sound around it," said Florence "I like the sound of recording on quite shitty microphones and bad computers, but sometimes it can get quite claustrophobic, so I was really looking for some air with the music and to make it sound like you were going into space!

"We used quite a lot of electronics and lots of weird vocals, and put some firework samples at the end. It's an organic song, but done with a lot of electronic atmosphere. It's got a lot of spark to it and electricity, and I think that's what that song should have – an electric feel! I always had this idea for a really big sound coming from all that clatter, and he managed to capture that on record in the best way."

Indeed, the success of how 'Cosmic Love' turned out convinced Florence that she wanted Epworth to work on the whole album, and thanks to his inclusion on Team Flo, Florence was able to realise another dream: to fill out the sound and make it slicker and more atmospheric. Up to now, she had affectionately described Florence + The Machine as a "highly creative collective all trying things out and clattering along together".

Epworth was in charge of pulling everything into a cohesive whole and pushing this group into an entirely new league. He was very much of the same mind – brain off, heart on – and he too was excited about trying musical ideas in new contexts. Soon Florence found herself recording not only in big, rather intimidating studios (in comparison to Isa's Shed) but also in abandoned synagogues, old swimming pools, studio kitchens… Florence loved hearing her voice bouncing around the walls of such acoustically interesting and untypical sites, and she would spend many hours layering up her voice to create the choral effect she wanted.

"I think it came from not being able to play many instruments," she confessed. "When it came to do the vocals the only thing I'd have at my disposal was creating these kind of choral vocals. It was so exciting to be able to create these soundscapes with my voice, you can build up these huge elaborate symphonies with your voice."

Plenty of time was spent at Epworth's small studio in Kensal Rise, West London, with just a Ludwig drum kit, a piano, two guitar amps, two sets of speakers, an array of keyboards, and samplers. The studio was originally taken on simply for use as a writing room several years before but, as he explained, "The nature of the work changed and we've acquired more gear, which is why it's so cluttered. Luckily, a lot of the more recent work I've been doing has been artists on their own, so there's little need to go into bigger studios."

Because the space was so limited, there was barely room for more than four people, and that intimacy was perfect for Florence. "It feels like a musician's environment, not a technical studio environment," continues Paul. "I would much rather create a record that's exciting, that feels good to listen to and also make, than strive for superiority with a need to use talkback systems or walking back and forth through a set of doors to communicate.

"[With Florence] we went, 'Let's make a noise-rock record like Crystal Castles or Fuck Buttons. Like a noise-rock band making a pagan record! Her playing drums and me programming beats and getting drums around it, or the reverse process, looking for a few key chord arrangements, lots of old circuit-bent keyboards. Just to be able to use audio creatively like a musician is something very useful.

"I had Florence singing into these old cheap samplers, most of the tracks we did we used field recordings in the background. I had her singing through circuit-bent equipment, we had out of tune honky-tonk pianos, we used all sorts of things. There's a very high-end technical approach to it and then there's the lo-fi… and Florence, the hardest thing with her is, she sings like it's the last thing she will ever do! She doesn't sing as loud as you might imagine, it's something about the feeling in her voice cuts through everything, you can actually hear her singing through a couple of soundproof walls!"

And as for his take on Florence? He couldn't believe her ability to bring even hardened studio engineers to tears with her voice. "I remember looking round at my engineer when she was singing and he was wiping his eyes! She's totally connected to that source that Frank Zappa talked about, the music's there, you just plug in, she's like 63 amps just plugged straight in. She's a total livewire and great fun to work with."

For Florence's part, she had already concluded that Paul Epworth was "a shaman. He's half spiritual guru and half lad. We got Indian headdresses from Soho fancy-dress shops, and I'd turn up in a big velvet cape and some chain-mail. He's got a studio full of deer heads and skull candles, and he really loves wolves." Just a normal day at the office...

More songs were being added to the *Lungs* pantheon, one of which was 'Howl', a primal, gothically visceral and very Florence song about being so madly in love with somebody that you become, in Florence's words, "like a beast, you want to possess them and you're possessed by that". The imagery of 'Howl' also conjures memories of Florence's morbid fascination with things that go bump in the night – werewolves, specifically.

"I still have to sleep with a light on. When I was a kid I used to draw crosses on my wall because I was convinced something was going to come and get me, that my parents were werewolves... troubled child!" All good songwriting fodder.

'Rabbit Heart', written towards the end of the album process, was just as elemental, redolent of a young girl coming of age, of racing hormones, of a springtime of the female soul, shining a light on what you stand to lose when you gain something special and unique – the "gift that comes with a price", as the lyrics go. But largely Florence was, with 'Rabbit Heart', trying to express how hard it could be, standing on the cusp of stardom, having the awareness that everything was about to change – and feeling far from brave.

"In this life you give up privacy, you give up your space, and almost a part of yourself, and you have to figure out why you're doing it," Florence explains of 'Rabbit Heart'. "It's a gift, it's amazing to do this, it's such an opportunity but you do sacrifice things as well and I was coming to terms with it in this song. It was a song to make me feel braver about the situation. Questioning I think."

The 'rabbit-hearted' quality Florence sings of was very real to her; far from feeling 'lion-hearted' about her quest, about the year ahead and the album she was creating, she felt scared and overwhelmed. Little did many people realise when they listened to 'Rabbit Heart' that these feelings of being 'frozen in the headlights' were very real, often paralysing, and would frequently wake her up at night.

"I don't think I could have felt any more pressured than I did on the first record," Florence would later tell BBC 6Music DJ Steve Lamacq. "It was my first experience of that, making my first record, and my first experience of press and media attention and it's all so frightening." One can only hope Florence has learned to enjoy it at least a little more, as the attention and adulation goes on unabated.

The video to 'Rabbit Heart' – which views like an, again, slightly pagan, elemental bacchanal – had rather higher production values than that of its predecessor for 'Dog Days Are Over': there would be catering, a choreographer, a food stylist and a grand total of 52 people on set, although it crucially retained directors Tabitha Denholm and Tom Beard at the helm, who injected a dose of *The Wicker Man* mingled with a pre-Raphaelite aesthetic into the proceedings. As always, it was all about "beauty and sadness" for Florence. Those were her core inspirations emotionally, and the pre-Raphaelites certainly had those qualities nailed.

"It's things that are beautiful and sad... like 'the model for Millais' Ophelia who [contracted] pneumonia from modelling in the bathtub, Lizzie Siddal. It's a really great back-story to that – she was like a muse for a lot of the pre-Raphaelites and they were all really into lithium, and she was doped up in the bath and the candle went out and she didn't want to move because he was so into his painting, and she got pneumonia." (Siddal later died, apparently of an overdose of laudanum.)

Home is where the heart is—Florence at the family home in Camberwell, where, at the time of writing, she still lives. *REX FEATURES*

An early shot of Florence (and her trusty drum) at the Camden Crawl, April 2008. LOLA PEACH/RETNA PICTURES

Florence + The Machine open for Courtney Love at the Bush Hall, west London in July 2007. Love was suitably impressed: "I played with her in London and she handed me my ass." WILLIAM E SHARP/RETNA PICTURES

One of Florence's famous stage-dives. This one took place at the O2 Academy, Birmingham on February 4, 2009 during the notorious Shockwaves NME Awards Tour. ANDY SHEPPARD/REDFERNS/GETTY IMAGES

Florence and Dizzee Rascal at the 30th Brit Awards ceremony at Earls Court, London, February 16, 2010, after performing their hotly-anticipated mash-up duet 'You've Got The Dirtee Love'. SUZANNE PLUNKETT/REUTERS/CORBIS

Florence Welch dazzles in the press room at the Brit Awards, Earls Court.

Mark Saunders, bassist with Florence + The Machine, during a gig in France in November 2009. DALLE/RETNA PICTUR

Tom Monger, harpist with Florence + The Machine, performs live with the group at Rough Trade, London, in July 2009, the same month that their debut album, *Lungs*, was released. JUSTIN DE DENEY/RETNA PICTURES

orence + The Machine rock Glastonbury Festival's Other Stage in 2010. Florence, clad in Maison Margiela, effortlessly drew not only the biggest crowd of the day, but also the biggest in the history of the Other Stage.

MARC LARKIN/LFI

nervy-looking Flo attends the announcement of the Brit Award nominations shortlist at the Round-house, London on January 20, 2009. Florence would receive the Critics' Choice award at the ceremony e following month. DAVE HOGAN/GETTY IMAGES

Florence poses at the Barclaycard Mercury Prize nominations, 2009 at the Hospital Club, London. (The winner would be rapper Speech Debelle). BRIAN RASIC/REX FEATURES

rence proudly holds aloft her Q Award at rosvenor House, London, 2010. DAVE HOGAN/GETTY IMAGES

Florence conjures up some magic of her own at the Voodoo Festival, New Orleans on October 30, 2010. It During this trip Florence broke into a graveyard. It was Halloween, after all. CHRIS SCHWEGLER/RETNA LTD/CORBIS

Florence channels her inner Loïe Fuller at the Hurricane Festival, Scheesel, Germany in June 2C

Thankfully Denholm and Beard, who have their own production company called Partizan, had steered clear of the lithium and no such risks would be taken. However, they too were inspired by Renaissance romanticism and were without a doubt the perfect people to direct Florence's videos. Friendship aside, their vision was absolutely in tune with Florence's, which made the unit, in Painshill Park, Surrey, an exciting place to be. And again, the promo was replete with a veritable mess of characters and a rich swirl of imagery, which includes a voluptuous banquet Henry VIII would be proud of. Minimalist it ain't.

"I like clutter and I'm quite visually greedy," said Florence. "I can't have things to be plain; I have to have things looking interesting ... maybe I'm just a frustrated interior designer stuck in a singing career. I've always been a bit of a decorator. I think if I wasn't a singer I'd probably be in stage setting or interior design or something."

The concept for the video was based on the Czech art film *Valerie's Week Of Wonders*. "It's amazing," Florence enthused. "It's basically about this girl having her period. She wanders around these woods in a white dress, and there are these men in black cloaks and women in white dresses, kind of sacrificial and weird."

The sacrificial element was certainly represented in the decadent, indulgent video for 'Rabbit Heart' – by the end of it, Florence is drifting away prettily on a lake in a flower-bedecked coffin as her chorus look on wistfully. This must have been like Christmas for Florence, acting out her most dramatic girlhood fantasies. But this was a long way from climbing the mulberry tree in Camberwell near her childhood home, playing 'Little House On The Prairie' with her little sister, Grace, or swirling around in the privacy of her bedroom in antique robes to music. Her play-acting, flights of fancy and 'dress-up' sessions would now be viewed by the critical, and in many cases worshipful, eyes of the record-buying public. The world was watching – and listening.

May 2009 saw the Radio 1 Big Weekend take place in Swindon, just a month before the release of *Lungs*. Florence + The Machine had to screw up their nerves, try to forget how rusty they felt after months in the studio and take to the stage, revealing some of the newer tracks on *Lungs* to thousands of people. They needn't have worried.

"It was quite a nerve-racking experience because I hadn't played the new stuff on the record before, except once at a club gig," Florence admitted. "We rehearsed as much as we possibly could but there's still a lot we need to work on. It was fun, but it was strange to not have played for ages because of recording and to then go from that to playing live in front of 6,000 people. I introduced the new stuff by telling the crowd, 'This is a new song... hope you like it' instead of just barraging them with lots of stuff. It seemed to go down pretty well!"

# CHAPTER NINE

*"I feel like I could go back to Camberwell and hand them the album and go, 'This is my project, can I have my degree please?'"*

The track 'Rabbit Heart (Raise It Up)' was released on June 22, 2009, the third single from *Lungs*. The album itself would be released a fortnight later on July 6, and within a week it would be certified a gold album. Not bad for a debut from a "rabbit-hearted girl", although Florence didn't exactly feel she was taking the process in her stride.

"It's a scary time, I'm nervous, I'm putting an album out there, it's like putting your baby up to be judged. It's like someone's gonna go: 'It's a fucking ugly baby.'"

"The release was so hard," Florence later confessed. "It was terrifying, because it was the first time doing everything. The first experiences of media exposure were almost paralysing. I spent a lot of time crying on the floor of the studio – it sent me a bit mad."

But, while Florence quaked in her room or had meltdowns in the studio, the album was swiftly capturing hearts the world over, from the very first track to the romantic artwork courtesy of Tabitha Denholm (and Flo herself), which featured an image of Florence looking suitably pre-Raphaelite and contemplative on the cover, her chain-mail top revealing that pair of red, gleaming lungs created for her by Maccabees frontman and fellow art student Orlando Weeks.

Existing fans thought the album was just about perfect – and new admirers were popping up all the time. Little did Florence know that, just as she used to take refuge in Billie Holiday and Etta James when she felt unhappy, thousands of people were doing exactly the same thing with *Lungs*. It's hard for those who are not Flo-heads to understand, but the effect she and her music with the Machine has had on hearts and minds the world over since the release of this album cannot be overestimated.

"I've had people tell me that they were going through a hard time and found comfort in the Florence album," says harpist Tom Monger.

Tom's only beef with the response was that some reviewers seemed to miss the fact that there was a harp on the album at all – the instrument was somehow referred to as a ukulele, a banjo, a piano... still, how Florence fanatics felt about the eventual product made it all worthwhile, and pushed any harp-related ignorance aside. "To have been part of something that does that for others is a wonderful thing."

Fan Emily Hussey puts it into words: "I've loved Florence + The Machine since I first bought *Lungs* in 2009. Whenever I've been feeling sad or upset, I'd just listen to 'Dog Days Are Over' to make me feel better. Just listening to the emotion she puts into her songs almost makes me feel like I'm feeling these emotions with her. Florence + The Machine's songs have had such an influence on me."

Fellow fan Shannon Lafferty shares these feelings. "As Florence once said, 'My music doesn't get stuck in your head, it gets stuck in your soul.' I believe that entirely and I agree. I find myself writing down the lyrics to Florence's songs whenever I'm happy or sad. Florence Welch taught me not to care about what anyone else thinks of me and to be my own person. She also taught me that we only live once, [so] we should make the most of life. Florence is such a great idol to look up to and her and the band's music gets me through any situation that I find hard."

So the fans were hooked, the record company was thrilled and Florence was, frankly, stunned. But while, with the exception of the temporary controversy surrounding 'Kiss With A Fist', Florence had managed to steer clear of scandal, the release of the single 'Rabbit Heart' itself would not be entirely straightforward.

It came to the attention of New York group Gang Gang Dance that part of the melody of 'Rabbit Heart' was strikingly familiar. It appeared that a sample of their 2008 tune 'House Jam' had been used, and also one of the song's lyrics, 'how quickly the glimmer fades' (in 'Rabbit Heart' it was changed to 'how quickly the glamour fades'), was a little too close for comfort in terms of similarity. There was no credit given to Gang Gang Dance in *Lungs*' liner notes, but, understandably due to the amount of radio play the track received, it did not escape their notice.

Island Records acknowledged infringement and agreed to pay Gang Gang Dance a share of the royalties, and Florence, for her part, accepted that a mistake had occurred and that she had simply wished to pay tribute to the group with the sample.

"Yeah, that's true, it's no secret," she said. "I've spoken about it in interviews before. I'm a massive fan of Gang Gang Dance and it was in homage to them."

The problem was the band hadn't been able to find any of the interviews in which they had been acknowledged. "I don't really have a problem with people wearing their influences on their sleeve. If she would have mentioned it in the beginning in the press, which we never saw, that would have definitely made a difference," Gang Gang Dance singer Liz Bougatsos told the website *Drowned In Sound*. "And if she was speaking of an homage at that point, that would have helped as well." However, Gang Gang Dance were happy with Florence's apology and, no doubt, the royalties Island agreed to share with them.

Just days after the release of 'Rabbit Heart', Florence + The Machine were preparing for two important gigs – one of which, of course, was Glastonbury 2009. But the day before Florence's Glasto appearance, she and her band appeared, along with Klaxons, in the support slot for Blur's big comeback gig at the MEN Arena in Manchester. Florence was already riding high, but this was a chance to convert a new audience to the Welch experience. It was also an opportunity for Flo and co to be converted to the Blur experience, not that harpist Tom needed much persuading.

"I liked Blur back in the day," he said. "The last time I'd seen them was playing Ipswich Corn Exchange in 1994, round about the time *Parklife* came out and just before they went absolutely supernova. So to go from that as my last memory of seeing Blur live, up to seeing them in the Manchester Arena, was amazing."

Florence was inclined to agree. "I didn't realise how big a fan of Blur I was until supported them at Manchester. I saw them and Klaxons and they were amazing. And Blur, you don't realise how much their music has affected you through your life until you see them. My favourite song of theirs is 'Beetlebum'."

The feeling was clearly mutual, as Florence went on to support the band at Hyde Park, just after the release of *Lungs* the following month – and the gig was memorable not just because of the sheer scale of the concert, the sea of faces and the sense of playing at the very heart of sweltering, summery London (it was so hot, in fact, that Florence had had to pour water on her own feet in bed the night before), but because the elements, appropriately, were on her side.

"There was a moment when the sun came out and the wind started to blow, it was like having the best special effects ever," she laughed. "You guys up there are doing a really good job! I love performing outside because it's as if the heavens are open and the elements become part of the stage show as well – you know, the wind and the rain and the thunder. It's almost as if there's a sense of invocation in performance."

There was certainly magic in the air, and life was sweet, not least because she and Stuart, her literary agent boyfriend from whom she had split during the making of the album, were reunited. Wonderful news, of course, but not a little awkward considering most of the songs on *Lungs* were written about him. Florence vowed never to speak about their relationship in the press, but the way she felt about him and the temporary break-up was plain to see if you listened to her lyrics, and he couldn't turn on the radio or walk into a shop without being blasted with yet another reminder of their previous split. However, they were in a different place now, even if Florence's constant travelling was not easy to cope with, and it wasn't just the absences that proved a challenge. Stuart occasionally had the opportunity to travel with Florence on tour, but he'd have to get used to 'touring Florence' as opposed to the 'home Florence' he was used to.

"It's quite hard, because you sort of work out a way of surviving on tour, don't you?" said Florence. "Be it through endless vintage-clothes shopping or endless shots of tequila. There are various coping mechanisms that you turn to. When Stuart arrives on tour, it's almost as if you have to be like, 'Darling, now this is what I've been doing to cope. I know you might think it's strange, but please can you handle it? Because this is what I'm going to be doing a lot...'

"Like any relationship, we have to work at things. I get worried when I go off on tour and then come back home. This business is so chaotic that it's easy to lose your bearings."

Not only was it easy to lose one's bearings, but it was even more easy to lose one's belongings – and other people's. On one occasion Florence was handed Mairead's mobile phone, and within a matter of minutes she became distracted and misplaced it. It's no wonder that Florence soon employed her little sister, Grace, as a part-time assistant and all-round moral supporter; just before Glastonbury, Florence was devastated to find that her suitcase, containing rather more than just some undies and a toothbrush, had gone missing on her way back from Athens.

"It contained all of my best clothes – shoes, jackets and jewellery," she lamented. "Now I'm going to have to start all over again. I know these things happen, but I've never lost so much stuff in one go. My life is sometimes too chaotic. Then again, I've never been very good at organising myself."

But, as Florence would later wryly observe, one of her favourite things about her life as a pop star is that, now at least, she doesn't have to worry about things like this any more. It's someone else's responsibility. "What's handy about the way I live is that lots of people organise things for you..." Handy indeed. But Florence was still staggered by the sheer amount of touring she suddenly had to do, and the logistics involved. She loved her job, there was no two ways about it, and was always quick to express how grateful and appreciative she is to be in such a privileged position. But still, when she was first starting out as a singer, she hadn't accounted for the amount of work she would have to do beyond writing songs and performing them.

"I think maybe I was quite naive about the amount of touring and gigging. When I looked at it on paper I was like, are you fucking serious?" she said. "I don't think you really realise how much you can do until you do it. There is no tour manager for your real life. So it can be quite odd. I used to be really excited about the idea of a tour bus but they are horrible. You can't share a bus with sweaty boys." Heaven forbid!

But sweaty boys and horrid tour buses (which, hopefully, became progressively less horrid the more successful she ultimately became) were not the only things to be considered. "You do a lot more press and work with publicists who are getting you out there," she continued. "With a major label you have to be willing to put in the work. You sing, but then you also have to be really committed to doing work beyond that." Take note, pop wannabes.

It was time for Florence + The Machine to head down to the West Country to the heaving, pulsing, Technicolor camp-site-turned-mudbath that is Glastonbury. Florence had appeared there twice before, but this year her performance would be a career-defining moment.

Her first appearance in 2007 saw Florence, complete with scuffed knees ("Who takes on a power-slide without trousers on of any kind?") take the Tiny Tea Tent stage at 11am and it was memorable for all the wrong reasons. She hadn't slept for two days and she was tearful and tense, not least because her guitarist had disappeared.

Thankfully, Madness singer Suggs noticed what was going on and told her not to worry, he'd handle it. A knight in shining armour indeed. Or rather, a knight in a comedy wig... Yes, apparently an "amazingly weird Mick Jagger impression" was the solution to this problem, complete with singing and a dance routine. All to buy Florence time. What a gent.

"That was pretty harsh," she told *The Daily Mail*'s Adrian Thrills. "I was still a bit hungover when I went onstage. To buy me some time, Suggs from Madness dressed up in a Mick Jagger wig and gave me a long, rambling introduction. In the end, I had to play the first half of the show unaccompanied. My guitarist eventually waded onstage, 30 minutes late, completely covered in mud."

By this time, Florence had already burst into tears, and her shame-faced guitarist attracted a chorus of boos when he finally did appear.

"My guitarist was in such a rage, I've never heard a crowd go from a boo to a 'yeah!' so quickly!" she added with a giggle. "They looked at him and saw the face on this guy and literally went 'boooOOOYEAAAH! You're here, amazing!' And then he got on the stage and all his guitar strings broke, he threw the guitar away... it was a festival moment. But Suggs, what a guy."

No doubt harpist extraordinaire Tom would have loved to be on that gig, although sadly it was a little before his time in the Machine – he credits Madness with changing his musical vision "from black and white to glorious Technicolor".

"It was 'Our House'," he recalled. "On the strength of me getting the single for Christmas, my dad went out and bought the album *The Rise & Fall* – which is a bit like Madness going slightly psychedelic. None of this 'Baggy Trousers' or 'House Of Fun' stuff; it was a little bit more bizarre than that. I just thought it was fantastic.

"I hadn't really listened to much pop music; it had been folk and classical – and the stuff I'd been listening to had been very straight. I think some of the folk artists I'd listened to had a touch of experimentation, but nothing in the way that this Madness album showed me what you could do in a recording studio."

Florence's sophomore Glasto appearance was more ceremonious – she had already attracted plenty of attention thanks to the recent release of 'Kiss With A Fist', and the crowd greeted a joyous Florence (clad in a clown outfit) and her ever-expanding Machine. So her third Glastonbury foray in 2009 was bound to be even greater. Florence adored the festival at Worthy Farm, Somerset, and admitted she often chanted 'Pyramid Stage, Pyramid Stage' in a bid to psychically secure herself a slot on the ultimate stage at the event. At the time of writing, this remains a dream...

So, no Pyramid this time, but Florence + The Machine took the respected John Peel Stage; Flo sporting a stunning bodysuit designed especially for her (with her input) by TopShop Unique, all roses and fringing. It was perfect for her highly kinetic stage performance.

"She's a born showgirl," said Topshop's head designer, Jacqui Markham. "She has a natural playfulness and innate quirkiness about her." Ever ahead of the curve, TopShop had Florence pegged as a style superstar before *Lungs* had even been released.

Florence had the audience rapt, *NME* described the experience as spellbinding, and everyone was talking about her version of 'You Got The Love', which she performed onstage at the same time as Kasabian sang their own cover of the song over on the Pyramid Stage.

Harpist Tom Monger was just blown away by the roar of the crowd. Glastonbury was a watershed for Florence + The Machine in terms of the sheer volume of adulation being beamed towards them. "We did 'Dog Days Are Over' and the crowd went ballistic," he remembers. "There are days when you think 'Hold on a sec; what's going on here?!' It is quite surreal at times. It's easy to be blasé about it, I suppose, but, then, when someone goes absolutely ape . . . it's nice."

"The atmosphere…" Florence recalled. "All those people singing along, and being on the John Peel Stage was a real dream for me. The album was coming out in a few weeks and I was really nervous but there was so much joy in that tent! It was an incredible feeling, I came off and I was absolutely walking on air.... So to go from there [the Tiny Tea Tent] to stepping out on the John Peel stage was like, 'Wow, this is real!' It's great to hear people singing back at you, like, 'Great, I'm not just abusing you with my songs!'" Meanwhile, *Lungs*, which had debuted at number two in the album charts, was to stay there for five weeks.

This particular Glastonbury was also memorable for another reason. There was a rumour circulating the gargantuan campsite that the undisputed King of Pop, Michael Jackson, had died from a drug overdose. Nobody could believe it at first, but soon it became clear that this tragic news was more than just hearsay. The collective feeling of sadness for Jackson was almost tangible, and his music was celebrated right across the site, as it was across the world, loudly. And in the twinkling of an eye, *The Essential Michael Jackson* album had shot straight to the top of the charts as people gorged themselves on his unique brand of soul-pop.

T In The Park up in Scotland was next on the Flo-genda, before the team flew out to Ireland for Oxegen festival, and after checking out Lady Gaga ("So tough and sexy… and a great bum," appraised Florence) and catching up with Katy Perry ("Such a sweet girl"), Florence was inevitably bombarded by questions from the media about how *Lungs* had been kept from the top of the album charts by *The Essential Michael Jackson*. Of course, Florence was simply thrilled that her album was as high in the charts as it was, she reiterated that she had not gone into music for chart positions and accolades, and besides, if you're going to be kept back at number two by anyone, it doesn't get much bigger than Michael Jackson.

"It was quite strange to be in the same chart as Michael Jackson, I would never have thought that would happen," she marvelled later. "I just was happy to have made an album and have it released, but to be just behind MJ, if someone had told me that would happen, I'd be like, 'What?'"

But like everyone else, Florence was shocked and saddened by the loss of one of the most seminal, and certainly most troubled, artists in pop. Florence admired his writing, and like him, strove to connect with others through her deeply personal lyrics.

As one former music industry executive who worked with Florence observed, "Florence inspires a very personal kind of response. It's not so much 'I fancy this person' or 'I want to be like this person' but more 'This person is speaking to me, articulating how I feel, thoughts that I've had.'"

There was no doubt that Florence's growing army of fans were keenly appreciative of how she seemed to set their feelings to music, and express emotions they'd felt themselves, but hadn't known how to put into words. Needless to say, the power of music is not to be underestimated when it comes to soothing the troubled beast.

Once the Glasto milestone had been ticked off, Florence, her band, management and friends could focus on something a little closer to home – the release party of *Lungs*. This meant costumes, stage-settings, garlands, bird cages (the original logo of the band – Florence has a bird-cage tattoo on her finger in honour of it) and Bumble and Bumble hair treatments to keep those famous red locks gleaming.

It had been decided that the launch would be held at the Rivoli Ballroom in Brockley, South East London, a place more often used for tea-dances than pop gigs. It had the perfect vintage feel.

"The Rivoli Ballroom in Brockley is an old gin palace, it's such a beautiful venue," Florence said on the day of the gig. "I like to bring a sense of drama or occasion to the gigs. I can get quite carried away! Tonight I've got this amazing old lace thing to wear, huge bell sleeves and a flowing train, might suit it!"

She was in close and constant contact with friend and *Vice* magazine fashion editor Aldene Johnson, who had been put in charge of her bursting wardrobe. "I just spoke to her on the phone," she gushed breathlessly. "[My wardrobe] is kind of a mix of disco and glitter, Age of Aquarius, and then it goes all the way to Madonna, black lace, death crow vibes! I've got a chain-mail headdress at home, I look good in chain-mail." Hold it right there, Florence, remember the 'lady of the lake' moment in Liverpool?

However, it didn't seem to matter how exciting life became, Florence's dark side always reined her in. Hopefully she had managed, with the help of Mairead and her friends, to keep the demons that threatened to sabotage her successes under control but, like so many artists, she still feared that, the higher her star rose, the more likely it was that she was going to come crashing down, or simply that she couldn't cope with the whirlwind velocity of the music business merry-go-round she'd found herself grafted onto. It certainly had its plusses, but no one could blame Florence for feeling overwhelmed.

"Yesterday I was coming home after an in-store gig and there was an amazing installation that said 'The Darkest Hour Is The Hour Before The Dawn' with loads of silver bunting, somewhere in East London. I felt like that yesterday, I felt like it was all getting on top of me, like, 'Oh, it's like a train and I can't get off!'"

Mike Walsh, XFM: "When the record was delivered to us by the label, we just thought, 'Yeah, this is really special.' Even then, I'd have to say, even then we had the feeling of 'This could be a million seller', and I've only ever felt that very strongly three times in the six or seven years I've been at XFM where the very early listens of an album you go 'There is no ceiling on this record's potential.' Florence was one, Adele was another, and Mumford and Sons."

Walsh's instincts were correct. *Lungs*, already at number two in the UK album charts, had sold over 100,000 copies in the UK within a matter of weeks. The fiery 'Drumming Song' and 'You Got The Love' were released as singles soon after, and a packed summer of festivals was already under way.

Florence always loved festivals, whether she was playing at them or not, and as the summers went by, she found herself rising higher and higher up the bill. But for Florence, while this was naturally gratifying, she was always going to have a good time, whether she was top of the bill or not. "Festivals are really fun," she said. "You get to play and then see other bands and run around together. It's like going to summer camp!"

For the first time, Florence would celebrate her birthday weekend as a bona fide pop star at the Reading and Leeds festivals, and this time the crowd that crammed itself into the *NME*/Radio 1 tent numbered more than 15,000 people. There would also be no need to dress up in a curtain – she had the stunning, vaguely fetishistic black bat-come-dominatrix outfit that features in her video for 'Drumming Song', the gothic song of obsession written with James Ford and Crispin Hunt.

The costume was almost as impressive as the song itself, and ensured that the video – and this performance – would be truly memorable. It was all thanks to Florence's new favourite designer Hannah Marshall, whom Florence remains a loyal supporter of to this day. "I worked with Hannah on a lot of stuff like power shoulders and leather, we wanted to make me look like a disco gargoyle!"

'Drumming Song' was, in Florence's words, "about horror and fear". Fortunately she didn't seem to be suffering from either of those qualities when she faced the crowd. It was her 22nd birthday, after all. It was time to celebrate, and while she was there to perform, there was plenty of time to drink, eat and hang out with bands such as Friendly Fires, the Big Pink and the XX, who would support her on her next tour.

As usual, the elements played their part in making Florence + The Machine's appearance even more rapturous and dramatic. In the middle of her performance at Leeds, there was a downpour of biblical proportions that hammered on the ceiling of the tent, piercing the roof and drenching Chris, the drummer. As one mesmerised writer from *The Collective Review* pondered, "Such is the majesty of the performance that, when the rain comes to Leeds, one cannot help but wonder if Florence made it happen."

Fortunately, the band remained unfazed. In fact, Florence was thrilled to bits. "They embrace the adversity," continues *The Collective Review,* "and there is a sense that it is almost welcome – an opportunity to be different, to give the crowd something unique. When the rain starts hitting the front of the stage, Florence literally embraces it, gamely joking about electrocution." What a pro.

Fan Molly Turnely remembers seeing her for the first time at this very gig, and admits that this set spurred her on to seeing Florence as many times as possible from then on. "She was the first live performer to engage me in such a fashion that everything around me disappeared, I am completely used to this fixation now [having seen her 10 times] but at the time it was like a new drug. Flo scaled the scaffolding on that stage and swung from it in six-inch heels singing 'Kiss With A Fist' – this was the beginning of our (one-sided) love affair…!"

Florence's manager, Mairead, had her Smash and Grab tent at the festival (Smash and Grab being the London party night organised by Queens of Noize) so Florence was looking forward to kicking back after her set, changing from her heels into her trusty brogues – complete with holes, hardly festival-wear – and heading over to Smash and Grab to listen to hip-hop. All in all, a good day and night's partying was guaranteed.

"I had to get up really early in the morning and play an acoustic set and I had this crowd of early-morning festival goers singing happy birthday," she told *NME*. "That was an amazing way to start my birthday! And later when I played the set, the crowd was so big I had to keep looking at the band, I couldn't keep looking at the crowd, it was amazing. There was a big present on the drum kit for me and the band had got me a megaphone. I think I'm the person who least needs to be louder! But it had a really cool alarm sound on it so I was walking around the stage playing that."

It wouldn't be right if her family wasn't there with her – most of them anyway: Evelyn watched the broadcast from home. But even the watchful presence of her loved ones couldn't stop Florence from behaving just as adventurously as she always did, climbing to the top of the lighting rig and scaring everyone to death. It wasn't planned, as Florence admitted: "I can't even plan what I'm doing in the next two hours…

"I hung out there for a bit but then I got banned from doing it as apparently my mum had watched it from behind the sofa nearly in tears. None of the band could watch it either, even though they knew I'd got down, the drummer Chris was like, 'I thought you were going to fall, I thought you were going to fall! Don't do that again.' But it was just an amazing birthday!"

Her day wasn't even spoiled by the fact that she'd jammed her thumb in the dressing room door and had to pay a visit to the medical tent. When she got there, she realised she wasn't alone. Half of her family were in there too. "My dad ended up in there for some reason! I don't know why. My sister was with me because I was crying and covered with blood… happy families in the medical tent at Reading!"

Of course, when you're Florence Welch, it doesn't have to be your birthday to be showered with gifts. When Absolute Radio DJ Geoff Lloyd discovered during an earlier interview that Florence adored *Little House On The Prairie* but had never seen *The Waltons*, he sent her every episode through the post, much to her delight.

Florence's favourite rituals when home from tour are as follows: shut the door, make a cup of tea, shout at her little brother, JJ, heat up some Heinz tomato soup (pure comfort) and then flop onto the sofa and escape into a box-set (her other favourite way to celebrate being home would be to "fold clothes" and potter about. Rock 'n' roll, eh? Folding is evidently the new champagne-quaffing).

So she revelled in watching *The Waltons* episodes back to back for two solid weeks – and when she caught up with Lloyd again at the Reading Festival, she was determined to give him a gift of comparable value: to his jubilation, Florence promised him an LP called *Psychedelic Pharmacy* by the band Lubricated Goat. She stood by that promise too.

After an ecstatic season of festivals, and once the sunburns had healed and the grass stains were washed out, it was time to return to London, which was also clamouring for the attention of Florence + The Machine, not least because she had been nominated for the prestigious Mercury Prize for *Lungs*, alongside La Roux, the Horrors, Bat For Lashes, Kasabian and Speech Debelle, much to her amazement (but not particularly to anyone else's).

"I'm so grateful and honoured to be a part of it," Florence said at the time. "You don't know what's going to happen so to have got this far is enough for me!

[This year's] been a blur. You're in a weird kind of cave when you're making the album and then you come out and it's like 'wooah!'"

Florence remained humble and down to earth, careful not to get too excited about the possible outcome. But it must have been hard to remain philosophical and feet-on-the-ground when she discovered she was the bookie's favourite to win the Mercury. Still, she remained contained, although the pressure was starting to show.

Florence had been up excruciatingly early (in rock 'n' roll terms at least) to appear on the breakfast TV show *GMTV* that morning, and had decided to grab some much-needed sleep in her hotel room afterwards. Her 40 winks were far from restful – she suffered repeated attacks of terrifying sleep paralysis, prompted by her anxiety. "It's so weird, like something's sitting on your chest," she shuddered. "I've had to be woken up because I'm screaming, I get it really badly."

Another recurring anxiety dream Florence would suffer from was that of not having revised for her history A-levels. "Like I'd be making the whole of the album and having to re-sit my history A-level," she told DJ Steve Lamacq, "and then I'd wake up and be like, 'Oh my God, I haven't revised! Oh... I've already done it! I got a C but I've already done it.'"

No one could have known when she hit the red carpet that evening, looking radiant in black, and freshly coiffured, that she had been in such a state. Florence has admitted that whenever the fear comes to call, she goes quiet, barely speaking to people until the cloud has lifted – but she was forced to talk seemingly endlessly to the press before the night's event, and having to stand in front of a bank of snapping paparazzi trying to look natural wasn't easy, despite the aplomb with which she pulled it off.

Forever looking for symbols, she noted that everyone who had arrived for the Mercurys that evening was clad similarly in black. "We've all come to our own funerals," she joked darkly.

Florence + The Machine gave a reliably euphoric performance of 'Dog Days' which delighted the tables of increasingly loud and drunken music industry executives, but the prize went to London rapper Speech Debelle.

"I didn't feel bummed [about the Mercury Prize]," Florence said graciously. "I was happy that the whole thing was over with! I didn't go into music to win awards, I went into it because I liked it." Fair enough.

Florence was also no doubt grateful that she could go to bed and try to get some quality sleep before preparing to zoom down to the Isle Of Wight for the boutique festival Bestival, where she would be performing on the main stage alongside her pals MGMT and Friendly Fires. Her outfit? Originally she had joked that she was going to go as the character Joe from *EastEnders*, with "tin-foil on my head" – sexy – but she eventually decided to plump for a "Barbarella-meets-Ziggy Stardust" look. Mairead, meanwhile, was keen to go as a Conehead (à la the eighties Dan Ackroyd film). Florence wasn't too convinced by that.

As the Mercury nominations reflected, it was certainly a bumper year for female talent, as the media would frequently report with their 'women in pop' or 'women in rock' features. How helpful was it that the music industry and press continually shove otherwise disparate artists together merely because of their gender? 'Twas ever thus, of course, but it missed the point. Florence wisely took it all with a pinch of salt.

"I have been compared to every single female artist ever," Florence laughed. "They might as well just call me Kate Nash for Lashes or something. Florence Kate Nash for Lashes Boots The Machine! Everyone's making such different music. I'm happy to be associated with other exciting female artists, but I think it is strange the way I have been compared to everybody. I can't be like Aretha Franklin *and* Kate Bush *and* this person and that person. But you know what? We all have tits."

If she'd had the choice, vocally she'd have loved to be compared to Etta James, Eva Cassidy or Alice Glass from Crystal Castles. "Her performances just blow me away," she enthused. "It's like this tiny little creature with such a demonic presence. She's completely mesmerising; terrifying and wonderful. She seems like this really strong female presence and again it's like that masculine and feminine conflict – taking yourself apart. A lot of my performance comes from watching male artists and punk bands; that sense of domination, of controlling the stage and it being your domain. So it's a real mix."

Which may explain why, interestingly, one of the artists Florence most wished she could emulate – or at least work with – wasn't a woman at all. It was Tom Waits, he of the growling, gravelly voice, the studied hipster persona and the brilliantly cranky, horror-tinged musicality. Like Florence, Waits surrounded himself with interesting musicians, such as the guitarist Marc Ribot. Waits' voice and Ribot's dissonant twangs were a killer combination that would capture people's imaginations and take them to a darker place, much in the same way as Florence's holler and the sound of Tom Monger's harp would send fans into raptures in quite a different way.

"Listening to Tom Waits makes me wish that I'd been drinking whisky and smoking cigarettes for 50 years and that I made all my music in a big scary barn somewhere in the country, basically," she said. "It makes me want to be an older gentleman who's been drinking and has lived this whisky and rain-soaked life. But damn, I'm a girl from South London." Them's the breaks…

Florence was booked to perform a residency at Shepherd's Bush Empire at the end of September, and there had been such huge demand, an extra night had to be added. A whole summer of performing live to huge, beer-soaked crowds under the beating sun had done Florence and her band a lot of good, because by the time of their residency they were better live, more accomplished and more exciting than they'd ever been before. But Florence was still keen to retain a sense of the unique chaotic creativity of her early gigs on the London college party scene.

"[In the early days] college parties, art projects and gigs were all mixed into one – and that's what I want it to feel like now," she explained. "It's all part of a ritual. You're trying to help the audience lose themselves, and you're trying to lose yourself."

Paul Epworth, Florence's producer and studio guru, loved the Shepherd's Bush residency, and felt it showed off her musicality perfectly. The gigs were fun too – at one point Florence split the audience into two parts, like in a pantomime, and encouraged fans to sing with her.

"The Shepherd's Bush shows were amazing," he recalled. "You have no idea of how good a pop writer she is either. She writes codas, and I'm like 'Hang on, coda outro?' I had to brush up. 'I was supposed to be brought in to help you!'"

*The Independent*'s Harriet Walker clearly agreed that those West London dates truly displayed Florence as a powerful force. She gave Florence a five-star review and was very much under the Welch spell, which had been whipped up by a combination of swirling diaphanous fabrics, shimmering lights, shamanic stomping and the kind of singing that seemed to come from a very deep, very strange place. "She is majestic," that word again, "like John William Waterhouse's Circe, with the awestruck audience as her swine." Charming. Florence also came out of the review as a "greenwood deity", a "flame-haired Boudicca", with the Machine described as "a well-oiled one".

The only question marks regarded Florence's habit of being "some might say, calculatedly overwhelmed" at the adulation she receives between songs, and also the decision to sing an *a capella* version of Etta James' 'Something's Got A Hold On Me', the song that brought her forcefully to Mairead Nash's attention three years earlier in that Soho toilet. While it displayed her range and power, it was, according to Walker, "hardly the most exciting song in the set-list". Maybe Florence didn't need covers any more. Many of the music industry insiders present believed she was beyond needing the safety of cover versions now, her own songs were strong – and she was arguably worthy of a bigger venue at this stage in her career too.

"At the time it felt like she could have done three or four nights at Brixton," said XFM's Mike Walsh. "She was on the radio, having hits, it felt like she was under-playing at the time I guess, regarding the venue size. That was when it was more realised visually as well, nicer costumes, the band, the bird cages onstage, her lightshow... it wasn't a festival bill, this was *her* headline production.

"Everything you wished her to be she became, this otherworldly Kate Bush-esque superstar. Seeing her at Shepherd's Bush, she was just hitting take-off really."

# CHAPTER TEN

*"What does the Machine look like? It would look like half an organic heart, held in half a real ribcage, half organic half machinery, bits of twigs and bird feathers, rusty metal, all clanking together... pretty much!"*

Florence to *NME*.

October 2009 was shaping up to be an exciting, globe-trotting month, starting off with a run of tour dates in Europe with Metronomy, Annasaid and Voicist, who would be supporting her. The 12-date tour would take Florence + The Machine to Germany, Holland, Belgium, Scandinavia, Italy, Austria and Switzerland before concluding with a date at London's Roundhouse. Days later, Florence and the band would be whisked away to the States for a Hallowe'eny coast-to-coast visit.

Yet again she had to pack her near-to exploding suitcases, select new costumes (not that that was much of a chore, what could be more fun?) and refresh her crimson locks which, fabulous as they look, fade quickly and often need an injection of her favourite Bumble and Bumble products to keep them bright – although this was often something that she had to do on the road, as time was so tight. On more than one occasion, Florence was running so late with her hair-colouring sessions that she'd slap dye all over her hair and then have to leave the house to be picked up by the tour bus still with cling film wrapped around her head. She'd later have to dash into a motorway service station to wash it off, much to the bemusement of staff, all the while sheepishly assuring them that there's "nothing wrong with me".

Another on-the-road ritual which was a little more fun and a little less embarrassing was lipstick-collecting. Whenever she had to go to an airport, which was an increasingly frequent occurrence, she would peruse the shiny, fragrant duty-free cosmetic counters in a bid to find the perfect red lipstick to suit her mood – and, as most ladies will appreciate, there are many, many different possibilities.

"They're just little luxuries that keep you going. It's a weird OCD thing, even though I've got so many," she told an interviewer. "The lipstick I'm wearing now is Estée Lauder Rich Currant, it's really nice, purpley nude, not too red…"

Lipsticks and hair dye aside, the October tour of northern Europe would be nothing if not eventful, not least because, while on the road from Norway to Denmark, disaster struck. But amazingly, given her sleep problems, Florence slumbered through the whole ordeal…

"Our bus caught fire when we were halfway down the autobahn between Oslo and Copenhagen, so for a while we were careering down the motorway with a big ball of flames attached to us and no one knew, we were asleep," Florence recalled. "The driver looked round when all these people started honking, and we realised we were dragging this flaming ball of instruments. He heroically stopped the bus and detached it somehow from the fire before it exploded. All the instruments went up in flames, you could hear the strings pinging; the idea of a harp on fire is just one of the saddest things, heaven and hell colliding."

Tom Monger was obviously heartbroken, and likened the incident to "losing a best friend". Florence's sound man, clearly a like-minded chap, took it upon himself to record the pinging sounds of the harp as its strings snapped in the heat for use in a song some day. Florence + The Machine certainly know how to make the best of a bad situation. They performed that night, despite the trauma of the fire and lack of equipment, borrowing the gear they needed and turning the gig into a joyous celebration that no one had been hurt. There was no merchandise for the fans, but they were just glad to see their heroes were safe and sound.

On a more positive note, this leg of the *Lungs* tour gave birth to a song that would find its way onto album number two, *Ceremonials*, which would see the light of day in October 2011. The song, recorded drunk with Isabella on an overnight journey from Belgium to Amsterdam, was 'No Light, No Light', and it was, in part, born of an idea that was sparked by the droning sound of the tour bus moving along the motorway.

"The intro was written at four in the morning," Florence told MTV. "We had gone out for [guitarist] Rob Ackroyd's birthday to an all-night restaurant in Brussels called Midnights. [Then] we got on the tour bus and everyone was a bit drunk and it was like, 'Yeah, let's write a song.' We recorded the sound of the bus moving, a real droney bass sound, and that's the intro."

Isabella: "We recorded the vocal on a line-in on my mic, wasted on a tour bus: she was singing at my laptop, it was so lo-fi."

As the bus made its way to the Dutch capital, and the joy of having written a new song en route sank in, Isabella and Florence decided 'No Light, No Light' was so good, they simply had to toast its arrival into the world, and so, once they had arrived in Amsterdam at around 7am, the hunt for an all-night bar commenced. They found one – a sports bar that would serve only Midori, a sweet, radioactive-coloured melon liqueur.

"So it was bright-green drinks and me and Isa kind of looking like crazy old ladies." Old ladies who knock back Midori at 7am in Amsterdam, that is. Now, most of us, if we'd been drinking heavily and suddenly decided to write a song whilst trying not to puke on a tour bus as it lurched along in the early hours of the morning, would probably wake up in the cold light of day, listen to the track and decide never to let anyone hear it for the good of their own ears. However, so musical are Florence and Isabella, that the melodramatic 'No Light, No Light', a desperate paean to lost love, wasn't just a decent track, it would be one of the strongest on the next album.

This tour-bus birth was just the beginning, of course. Once they were back home, Isabella had to get to work in the studio and come up with ideas for how the song could develop – and Florence and Isabella didn't always see eye to eye.

"We had a big choral 'Like A Prayer' thing that has a really nasty beat in it," said Isabella. "I used the choir sound on my keyboard. I was struggling with this idea for ages. There's another which Flo is a bit afraid of it, she's like, 'Oh, it sounds like Take That should sing on it! It's too nice, I have to sing something nasty over the top of it,' and I was like 'No you don't! Do something really lovely. I finally persuaded her."

Florence + The Machine were now on the top of everybody's wish list, and it was no surprise that, in October 2009, Absolute Radio, which had been supporting Florence since she first emerged on the London pub gig circuit, would invite her to be part of its high-profile first birthday celebrations. Other stars offering good vibes and exclusive performances would be Bon Jovi, Madness and Elbow. For Florence's part, she would be recording her song for the radio station at a secret location: Studio 2 at Abbey Road Studios in London.

Florence had been to Abbey Road before, but noted that every visit to this historic place was special, and, naturally, picked up on its more reverent qualities. "It is semi-devotional here," she whispered mysteriously. "There's a church-like atmosphere, the high ceilings, the quiet, and everything that happened here. It's a really special place to perform, you always do a good performance here." Well, if it was good enough for the Beatles…

Florence + The Machine's Absolute Radio/Abbey Road set consisted of 'Between Two Lungs', a blast from the past with 'My Boy Builds Coffins', 'Kiss With A Fist', 'Hurricane Drunk', 'Cosmic Love', 'Dog Days Are Over', 'Drumming Song', 'You Got The Love' and 'Rabbit Heart (Raise It Up)'. They also paid tribute to the Beatles' *Abbey Road* album, which was recorded in this very room, by playing a cover of 'Oh! Darling'.

Absolute Radio was originally known as Virgin Radio, but changed its name in 2008 and was now bigger than ever. Geoff Lloyd, one of its star DJs and, as you may remember from a previous chapter, the lucky recipient of a Lubricated Goat album from Florence in return for a box-set of *The Waltons*, had long been a particularly vociferous fan of Florence + The Machine, and it was worth noting that the station's inception as Absolute and Florence's first foray as a professional musician were both one year old, give or take a few months. But of course, in both cases there was more to it than that. Just because Florence had only been in the public eye for 18 months didn't mean that, up to that point, she hadn't been doing anything – on the contrary.

"The first album was 23 years in the making, but at the same time I've been working really hard for about two years, it's gone through so many different stages. It started out with just me singing with no band, so to go from there to having a six-piece band and be at Abbey Road is amazing."

With four American dates lined up for the end of the month, Florence was preparing herself for a full week's worth of explaining that she didn't just spring out of nowhere, because she found that, when she was in the States, people had even more of a belief that she was an overnight success, not having had the benefit of seeing her grow organically at smaller London gigs.

"When I come to America, people always say, 'Wow, it happened so quickly!'" she laughed. "And I'm like, 'Not really! I was working for about two years solidly, from just being me and an acoustic guitar."

But those in the know were desperate to get Florence Stateside. Hole frontwoman and the Twitterverse's compelling microblogger Courtney Love had already expressed her desire to "unleash" Florence + The Machine on America herself after the pair briefly shared a stage in London that year. In Courtney's words: "I played with her in London and she handed me my ass." High praise indeed.

Florence's short American run began with a gig at the legendary Bowery Ballroom – just a stone's throw from her American mother's stamping ground – in New York on October 27, before a jaunt to the opposite coast for a show at the equally iconic Troubadour in Los Angeles. They then travelled up to Canada for a gig at Cabaret, Montreal, and the Mod Club in Toronto. Florence also had appearances on *The Late Show With David Letterman* and *Jimmy Kimmel Live* scheduled.

This was a short but high-pressure stint of make-or-break US appearances. America is a famously tough nut to crack for British artists – the States hadn't particularly warmed to Lily Allen or Robbie Williams, so what would Americans make of this very British eccentric? Thankfully, they fell head over heels in love. Could it have been her peculiar Englishness and awkward charm that captured their hearts? Or her sartorial resemblance and similar stage-craft to their own witchy rock queen Stevie Nicks?

Whatever the clincher was, everyone from Katy Perry to Nicole Richie was a fan. *Gossip Girl* TV star Blake Lively also made a beeline for Florence when she was at the Bowery, and the pair remain firm friends to this day. "Blake is just so nice," Florence said. "She came to my very first New York gig and has been a huge support in the States. Her mum and brother have come to the shows [too]."

Thanks to Blake, Florence would even land a cameo appearance on *Gossip Girl* in the episode 'Panic Room-mate', which went out on February 7, 2011. Florence, clad in a floaty monochrome number and looking winsome as always, performed an acoustic version of 'Cosmic Love'. This can't have hurt her profile in the States.

"She's done astonishingly well," says a music industry insider. "The US tour, that's what traditionally killed UK acts in the past out there. She's not a UK artist trying to be a US artist. She's been very well received by a lot of the right people over there. She's unique. She's a little bit eccentric maybe, attractive in an English way, she's not plucked and styled, she's ginger and diaphanous.

"The closest contemporary she's got is Ellie Goulding, who won the Breakthrough Brit the year after Florence. Completely different people of course. The music is in the same ball-park, but there's nobody quite like Florence. She's got no choice but to be the kind of artist she is."

No one could blame Florence for being a little nervous. She was entering a new phase in her career, an important one at that. Every performance counted, and with huge audiences across America watching her appearances on TV shows, she had to find a way to quell the nerves. Her solution? To dance stupidly in her pants. Not on camera, it should be clarified, but in the safety and privacy of her dressing room, pre-show.

"In the middle of getting changed into stage clothes there's normally a moment I just wear pants, so I just do some sort of strange dancing in my pants," she said. "I find that lets my inhibitions go and then I can go out. If you don't mind dancing in a silly way in underwear, you probably won't mind going out performing." Another slightly more OCD 'ritual', if you can call it that, is even less poetic. "I have to have so many little wees, it's ridiculous."

What with Florence being in America around the time of Hallowe'en, this was a perfect opportunity to dress up… not that Florence, Isabella and co needed an excuse for that. But this spooky time of year is celebrated rather more in the US than it is in the UK, and they certainly made the most of it. Not only did they make their LA show entirely All Hallows-themed and attend a Hallowe'en party dressed as the eighties cartoon characters Calvin (Isabella) and Hobbes (Florence) – "because I'm tall and orange…" – but Florence, intuitive as ever, saw a ghost in her hotel in New York. Sinister music, maestro, if you please; Florence is going to tell us all about it:

"It was in one of those old twenties red-brick buildings in New York. I was having these weird nightmares about people looking over me while I was sleeping and then I woke up and saw something sitting on the end of my bed. I screamed this blood-curdling scream and tried to punch it and it disappeared. I was worried that people thought I was being murdered… but it was a ghost."

And that wouldn't be the only spectral presence that Florence would encounter during her time in New York. On one of many shopping trips with Isabella at the countless antique stores and flea markets in New York, Florence found a very special dress. It was perfect for Florence's stage performances, and as Stevie Nicks often said, and Florence quoted, "You should wear something long and floaty. It's nice to think your dress is doing a performance too…" And this dress definitely had a mind of its own.

"It was a party dress from the thirties in the basement of [a vintage store in New York] and it was flood damaged so they weren't going to sell it. It was just going to go to rot," said Florence. "But we rescued it and restored it, and when we played, it sort of came to life around me as if the dress was fulfilling some sort of past dream."

Only Florence could describe it like that. The idea that vintage clothes all have a story, a past life and a history is one that Florence loved to ponder as she built up her antique wardrobe of elderly threads with stories to tell. She imagined the people who used to wear them, the places those people would go and the experiences they would have in them, and this might explain why, during down-time, when the rest of the group and entourage were seeing the sights and exploring, she would be alone in her hotel room, in a world of her own, playing dress-up with her latest magical finds.

"I like to swan around in my room in a kimono and listen to blues and classical music, float about," she said. "I always end up playing fancy dress with myself. I'm such a parody of myself.

"I went to see my manager when I had two hours off in a hotel. She was like, 'What have you been doing?' 'Well, I put this new headpiece on and I was twirling around in this new peach chiffon dressing gown I bought...' and she was like, 'What, so you've just been performing by yourself for two hours?'"

Florence wasn't always such a harmless hotel guest, however – she often had people in the neighbouring rooms climbing the walls with fury, although it was all in the name of art. She "keeps sane by writing", and where better to try to escape into your own world than in an anonymous hotel room? Florence would do her best to customise her dressing and hotel rooms by hanging up scarves and shawls, and generally Welchifying her surroundings, and before too long she would have created enough of an atmosphere that she'd be ready and inspired to start writing songs. She didn't wait until she was in the studio to record them either. Time was of the essence – she'd record them in the hotel if she had to.

"We have makeshift studios. We've used hotel sinks as drums," said Florence. "Bad idea is to use a hotel partition wall, because the people banging back, they're not playing along, they're just angry!" Needs must… and if you can record and use this impromptu percussion, so much the better.

Back home, Florence + The Machine's successful conquering of America had not escaped the notice of the music press, notably *NME*, which celebrated with what was, in Florence's eyes, a rather startling cover feature titled 'Florence Takes America'. From Florence's point of view this was thrilling, but unnerving too. "I'd never had a feature that big," she confesses. "The 'Florence Takes America' one still scares me! But you learn to take things less seriously and not to be so freaked out."

America, meanwhile, was still recovering from the chiffon-swathed whirlwind that had just whipped from coast to coast and left everybody reeling. "I think Americans are slightly more reserved because they're still getting into it," said Florence. "But everyone's still singing along and there's still a huge amount of support over here, which is really amazing to me. I'm not here that often. It feels really good."

As well as firing up audiences with her voice and stage presence, Florence was, of course, fast becoming a style icon of serious proportions. She initially felt the fashion world that was soon to embrace her was "terrifying", telling *The Guardian* that "if you're in fashion you can go out of fashion. If you keep trying to move away from fashion … it'll keep following you!" But she had been expressing herself quite naturally through her clothes in curious and creative ways since she was a little girl.

Florence had already admitted she was more likely to be found reading a fashion magazine than a copy of *NME* when she was a teenager and her adoration of vintage markets, thrift shops and quirky designers meant that not only her own wardrobe was under some considerable strain, but her manager Mairead's office, then above the Albert and Pearl pub in Islington (which serves punch in teapots and has a bar in a wardrobe – how impossibly Florence), was crammed to the gills with designer clothes.

If Florence wanted to cheer up a dressing room, she'd hang up some of her most beautiful costumes around the space and transform it, lifting her spirits and creating a very 'Florence' atmosphere. But ultimately, as

Florence said, "The music dictates the look as opposed to the other way around."

Florence loves Chanel, Chloé and Cacharel (and no doubt many other designers that don't begin with a 'C') but she has always made a point of working with up-and-coming, more under-radar designers such as Opening Ceremony and Hannah Marshall, who famously created the raunchy black outfit for the 'Drumming Song' video. It means a lot to Florence to collaborate with designers she can get to know and support, and have a personal connection with. Another sartorial figure who has loomed large in Florence's life since 2009 is, of course, stylist and *Vice* fashion editor Aldene Johnson. One of the joys of working with Florence is, according to Johnson, that she is "brave, up for trying things".

When asked whether she wanted to create her own fashion line, however, Florence is typically self-effacing: "I'm not entirely sure anybody would want the sort of things I'd want to design," she laughed. "The other day I was designing this outfit. It was a fitted frock-coat waistcoat with a thick black brocade material and a maroon paisley lining. I don't think anyone would want that at all." Oh, you'd be surprised, Florence.

"The process of working with Flo has evolved," Aldene Johnson told the *New York Times*. "The bigger she's got, the more we can do different things than what we could do in the beginning. On stage, it's about two sides. It's always this ethereal white witch meets darkly sexy vamp character. For red carpet, it's classic and glamorous and never trashy."

You would never find Florence flashing the flesh in overtly sexy ways like Rihanna or Christina Aguilera – there was more to this pop queen in the making than having to resort to over-sexualisation, whether on stage, in her videos or at events. She just isn't that kind of artist; in fact, as Florence has often said herself, her natural style is somewhat masculine. She spent most of her time at art college partying in a customised tuxedo after all, but her favourite piece of clothing? The chiffon ball gown her American debutante mother came out in. Again, it's a garment with a story, and that makes it all the more appealing, fascinating and poignant to Florence.

This isn't to say that she hadn't already had her first brushes with the world of haute couture – even if she was initially incognito. The previous year, the Queens of Noize had been booked to DJ at the lavish Milanese mansion of Donatella Versace, no less. There was just one problem: Tabitha Denholm, Mairead's partner in crime, was unwell. So Mairead had to improvise – there was no way she was missing that party – and Florence was whisked over to Italy to pretend to be Tabitha and be a Queen of Noize for the night. She couldn't believe what she was surrounded by. Was it weird? Yes. Glitzy? Of course. And to say it was star-studded would be an understatement.

"Jay-Z and Beyoncé turned up!" she recalled excitedly. "We played 'Ah got a woman way over town that digs on me!' (Ray Charles's 'I Got A Woman') and Jay-Z leaned over the decks and went, 'Yeeeaaah!' and him and Beyoncé were dancing with the weird Versace crowd and I was like, 'This! Is! Ah-May-Ziiiing!'" Little did she realise that one day she would be invited as a guest of honour herself to parties hosted by Jay-Z and his bling-encrusted pals. The days of being sneaked into celebrity parties under someone else's name were numbered.

Florence had huge amounts of fun, almost in spite of herself. It was never a dream of hers to be partying with A-listers, although she was certainly going to enjoy it. "I'm slightly unambitious," she pondered. "I'm quite happy to bimble around in the Twilight Zone, and go off on a tangent. And think, 'I saw a really great pigeon today!'"

Ultimately though, great pigeons aside, Florence would have to get used to being in the spotlight and not just for her music. Plenty of time would be spent being photographed in various outfits and in various locations. At least sometimes the location would be in her house. One shoot involved Florence doing no more than lying in her bed drinking tea. Others wouldn't be quite so straightforward. But Florence was learning how to use these shoots as times to focus on other things.

"Photoshoots are almost like meditating in a weird way," she said. "Sometimes you have to stay really still, even keep your facial position still, so it's almost like doing a weird musical statues yoga or something! The mind does tend to wander."

Florence was getting used to being interviewed too. Talking had never seemed to be a problem, despite her deep core of shyness. She had always managed to be entertaining and charming and humble in interviews, right from the first interview she had ever done, and her interviews today are as quirky and open (to a point) as ever. You can always expect something a little off-kilter too, whether she's gushing about Scottish broadswords and werewolves, ghosts or the delights of eccentric eating.

"I love weird food," she told one interviewer as she tucked into some unappetising-looking cockles and whelks. "I discovered wasabi peas long before any gastro-pub ever did." Maybe not a front-page headline, but certainly an out-of-the-ordinary start to an interview, which makes a change from the beige, monosyllabic, or simply disengaged retorts of some artists. Put simply, it's all about the joie de vivre, it's all about feeling things, whether those things are fearful, delicious, woeful or surprising. Florence is nothing if not a sensualist and her life, even if you took pop stardom away, could never be dull.

After her trip to the States, Florence was summoned to perform a special gig that October for XFM, another radio station that had supported her from the off. Clad in floaty autumnal colours and wearing a gothic slash of glossy black lipstick, she and her faithful Machine headed to the intimate, crimson womb of London rock 'n' roll, the iconic 100 Club on Oxford Street (complete with tiny graffitied dressing room – on one wall an anonymous musician armed with a marker pen has scrawled the classic line, 'Champagne for my real friends, real pain for my sham friends' alongside the inevitable drawings of penises). Yes, there was always something good to read at the 100 Club.

This sweaty, much-loved venue had played host to many seminal acts over the decades – from trad-jazz stalwarts to the Rolling Stones to the infamous 'Punk Festival' of the late seventies, which starred the Sex Pistols and an early incarnation of Siouxsie & The Banshees. It was partly in tribute to goth queen Siouxsie that Florence decided on the black lipstick, and she gave her all that night, even inspiring an all-female stage invasion during 'Rabbit Heart'. Florence insisted that, despite the gig's size in comparison to the venues she had been playing in recent months, that this was a significant night for Florence + The Machine.

"I loved doing the XFM 100 Club gig," she said. "I was definitely going through a strong black lipstick phase at the time, black leggings, the Siouxsie link! Having grown up listening to XFM to doing that gig, it was a big gig for us.

"XFM is usually the place where I hear my songs most, I'm really grateful. I think my songs aren't the most commercial things – they're pop of course, but I don't think it's always that easy to get radio-play. I think it was 'Dog Days' that I first heard on the radio; I probably immediately jumped to turn it off because it's very frightening hearing your song on the radio!"

As she said in the lyrics of 'Dog Days' itself, 'The horses are comin' so you'd better run...' Success continued to gallop towards her, and she couldn't out-run it.

XFM's Mike Walsh remembers the night fondly, not least because it felt like an acknowledgement to the station for the loyalty they'd shown. "She was already flying by then to be fair. We had the 100 Club gig and she totally smashed it. We broadcast it on the radio and it was a great moment for us to feel we'd had that 'Thank you.'"

So this was it: Florence was now officially famous, officially a star. It was magical, exciting and nerve-jangling all at once. Christmas 2009 would be the first festive season that Florence would really start to feel that she was a public figure – she'd even recorded a version of the Pogues and Kirsty MacColl's Yuletide classic 'Fairytale Of New York' with Billy Bragg for Rob Da Bank's show on BBC Radio 1 – complete with Tom on harp. This kind of thing just didn't happen. Or did it? Well, increasingly it would, and then some.

It wasn't even as if Florence had particularly dreamed of being a celebrity as a teenager, as so many young girls do. She'd visualised making music and art her life, yes, but the reality TV-style hunger for sheer recognition at any cost was simply not on Florence's agenda. It wouldn't hit her until people in the street started to recognise her that life really had changed for good.

"I only realised I was famous when people started shouting at me," she said. "I didn't think of myself as a celebrity. I still think I'm this girl going to charity shops or hanging out at festivals and wondering about going back to university. But then I go somewhere and a guy in a white van shouts out 'Hey, Florence,' or I hear my song on *EastEnders* and think, 'That's so weird.' That has way more impact than playing in front of thousands.

"I really like men in white vans now."

# CHAPTER ELEVEN

*"I like the idea of the name being something hard for people to decipher. Is it me versus the machine or me and the machine? You don't quite know."*

Florence to *NME*.

"I'm so excited about coming to Australia! I'm going to have to wear a lot of sunscreen…" Yes, Florence + The Machine were booked to go down under for the first time in January and February of 2010 for the sprawling Laneway Festival in Melbourne, Sydney and New Zealand, alongside an array of stars including post-punk legends Echo & The Bunnymen, Deep South garage loons the Black Lips and the XX, who would support Florence on her subsequent Asian dates.

Despite the confusion of it being the height of summer in Australia and the depths of winter back home, Florence was probably the only artist on that bill threatening to bring a parasol to shield her translucent complexion, but it was the perfect antidote to a British January, particularly as Christmas and New Year always leave her feeling downright depressed. "I think a lot of people [feel depressed around Christmas]," she pondered. "You start questioning everything, like 'Where is this going?' And 'What am I doing?' But I feel great now I'm getting back into the swing of things."

She could be forgiven for taking the New Year off, for putting her trusty notebook into a drawer and kicking back before her Australian trip (during which Florence did manage to grab some hard-won free time to relax on the beach and enjoy impromptu cocktails in the pool with members of the XX, as you do). But even if she'd tried to, you can't pack that imagination away; Florence's right brain is never on holiday. Just days before they packed their bags and headed out of grey, gloomy London to play to fans in sunnier climes, Florence, who had spent two weeks with Paul Epworth in his studio, working on new ideas, had conjured up a beautiful new song with an oh so Flo title: 'Strangeness And Charm'.

"It's based around these two atomic particles called 'strangeness and charm'," Florence explained. "I thought they were the most beautiful names for something so scientific. Me and my dad had this conversation about subatomic particles very late at night and he was telling me about these atoms called strangeness and charm. There's quarks, and then strangeness and charm and they're the smallest atoms. It's so cool! They're the smallest particles of an atom and we can't see them, but we know that they exist because of their effects. That was a good starting point for a song, so I kind of wrote a strange song about that, like a love song about atoms!

"Me and Isa also used to challenge ourselves to write 10-minute songs about objects in the room so it would end up being about stationery and D12 LPs..." Surely Björk, who was working on her science and nature-inspired album *Biophilia* at the time, would have approved.

"I'm so anatomically fixated, and everything is quite visceral," said Florence. "Blood and teeth, ribs, body parts, lungs. Lyrically, I've been focusing on things outside the body now. Or maybe even things that just encompass everything! But now there's 'Strangeness and Charm', and then I wrote another song called 'Spectrum', so it seems to me it's more chemical, it's more science based. I've done the arts, now I'm moving into science and then I'm going to make an album about PE!"

But despite Florence's move into spacier territory, she still couldn't resist a bit of blood and guts. Even in the gorgeous and uplifting track

'Heartlines', which would appear on the album, there is mention of "entrails".

"In 'Heartlines' I was thinking about soothsaying. 'Heartlines' is about being tied to someone emotionally, so this soothsaying imagery came into my head. I like how soothsayers read the future in things like animal entrails. I was trying to go for more themes of light, but I always end up bringing it back to a darker side."

So, album two was starting to take shape, even if work on what would be an epic new release was intermittent due to touring commitments. Florence already had a raft of material to include, and, as we know, demo sessions with Paul Epworth had taken place. The choppy stop-start nature of the process wasn't necessarily a problem, however, as when Florence returned home, she would find that Paul had prepared ideas, sounds, "reverential organ chords" and drum patterns for her consideration. In fact it was that powerful organ sound that inspired the "heaven and hell" imagery which would define the album we now know as *Ceremonials*. Other producers were keen to work with Florence but she and Epworth were already something of a dream team. If it ain't broke…

"I was really lucky to be able to work with people like Paul," said Florence. "He was so inspiring. I'd come back from my tour and he'd have an amazing drum pattern or chords ready for me. When someone is constantly feeding you with inspiration, it makes the whole process quite easy because you start to see images and can form lyrics quite quickly. I also read, walked a lot and went to galleries as much as possible for inspiration. It's important to keep yourself in touch with the world.

"Listening to chords and drum patterns it's almost like you have to feel what the music is saying. Like there's a drum pattern on 'Only If For A Night' which to me sounds like rolling hooves and clashing swords, like a medieval battle," Florence mused. "I had this Joan of Arc imagery coming into my head, and I was thinking about things that come to you in visions and dreams. There's the line, 'While I was burning, you're the only light.' I was thinking of tragedy mixed with that kind of strength. It's about Joan of Arc and my dead grandmother."

Back during her touring days with MGMT in 2008, as we know, Florence had dreamt that her grandmother had appeared to her as a ghost. "That was what it was like," Florence insisted. "I threw my arms round her legs and she actually said, 'Concentrate'. It was strangely practical advice for a dead person. It was the first time I'd seen her since she died when I was 11. I was having a regular dream and then she was just there. There's this amazing Thom Gunn poem about seeing a dead lover in a dream, and he says it was as if death was undone."

What is particularly poignant about 'Only If For A Night' is that, when it was released as a vinyl special edition in 2012, it would form a very special tribute to a young Florence fan called Natalie Roberts, who tragically died of a rare form of cancer in 2010 aged just 20. Natalie had listened to Florence's music constantly on her iPod while undergoing treatment in hospital, as she felt it eased her pain and had therapeutic qualities for her. The following year, her best friend, Louise Clifford, painted a beautiful watercolour portrait of her – and that portrait would feature on the cover of this special edition Florence + The Machine seven-inch.

Louise had painted the picture for Natalie's mother, but she saw a competition on Twitter, organised by the Teenage Cancer Trust, asking entrants to draw a picture to feature on the cover of a track by Florence, a patron of the charity. Florence had also spent time with Natalie at a Teenage Cancer Trust event at the Royal Albert Hall. When she and her team heard about the portrait of Natalie, there was no contest.

"The song is all about a celestial being – someone who's passed away – and Florence felt inspired by them in the same way I was inspired by Natalie," said Louise. Natalie's mother would describe the tribute as being like a huge present to her late daughter, who would have been so thrilled by the gesture.

The track 'Breaking Down', meanwhile, has a very different feel from anything Florence had done previously. "It has this masculine energy. As I was singing it, I was trying to be David Bowie," Florence explained. Fans could expect something very different from *Lungs*, something bigger, stronger and more intense and potent. Earthed, if you like, rather than floating and airy. Plus, Florence was drawing on different influences, soul, blues and sixties music. In the process, she appeared to have created her own genre...

"I think there's a lot of chamber-soul, if that exists!" she laughed. (When trying to describe the sound of *Lungs* on the other hand to *The New York Post,* Florence coined the term "choral choir crash, like nuns falling down an elevator," which sums it up neatly.) "I was listening to a lot of Otis Redding so some of that came through, I think.

"With 'Lover To Lover' I did set out to write a masculine, aggressive soul song. I'd been listening to a lot of Marvin Gaye [too]." Redding's 'Try A Little Tenderness' had been a favourite of Florence's since she'd heard it on the *Pretty In Pink* soundtrack some years earlier, and singing her own version live was always a thrill. Her own song 'Lover To Lover', on the other hand, would become a favourite track for Florence to wake up to.

"I listen to it in the morning when I'm feeling a bit sleepy because it's so aggressive..." Florence's boyfriend, Stuart, would jokingly despair at Florence's musical decisions, which might not seem to be particularly commercially minded, at least at the outset. "He said, 'Still not gagging for that number one, are you? Still not rushing towards commercially viable music with epic one-minute drum breaks and crazy, backwards whispering, huh?" But Florence was clearly right to follow her heart.

Paul Epworth: "We decided, way before getting to the studio, that we'd use only organ for the bass sound, which resulted in a heavier sound that was slightly synthetic. I think the only thing on that record that sounds like a bass is actually a guitar that we pitched down an octave for a twangy, slack and detuned effect."

Florence had initially considered working with a different producer for *Ceremonials,* an American one, to be specific, for a big, epic Hollywood sound. The one thing Florence was sure of was that she wanted her next album to sound *big.* The studio was booked in LA, but just two weeks before she decided she couldn't go through with it.

"I thought it would be a strange way to start, all of a sudden you completely change what the essence of the first record was about," she later explained. "I just went back to the little studio in Crystal Palace. We did 'No Light, No Light' there and I did some writing with Paul in Soho, so I really wanted to stay with the people I'd worked really closely with on the first record. I didn't want it to suddenly change, I just wanted it to move forward."

Not that Florence would rule out working with American writers and producers in the future – she admits she will never stop being impressed by the "big massive pop songs" that America seems to do so well. The time just wasn't right on this occasion. "I love those songs. Those songs are almost chemically engineered to make you feel something. I've always been a sucker for it.

"I love Lady Gaga and I love Katy Perry and R&B and rap music... So the label said, 'Do you want to go over to America to work in that scene?' And I was like, 'Yeah, maybe I could bring my own take on it.'

"[But] I saw it in the diary... and all of a sudden, I was like, oh my God, I don't think I can do this," she said. "This is too far removed from everything that I've come from, and I'm going to be away and I won't be with my family. You don't want to completely alienate your fans.

"I think this time round I was slightly calmer and I knew what I wanted to do, I had more of a plan, I wanted to do it all in one place with one producer."

Florence had previously pondered on the possibility of working with TV On The Radio star Dave Sitek for the album, but Paul, with his Midas touch, was always her go-to man. Florence needed someone who understood how they reached their musical destination before in order to take the next step, which would be heavier, darker, with big drums and big bass and a more cohesive sound – those were the elements that Florence knew she wanted.

But work on this new album would, ironically, be a disjointed process at times, simply because *Lungs* was becoming more and more popular Stateside, and Florence would be greeting her public across the pond once more in the form of a gruelling but thrilling tour later in the year. What would become *Ceremonials* would have to wait. But in the grand scheme of things, as Tom Monger observed, it didn't really matter how tiring life on the road could get, or how much they were expected to do: everyone concerned knew exactly how fortunate they were to be in the position they were in, even if, from time to time, the pressures and daily difficulties sometimes got them down.

"I know how lucky I am," said Tom. "I might complain about it from time to time, but I feel bad about it because there are people [musicians] out there who've been slogging away and will never be doing what I'm doing. So I do feel tremendously privileged. I do realise that, most of the time!"

Guitarist Rob Ackroyd agrees whole-heartedly. "It's an incredible privilege to be able to play live in so many different countries. We have been lucky enough to play some incredible venues too, from a 2,000-year-old amphitheatre in Nimes to a car park in Auckland! Playing guitar for a living can feel a bit like getting away with murder."

It was, naturally, more than a little different for Florence. She was the one everyone wanted to talk to, the one the buck stopped with, and the one who had to create the material. "There was a bit in the middle [of the tour] that I was, like, totally over it," she said. "I remember I was in Ibiza and I was just a totally broken person. Everyone was relaxing in the sun, and I was shaking in my bedroom refusing to come out.

"But then when I started going back out to America, it was fine. I never once got bored of the record. It's just been a sort of tidal wave that hasn't stopped. Every week it seemed like there was something really massive to do. You just go into this weird sense of almost battle mode."

And so, while Florence was on tour, she and Epworth would work separately towards the same goal, Paul developing tracks in his London studio and Florence recording vocals in studios abroad during days off. The pair would end up finishing an impressive 40 tracks. This vast haul would need whittling down, and just 12 songs would ultimately make it onto the release itself, with an extra eight added for a subsequent deluxe edition.

"I'm pretty surprised at how prolific I've been, to be honest," said Florence. "When making the first album, I think I wrote a song about every six months. The first album was so much about the vocals carrying it. This time I really wanted to give the music space to breathe and for the band to be able to experiment."

Early songs from this stage of the process, such as 'Strangeness And Charm', were, of course, not yet ready to be unveiled to the good people of Australasia, but it wouldn't be long before they crept into the set a little later in the year, and Florence was already champing at the bit to freshen up her set with new material, even if the audience was simply clamouring to hear *Lungs*. There'd be plenty of time to work new songs up to a high standard for the album and play around with what worked and what didn't, because Florence had an incredibly intense concert schedule with only a week between legs, so to speak, of the upcoming European tour, and just a fortnight between the last date in March in Portugal and the first day of her headline tour of North America in April.

As a result, it's hardly surprising that there was no time to sit down at a computer and blog, but if there was just one thing that many of Florence's fans – and members of her team – would have loved the singer to do more, it was engage in social media. It might not have seemed a very 'Florence' thing to do – where's the mystique, for a start? – but in this digital age, it seemed that everyone who was anyone was tweeting, Facebooking and posting up pictures of their dinner for all to admire. No chance of this with Flo.

"I can only manage about one [tweet] a month," she said. "It's not that I don't want to, it's just that when I am in a situation where I am doing something amazing it's a shame, and rather rude, to bring out my phone and start tweeting." Very true.

"I think a lot of people miss out on enjoying the moment because they are so busy trying to communicate it to the world. And I want to keep some moments to myself. I'm not cut out for the hi-tech age. I don't email, I use a Walkman and my preferred method of transport is by foot. I'm nervous on planes, which isn't great as I spend my life on them, but I'm getting better."

As we know, even when Florence was trying to use MySpace, she had to borrow her sister, Grace's, account to get started. The last post on Florence's Florrible and Misrabella MySpace account (a post sent in 2008 declaring 'I have no friends!' accompanied with a 'betrayed' emoticon) seems dramatic enough to have been posted by Florence, so considering this tendency to openness, perhaps it is just as well that the air of enigma and mystery is retained by a lack of plaintive updates, possibly posted while, erm, 'tired and emotional'.

"We'd love her to tweet more but she doesn't," admits a former member of Florence's team. "There are some acts who have people tweeting on their behalf, but unless it's specified as coming from an HQ or 'team' it's a bit weird to think of people like, say, Pixie Lott and there's some misanthropic bearded bloke tweeting convincingly on her behalf.

"Anyway, Flo seems quite private, it doesn't seem like she aspires to be this massive public figure à la Katy Perry, which is not to say she isn't lovely or delightful with her fans. Her fans are one of the nicer fanbases, I think, because there are a lot of girls who like Florence and girls are generally nicer than boys, especially on the Internet.

"She gets written about a lot on fashion blogs and in fashion magazines, but you can't imagine her thinking, 'What's going to get me written about in the fashion press today?'"

Admittedly, that sense of self-contained composure may help to retain some sense of star 'otherness' – while other celebrities break down the fourth wall by venting their emotions online, even having spats with other public figures for all to see, much to the slavering glee of the press, Florence remains dignified and, in the nicest possible way, distant, and thus special. Can you imagine Marilyn Monroe blogging? Elvis Presley? David Bowie? It wouldn't seem right somehow, like eating all of our sweets in one go. Any overdose of the very thing we want is what in turn causes the novelty to fade.

The lack of online engagement may not have been a conscious decision, but this distance is actually vital to Florence's survival as a pop star, not merely to protect her mystique, but also because the perils of social media when you are a celebrity can be 100 times as difficult to deal with when you are already trying to keep your head above water amid a torrent of press interview demands, TV appearances and shows. Not to mention trying to keep your mind clear and receptive to inspiration.

XFM's Mike Walsh agrees. "When you think of the aura around certain artists and stars, less is more. I'm aware I'm part of the media machine that is constantly asking artists to do more and give more of themselves but at the end of the day we're conscious that if we had too much access, the sheen of the star can fade.

"There has to be an element of mystery, otherworldliness almost. It goes back to the David Bowie thing, is he actually an alien? He's so extraordinary, what's the story? In the information age, we can lose some of that. [Florence's] self-contained nature may have been part of the success. Adele is far more open, you meet her for two minutes and you feel like you've known her all her life! She's this wonderful character, incredibly down to earth and really open. But she's very smart and her team do a great job, there's this emotional lockdown as a result of that, and so her star is undiminished. People perceive her as the likable girl next door but at the same time we don't know too much. In that sense maybe Florence and Adele have got it right, and maybe Lily [Allen] got it a bit wrong."

So Florence might not have had the time or inclination to spill her guts on Twitter and Facebook, but that didn't stop her fans from uploading their thoughts and feelings and messages of love. One fan who was particularly enamoured of Florence met his heroine outside a show and asked her to sign his forearm with a biro, presumably ignoring all of those warnings you get at school about blood poisoning via biro scribblings on skin. Florence was evidently more important.

But what happens when he goes in the shower, I hear you ask? Well, he'd thought of that. Soon after getting his treasured autograph, he went straight to the local tattoo studio and had a tattoo made of the signature. And, before the bleeding had even stopped, you guessed it, he posted a picture of it on Facebook. Told about this intriguing picture, Florence was flattered if somewhat bemused, although she naturally made no comment on the Facebook page. Still, top marks for commitment, that man! No one could say Florence's fans aren't loyal.

"I've got a supportive and amazing fanbase," admitted Florence. "Everybody sings all the words to the songs at the gigs. I've got really amazing fans." And some quite unusual ones too.

One admirer observed that it wasn't just online that Florence preferred to stay discreet. She was excited to see Florence at a nearby table at the sophisticated Quo Vadis restaurant in Soho's Dean Street, but intrigued to see that, possibly due to a throat problem, she had to rely on her companion to relay her drinks order to the staff.

"The barman asked what she fancied and she somewhat eccentrically whispered her preference to her friend, who then had to repeat the request more audibly to the barman!" said the observer. "Mind you, it was after a show, so perhaps she had lost her voice, rather than this being a diva type thing, like 'stars can't be seen to order their own drinks'…"

Could Florence have been being a diva? Who can say. Fans, no doubt, would find this hard to believe given her impressive strike rate of being kind to her followers, and Florence insists she's always been very aware that she is surrounded by instrumental people who have helped her to get to where she is now. "People think that being in a band means bad behaviour, but I think I'd be a lot worse if I wasn't." Still, Florence freely confesses that she can also be a "pain in the ass".

"I can be crazily egotistical," she admits. "For instance, I hate flying and all the time I am up I am not thinking about the people around me if we go down, I am thinking that there are only a few good demos out there! Please, universe, don't take me yet!"

Another great by-product of discretion, particularly in the form of shying away from the addictive lure of social networking is, of course, enhanced productivity – and Florence, while touring *Lungs*, had been working hard on new songs. Admittedly, as many artists find, the second album is harder than the first to write because the first is a piece of work which has been developing for many years, a whole life even, while the second is required quickly by the record company in the light of the debut's success, and as a result it doesn't always have the material or depth of the first.

This was not the case for Florence. She knew exactly what she wanted for album number two: while *Lungs* was a scrapbook of her life so far, bringing together different periods of her life as she was growing and changing, album number two, *Ceremonials*, was already taking shape in her head. It would be darker, even more potent but in a different way, embracing love, death and violent emotions… And Florence certainly didn't have writer's block…By the end of year she would have amassed an incredible 53 songs for the album. What to choose? The songs that were, well, the most 'violent'…

"Oh, the violence. Mmm. The word itself I'm obsessed with," she said. "I wanted to call this whole record just *Violence.* You can feel things violently. It's a beautiful word.

"I wanted to make an album that sounded like the soundtrack to Baz Luhrmann's *Romeo + Juliet,* the violence mixed with the classical Shakespearean drama mixed with the pop and the pulp…"

Perhaps Florence's fascination with intense, dark emotions, obsessions and the kind of mad love that leads to crimes of passion stems from the fact that, actually, Florence is a totally non-violent person. She admits she "can't even argue". It's that inherent peaceable quality in her nature that draws her inevitably to lift up the stone and peer underneath at the dark side of life, and we're not just talking about Hammer Horror and Edgar Allan Poe. Her true fascination lay with the real stuff, the issues that, like it or not, we all have to face in life, in some form or another.

"Love, death, sex, and violence are never going to be irrelevant," said Florence. "Death is inevitable. There will never be a new version of death." Those gothic childhood fantasies and premature experiences of loss still informed so much of Florence's output. It was, in some ways, surely a kind of personal catharsis, but one which people the world over could relate to strongly, hence the cast-iron loyalty Florence fans have for her.

And to prove that point, fan Tyler Mellins puts it into words: "I find sanctuary in the knowledge that no matter what the situation, there's always a Florence song that fits my mood. If I'm lonely and upset, I have 'Never Let Me Go'. If I'm happy and excited for the future, I have 'Shake It Out'. If I'm angry, I have 'No Light, No Light'. If I feel insane (which happens), I have 'Breaking Down'. I have 'Heartlines' to remind me of good times and keep me looking towards the future. I have 'All This And Heaven Too' to remind me that I'm not alone. Florence is just always there to say the right thing."

When it came to songwriting, Florence's methods were largely the same as they'd been for *Lungs.* Simply remain open, aware and sensitive to whatever is around you, go beyond the surface and remember that not everything is as it seems. Simply wandering through London was enough to spark a rush of new ideas – now Florence had the whole world to draw from, but as always, it would be the strange little details, odd slogans and hidden emotions that would fire her up. Once she got in the studio with the rest of the band, that communal feeling of making music together and bouncing ideas around would help the process flow, no pun intended.

"I have a notebook, and it's whatever phrases I see, whatever comes into my head... songs tend to write themselves that way, bit by bit. Sometimes one will come all at once when I'm in the studio and really focused...Then I put in characters, like a bird or a donkey... It sounds like an escape. Things falling down, a demolition, but one of those demolitions that happens from the inside... a reverse demolition!"

2010 would be a highly creative time for Florence + The Machine. The festive season had barely come and gone and Florence had, since January, been trying to grab moments to head to the studio to record some demos with Paul Epworth. But hard graft aside, 2010 would also be a year of celebration for Florence + The Machine: just days into the new year, Florence, who was away in Italy filming a TV appearance, would receive the news that *Lungs* had reached the top of the UK album charts.

Admittedly Florence wasn't feeling quite herself when she received the news, so her initial reaction might not have been exactly what Mairead had expected. "I was lying face down on the floor of an Italian TV studio when my manager told me," said Florence. "I had drunk far, far too much the night before. All I could manage to say was, 'That's great, can someone please get me an ibuprofen?' I'd had a little pre-number one celebration the night before and it had got out of hand."

Another reason to celebrate was around the corner: Florence had been nominated for three Brit Awards – British Female Solo Artist, British Breakthrough Act and the Mastercard British Album award for *Lungs* – and the ceremony was just weeks away. She could barely take in the fact that she was up for a clutch of gongs because there were so many things to do in the lead-up to the ceremony, as she would be performing too –

this time with grime star Dizzee Rascal, a unique mash-up of 'You Got The Love' and Dizzee's track 'Dirtee Cash'. Their duet would be called 'You Got The Dirtee Love' – see what they did there?

Pelted with questions from eager journalists keen to ask "how she felt" to be up for so many Brits just one year after bagging the Critic's Choice honour, she could only say that it still felt like "a blur", that it would only really sink in when the names of the nominees were being read out.

She had competition in the Best Female category from a diverse group of pop stars: Lily Allen, Bat for Lashes, *X Factor* star Leona Lewis and cutesy Pixie Lott. Her fellow Breakthrough nominees were her friends and contemporaries Friendly Fires, who were also up for Best British Group, La Roux, Pixie Lott and *X Factor* boy band JLS – yes, Cowell's presence was felt here. However, Florence wasn't above showing her appreciation for *X Factor*, the idea of someone performing one of her songs on the show would be "amazing!" she trilled. "I would love to be mainstream enough to be on those shows. I, like the rest of my family, am obsessed with them, though I find it quite hard to watch people be so vulnerable. Those talent shows are emotional public humiliation. I find them really hard to watch, but I still do!"

Fellow Best Female nominee Lily Allen would also compete with Florence in the album category with her cheeky *It's Not Me, It's You* album, the last she would release before her 'retirement'. Paolo Nutini was also up for the award with his album *Sunny Side Up,* as was the Leicester band Kasabian for the snappily titled *West Ryder Pauper Lunatic Asylum,* and finally her collaborator for the evening, Dizzee Rascal, was also nominated for his release *Tongue 'n' Cheek.*

But as Florence said, there was plenty for her to think about in the run-up to the event, not least rehearsing with Dizzee, although in the end the pair managed only three days working together in total. But they were confident; Dizzee promised viewers a "pleasant surprise" and they had plenty up their sleeves for the big night. One idea was that they planned to shower the audience with 'money'. Recession, be damned!

"I've no plan for one of those Shakespearean massive performances,"

Dizzee smirked. "It won't be one of those Robin Hood things with lots of twirling – unless I'm drunk! But we do have a few tricks. It sounds good and it's going to look good as well."

Florence also delighted in teasing the fans. "I'm going to be rapping and he's going to be singing! Not really... It's a mash-up of 'You Got The Love' and 'Dirtee Cash', so it's You Got The Dirtee Love. Or it could be You Got The Lovely Cash... It'll be a harp-filled hip-hop bonanza."

Whatever they had planned, it was going to be a riot, and crucially the song was to be recorded live and subsequently released the following day as a charity download. Dizzee even auctioned his suit off too. The charity benefiting from the proceeds was to be The Brit Trust, renowned for its contributions to The BRIT School and Nordoff Robbins Music Therapy with its mission 'to support young people in music and education', and this year the funds would also benefit the War Child fund and the Haiti Earthquake Appeal.

As the fateful night of February 16 drew ever closer, with its promise of glitz, glamour and, in Dizzee and Flo's case, gothic grime, the up to now relatively cool Florence started to get nervous. So much for it only sinking in when the nominations are read out. Florence was already terrified, and not just because of the Brit Awards; everything was getting on top of her. Thankfully, her family was on hand when she returned home from tour to restore her equilibrium.

"I just feel a bit shell-shocked and tired. Before the Brits I was in Japan, and travelling through every country," she said. "I've had times when I've just turned up in a hotel in Stockholm and gone into a meltdown. Crying and feeling lonely. My dad is fantastically good at calming me down and making me see straight. I think it's just a feeling of being overwhelmed. There's a big part of me that never thought all this would happen. It's wonderful, but it can be scary."

It's hardly any wonder, considering the many directions in which Florence was being pulled. She'd gone from being a drifting art student to someone who was seriously in demand, honouring tour dates, TV appearances, gigs, press interviews and also, by the way, having to write her next album amid all of the madness. But as February wore on and the

Brits ceremony approached, the terror zoned in and was encapsulated by one thing: the red carpet.

"I am so scared," she said. "I've been having anxiety dreams about running down the red carpet in my pyjamas going the wrong way, screaming, trying to hide my face... it's really scary on the red carpet."

However, as usual, no matter how 'scary' Florence found it, she managed to conquer that fear to the point that she looked like the most courageous person skipping down it that evening. She certainly wasn't afraid to flash some flesh: while Lily Allen sported a full-length gown and capelet, Pixie Lott cosied up in opaque tights and even Kylie Minogue, still a hotpants fan in her forties, covered up with a lacy black maxi-dress, Florence had slicked on one of her many red lippies and bravely shimmied into a minuscule glittering white dress for the occasion. It was short *and* low-cut. Surely it should have broken all the rules, but with her scarlet hair, lily-white skin and endless legs, Florence still looked fantastic and classy. No pyjamas on the red carpet for her.

There would be costume changes, of course – from a long asymmetrical black number in silk and lace, designed by Roksanda Ilincic, to a fish-tail white gown for her performance with Dizzee. And she wasn't lying about the performance being "harp-filled hip-hop". There were harps *everywhere*, not to mention a huge glitter-ball, out of which Florence emerged with a voice big enough to match any ego in the house that night. Dizzee and Florence rocked it.

Gracious as ever, Florence told reporters how excited she was to see her fellow artists performing that night, not least Lily Allen – the West London popstrel would descend to the stage scantily clad and on a rocket ship, and would later pick up the Best Female award sporting a bright orange comedy wig; a fine example of not taking the music industry and its trappings too seriously. Behind the scenes things were just as much fun, with everyone making a special effort not to let the pressure get under their skin.

"It's amazing backstage because you can hear everyone rehearsing," Florence said. "You've got Robbie Williams blasting through the dressing room walls and Lily Allen and Gaga passing each other in the hallway. But it's quite relaxed, everyone's just trying to be calm.

146

"It always feels to me that the Brits is a great British musical," pondered Florence. "Everyone's running around backstage, half-dressed. Gaga's going in one room, Dizzee's in another, and there's me in some funny brocade dressing gown, barefoot, chatting to everyone. It does have that sense of a celebration. I guess I think about it in that way to help myself process it. I understand musicals."

While Florence might have lost out on the British Female award to Lily, and the Breakthrough to JLS, it was still set to be a special night for her. Much to the delight of her entourage, which included, of course, her manager, Mairead, members of Toast Press who had done a sterling job on Florence's publicity and celebrity pals including the presenter Nick Grimshaw, Florence would be picking up the Best Album award that night. She thanked fans and her team through a veil of happy tears. Before the night was through, album sales of *Lungs* had increased by 1,550 per cent. Her bone-shaking performance with Dizzee had certainly played its part.

"Each year featured Brits artists can always expect a huge lift in sales of their recordings – both in the run-up to the ceremony itself and then immediately after, when their media profile is at its greatest," explained HMV spokesman Gennaro Castaldo to *The Telegraph*. "The biggest gainers are those that give show-stealing performances on the night or who grab the headlines by winning multiple awards. Such artists can easily experience a doubling or even a trebling of sales overnight, especially in these days of instant downloads, while a further boost can be expected at the weekend, when people are out shopping."

"The Brits 2010 was just incredible," said Mike Walsh, of XFM. "A weird memory of that night: I remember sitting in a car on our way from the Brits to the Universal Music after-party with the two MDs of Island, Darcus and Ted. We were driving past all these electronic billboards that had *Lungs* winning the Brit Award – she'd only won an hour or so ago…. I remember thinking, 'That's the future of advertising!' in my pissed state.

"It felt like your team had won the World Cup – an artist you'd felt passionate about since day one had obviously had the sales but had also bagged the award *and* nailed one of the most incredible performances with Dizzee; it was a proper collaboration, but she just blew everybody away."

Florence might not have scooped the gong in every category she was included in that night, but the Brit effect lasted far longer than the thrill of that special night. Florence was now a bona-fide star, and Florence + The Machine was a brand that her label wasted no time in making the most of. Her stratospheric rise to fame was unusually fast and, even more unusually, untainted, if you ignore the 'Kiss With A Fist'/domestic violence speculation, which was soon dissolved. In short, Florence was a prize, and her team couldn't believe their luck.

"It's not unique but it's certainly rare," says a one music executive. "Paolo Nutini is a good comparison: his debut really kicked off and inspired a lot of emotion, and he has a very active fan community. He's been successful but managed to retain some credibility. There haven't been any 'drunken Florence' stories or 'Florence cancelling a gig' stories, she's managed to avoid all of that.

"She's been one of the first acts to break that campaign cycle. Until relatively recently you'd have campaign, campaign, campaign, single, album, two more singles, maybe another if things are going well and then off you go, write the next album sitting in a bunker for the next 18 months.

"But she's got that combination of being very prolific and also hugely successful. There's never nothing to do on that job even when she was writing or recording, there's just so much stuff going on around her. There were about five editions of the album – that's another hallmark of the way the industry operates now: money's getting tighter so they want to flog things in about 20 different flavours. But there was that super mega deluxe box-set that I think had a lock of her hair in it, hand-written notes… I think it was a limited run of about 100 but that's still a fair bit of hair."

No one could say that Florence wasn't prepared to make sacrifices for her fans. When she was a little girl she used to make offerings to the sea or the river, throwing rocks into the water ceremoniously, no doubt accompanied with a little incantation. Now she was making offerings to her fans, who had blessed her with success she never could have dreamed of.

There was one thing that Florence did dream of: marriage and a stable family life of her own, at least at some point. However, she wistfully admitted that the flipside of her fabulous new existence was that any chance of cosy domesticity was not on the cards for the immediate future. Florence seemed to spend half of her time living in hotel rooms trying to remember which city she was in and the other half in the studio. "I didn't have much time for contemplation," she confessed.

"I have a ridiculous life. This is all consuming. You have to shelve things. You live for that moment on stage when none of that matters, whether you'll ever have a normal life."

# CHAPTER TWELVE

*"I was going to make a concept album called This Time Machine Sucks*
*and the album artwork was just going to be me looking moody standing in*
*a cardboard box. They weren't so keen on it..."*

After a euphoric whirlwind tour of North America, which included the festival Coachella, Florence had a couple of weeks to take stock, recover from jet-lag and consume plenty of tea and box-sets before packing her suitcase yet again. Was there any point in unpacking it? Maybe not. But in the light of the incredible success of *Lungs*, Florence's team announced a short run of tour dates in the UK and Ireland, titled the *Cosmic Love* tour, which would conclude at London's Hammersmith Apollo, and featured Babe Shadow and Brooklyn band the Drums in support. It was also confirmed around this time that Florence + The Machine would be headlining their first festival in July – Latitude in Southwold, Suffolk. Florence had a super-impressive billowing sheer black outfit lined up for that one, designed by Alex Noble, designer for Cirque Du Soleil and Lady Gaga, no less. It was never going to be an outfit for a shrinking violet.

'Strangeness And Charm', that special new track of Florence's that was just four months old, inspired by a late-night conversation with her father, was debuted at the first concert of the tour at the Olympia Theatre in Dublin on May 2, 2010. It's fair to say, her fans adored its pulsating rhythms, relentless, fast-paced harp and hard-edged, strong vocals.

Just days later, fans would be delighted further by the news that Florence + The Machine would provide a track, namely the brooding 'Heavy In Your Arms', for the soundtrack to *The Twilight Saga: Eclipse*, the third film of the hugely successful teenage vampire movie series *The Twilight Saga*, based on the Stephanie Meyer books of the same name. *Eclipse* was released in cinemas in June 2010, to be devoured by a swooning and largely female public. An entirely black and white music video for 'Heavy In Your Arms', again directed by the visionary Tabitha and Tom, was released the following month.

It amused Florence, and of course seemed perfectly fitting, that she would be chosen to contribute to *Twilight* musically. "I'm the soundtrack to a spook generation!" she giggled. "Apocalyptic-pop.

"'Heavy In Your Arms' is about the weight of love, and how sometimes it can be a burden between two people," Florence explained on her website. "I felt this was a strong theme in the *Twilight* series – is someone being rescued or are they being condemned, and is the love you carry bringing you down?

"I recorded it with Paul one evening, using a lot of strange reversed vocal samples and big hip-hop piano. It's basically inspired by nineties hip-hop and gospel choirs, like most of my songs."

Florence and her sister, Grace, had made a point of getting stuck into *Twilight* whilst on holiday to get into the mood. They weren't disappointed. How could they be? Vampires, darkness, romance and doom… it's pure Flo.

"I went on holiday with my family, me and Grace only had one book between us," she said. "We were sharing a room and we'd be reading *Twilight* to each other at night. She'd fall asleep and be like 'You can't read ahead of me!' And I'd be secretly reading faster than her."

Florence + The Machine would also be featured on the trailer for the Julia Roberts movie *Eat, Pray, Love*, based on the book of the same name by the US author Elizabeth Gilbert. The song used was 'Dog Days Are Over'. It combined perfectly with the concept of the movie, which was about a divorcée on a quest for joy and inner peace.

"I thought [the trailer] was beautiful, and fitted well with the song," said Florence. "We say no to so much stuff, something really has to work for me to OK it, and when I was deciding whether or not to do it I was in Miami and found a copy of the book completely by accident in the back of a taxi, so I took that as a sign.

"[Then] when we did the trailer, I was like, 'OK, so that means Julia Roberts and I are like friends, right?' Isn't that what that means? To me the movie world seems like a whole fantasy world!"

Another thrilling project was also under way, this time a collaboration with legendary Talking Heads frontman David Byrne, an enduring icon of New York's post-punk scene, and the DJ and producer Fatboy Slim. The project was titled *Here Lies Love*, and was, rather intriguingly, a concept album-come-rock-musical about Imelda Marcos, former first lady of the Philippines, she of the incredible shoe collection. The title came from Marcos' desire to have 'Here lies love' enscribed on her tombstone.

David Byrne: "The story I am interested in is about asking what drives a powerful person – what makes them tick? How do they make and then remake themselves? I thought to myself, wouldn't it be great if – as this piece would be principally composed of clubby dance music – one could experience it in a club setting? Could one bring a 'story' and a kind of theatre to the disco? Was that possible? If so, wouldn't that be amazing?"

Byrne invited Florence to provide vocals for the album, alongside Cyndi Lauper, Tori Amos, Santigold, Martha Wainwright, Roisin Murphy and many others, all alternately playing the role of Imelda Marcos and the woman who raised her, Estrella Cumpas. Florence sang on the title track. She didn't need too much information about what he wanted her to do – the title would have been enough to intrigue this incorrigibly dark romantic – but there was never any doubt that she would agree to working with Byrne.

"Well, he just asked to work with me, and when David Byrne asks to work with you, it's 'Yes! Anything!'" she said. "We spent the day in the studio together. It was fun. I didn't know much about the project, but like I said, he's my hero. He could have asked me to sing the alphabet backwards and I would have said yes.

"He was so nice, we just went into a studio in South London and he told me about the back-story of the song. I didn't actually meet Fatboy Slim."

Success was certainly flooding into Florence's life in great abundance, and some might argue that it was bringing out, shall we say, the eccentric side of the singer even more. In June, Florence + The Machine would head to Swansea in Wales with the band Clement Marfo and the Frontline in tow, a gig memorable for the support band because of Florence's apparent rider requests. In short, according to Clement, everything had to be black. "Black straws, black tissues, black curtains – everything black," he told the site *TaleTela*. "We were like 'Alright, love.'" Whatever works…

A full-on summer of festivals was unfolding too, including an appearance at the idyllic Somerset House's Summer Series, T In The Park, Oxegen and the historic Isle Of Wight festival – which was particularly exciting for Florence, as it would be the first time she and the band had taken the main stage there.

"Two years ago I was just here to do one DJ set," she said. "I stayed for the whole weekend and I can't remember anything about my DJ set except for the fact that I *may* have crowd-surfed at the end, and maybe I tried to break into the cider tent. I remember how I started it too, I started it with the *William Tell Overture*. This year it feels quite nice to be playing the main stage."

Quite nice was an understatement. Florence was made up to be "warming up" the festival for the rapper Jay-Z, who would be headlining the opening night. She admitted she was amazed and honoured to be asked to do it, not least because it seemed like yesterday that she was an unknown artist behind the decks.

"When I hear about these sets I do ask, 'Are you sure?'," she said. "I'm not sure we're big enough to play the slots we're doing." Rest assured, no one else shared this feeling. After a few stretches to warm up, she thrilled the crowd with her blistering set, leaping up and down on top of a speaker as the audience danced at her feet and her band – which included a choral and string section – rocked that little island with their wall of cosmic sound.

Backstage was every bit as exciting as being out front. She bumped into Beyoncé and Kanye West, as you do, which led to something of a mutual appreciation society toast-athon, as glasses of champagne were raised and gushes exchanged.

"I was on just before Jay-Z and [Beyoncé] passed me and went, 'Ah!' And I went, 'Ah!' And she was like, 'It's such an honour to meet you!' And I was like, 'Oh my gosh, it's such an honour to meet you!' Then she, Kanye and I went 'Cheers!' It was so surreal."

On June 25, Florence was back at Glastonbury with her band and her siblings. Her mother, Evelyn, had expressly told Florence to look after her little brother, JJ, at the festival, but it wasn't as if she'd have time to do any brother-sitting… "My mum's like, 'You can't let him get into any trouble!' I'm going to be on stage! I'll probably see him crowd-surfing with my Brit award and a couple of his friends wearing my clothes…"

Florence would not yet be playing her dream stage, the Pyramid, but this time she and the Machine would be taking the Other Stage. Clad in a Maison Margiela creation that, again, would make Björk, not to mention Lady Gaga, proud – a swan-like, ballerina-esque bodysuit with a lace sleeve – she effortlessly drew not only one of the biggest crowds of the day, but one of the biggest in the history of the Other Stage. The tremendous significance of this was not lost on her, and she broke down in tears several times on stage, notably in the middle of the ecstatic 'Dog Days', which caused the crowd to practically combust with joy. "This is a pretty big moment for me," she told the audience through her sniffles. "To start in a tent and then be here… it means a lot to be on this stage in front of you. I never want to leave."

Defining moments? 'You Got The Love', no doubt, which she famously took the opportunity to sing frequently around the festival site, and her dramatic cover of Fleetwood Mac's 'The Chain'. Florence had hoped that Fleetwood Mac would be at the festival to hear her rendition of their seminal hit. They weren't, sadly, but for one night only, Florence + The Machine played their arrangement of the song before thousands of thrilled festival-goers.

"This is pretty much my favourite song of all time," Florence told them. "All my heroes are in this band and I thought they were going to be here but they're not. We're never going to play it again. We hope you enjoy it Glastonbury, this one's just for you."

"I remember that glorious year when she did 'The Chain'," says XFM's Mike Walsh. "I remember watching that and thinking, 'Could you get any better?' That kind of 'how many stars can you have in one band?' question came into my head, I love Fleetwood Mac but that was a band with too many personalities – Florence is a one-woman Fleetwood Mac, really. All that creativity and passion and genius isn't spread across four or five powerful individuals, it's rolled into one person."

Admittedly, the ubiquity of 'You Got The Love' at Glastonbury, with Florence appearing onstage with the XX to sing it and also with Dizzee Rascal, started to pall for some critics present.

"You couldn't move five metres in any direction without hearing her cover of 'You Got The Love' partly because Florence Welch herself kept popping up unexpectedly and singing it," sighed *GQ* magazine. "You started to wonder if those people you saw in the early hours, gingerly approaching the Portaloos, torch in hand, were worried about the notorious state of the facilities or simply concerned that she was in there as well, ready to deliver her lung-busting version of the old Candi Staton hit."

Still, as *The Guardian* observed, "She's got the sun-scarred crowd around her pinkie. Expect her fifth Glastonbury appearance to top the Pyramid."

Fully charged with Glastonbury magic, Florence would make a triumphant return to Australia just weeks later, kicking things off at the brilliantly named Splendour In The Grass three-day festival in Queensland. The gig took place in a huge open-air amphitheatre, which apparently wasn't big enough for the number of people clamouring to see Florence, who was clad in billowing, angelic white and looked impossibly cool in the intense heat. In fact, 28,000 of the 33,000 people attending were there to see Florence, and she and her band drew one of the biggest crowds of the festival, to the point that the amphitheatre had to be temporarily closed by security due to safety fears as fans rushed to see her.

Their performance was "mesmerising", according to a reviewer for ABC.net, "joyous". One member of the audience was even inspired to strip off all of his clothes, before he persuaded fellow festival-goers to lift him up above the crowd as he pretended to be a Greek statue.

It was only a matter of time until Florence's unique sense of style and effortless sartorialism caught the attention of the world of haute couture. Yes, she was increasingly being lent gorgeous gowns by world famous designers keen to have a bit of Florence cachet as she glided down the red carpet at yet another event or awards ceremony. But that autumn, both Valentino and Dries Van Noten used Florence songs for their spring 2011 runway shows, and Mulberry actually hired Flo to perform at its after-party. It even seemed to have paid tribute to Florence on the catwalk itself, with a series of flame-haired models slinking back and forth. This was, admittedly, a happy accident...

"It was a perfect colliding of inspirations," Mulberry designer Emma Hill told *The New York Times*. "I like to design with one girl in mind to have a consistency to the collection, and we found this gorgeous girl from Finland, Julia Johansen, who opened our show. Coincidentally, she has red hair like Florence and we liked the idea that all the other girls would be mirror images of Julia with red wigs and all. It was bizarre."

Florence was there at the New York show, clad in a Mulberry skirt and boots with a sheer black shirt, watching from the front row alongside fellow style icon Alexa Chung. Florence laughed as her friend urged her to get up onto the catwalk herself. "She was like: 'You should be walking off the runway, too. Go join your fellow girls in the land of ginger.'"

It was nice to know that ladies of the flame-coloured locks were being celebrated, not least because some people still had enough of the school bully about them to single 'gingers' out in less flattering ways. "As for cool people," Florence mused, "Liam Gallagher was really rude to me for no other reason than I have ginger hair – what does that tell you?" Quite. A dignified response to an unfathomable snipe from the former Oasis singer.

And, for the record, Liam's actual quote? "I'm not having someone with ginger hair making music. I'm not going down that road." But this is someone who also can't bear his own flesh and blood (Noel, that is), and also revealed that he didn't even like the name 'Oasis' (undoubtedly one of the most successful Beatles tribute groups in the world).

Having the world's spotlight on her, not just for her songs and performances but for her style, gave Florence an opportunity to shine *her* spotlight in turn on the designers she loved to support. She loved Alex Noble, always praised Hannah Marshall, whose designs she continues to wear, and she made a point of crediting Verity Pemberton when it came to stage-wear: "[She] designs bodysuits, stuff I can jump around in." It was crucial not only to have a costume that would be an extension of Florence's self-expression, but also to have one that wasn't going to fall apart, trip her up or tear if she had the sudden yen to climb a lighting rig or jump on a speaker stack. And as Florence fans knew, this was not out of the question.

"I really like this outfit I wore for T4 On The Beach, which is like half-witch/half-sea monster," Florence enthused. "[It's] like one big string vest, all black fringing coming all the way down and sparkly hotpants and a shiny leather-effect body. I looked really like something that had been dredged up. I was performing on the beach in front of all these kids wearing neon sunglasses and I was really hoping I was scaring them."

Offstage, her tastes were, perhaps, a little less sea monster and a little more Annie Hall, as she enjoyed rooting around in treasure trove second-hand shops and festival stalls rather than floating about in haute couture all the time. For a while Florence favoured wide-brimmed felt hats, waistcoats and shirts, tapered trousers... "I want to look like Blossom all the time!" she joked.

"I spend half my life in Beyond Retro [a vintage shop]. I mix vintage with my grandmother's old clothes and stuff I get from the high street. There's a lot of stuff I get from festivals, Bestival especially, they have a lot of vintage shops there and I'm like, 'Ooh, shopping at a festival!'

"I'm still going in and out of my little old lady phase, I have extremes of frumpiness, I either look like Little Lord Fauntleroy or Anne Frank. A mix of First World War evacuee and a page boy. I'm drifting in and out of that, I veer into punk but I always come back." Whatever she seemed to choose, Florence captured attention. She could just pull off any look – well, almost any look. She cheerfully admits that her sure-fire "man-repellent" is her all-in-one paisley suit and loafers combo. But that didn't matter, as long as she was trying new things and expressing herself through her clothes, she was happy – and there was a whole world of fashion out there, old and new, for her to discover and enjoy.

"I used to dress like an eight-year-old boy," said Florence. "Travelling has inspired me to be more experimental."

Despite the (almost) across-the-board adulation and near-constant validation, not to mention emulation, from adoring fans, smitten designers and mesmerised columnists of both the music and fashion persuasion, Florence still swung from feeling ecstatic and delighted to unsteady, weepy, fearful and confused. Partly this may have been to do with fatigue and jet-lag, constantly having to adjust to different time zones and new places, but part of it was also down to simply not having as much confidence in herself as many might have believed. While the attention and near-hero worship she received was appreciated, Florence still felt, as so many artists do, that she probably wasn't entirely worthy of it, particularly when she awoke the morning after a blistering gig during which the world seemed to be in the palm of her hand.

"You've still got your internal voice telling you you're a dick!" she laughed. "You just wake up and it's like, 'Oh, I'm me again … Still me.'"

This lack of confidence, panic, in fact, loomed forth just before another career-defining moment – the MTV VMAs (Video Music Awards) in October 2010. In fact this would be the appearance that would seal the deal with America and make her a true-blue superstar on both sides of the Atlantic, and yet she was so terrified the day before the ceremony that she spent hours tied up in knots, could barely sleep and cried fitfully. It didn't help that, during a pre-show rehearsal of 'Dog Days Are Over', in a thrilling routine directed by *So You Think You*

*Can Dance* choreographer Travis Wall based on her fantastical video for the track, she was required to prance about on a rotating platform with an army of very energetic dancers. It wasn't as easy as it looked, and it didn't actually look that easy. Fans might assume everything Florence does is effortless, but certainly in this case, it was not.

"I was really honoured, I really didn't want to fuck it up!" she admitted. "The live performance, I just wanted to re-create what the video was about, obviously there's so much going on in there but it was great, we had the blue ladies and all the different characters, it was fantastic to see the dancers, how they would interpret the song."

The only thing they couldn't manage was "having exploding people" in the performance. That would have been a health and safety nightmare.

"We were up for an award for Best Video, so they allowed us to go full throttle. That was brave of them – we were a really unknown act in America. And to give us this huge scale of a performance with all the bells and whistles – well, it could have gone one of two ways: 'Oh my God, this crazy English girl... go back home!' Or they could embrace it.

"So we arrived at the VMAs, painted 27 people blue, massive psychedelic choir, spinning podium, drummers, Busby Berkeley dancers, me in a kind of Grecian, pink extravaganza with no shoes on, lying on this podium, waiting for it all to start, looking at the ceiling thinking: 'What am I doing here?'

"Afterwards it didn't really hit me what had just happened. There's always five minutes after I do an awards thing where I'm like, 'Was it OK? Did I sing? Did words come out of my mouth? Was I waving my hands?'"

Despite her fears, this "Busby Berkeley on acid" performance was hailed as one of the highlights of the night, and *Lungs* immediately shot to number two on the iTunes albums chart, while 'Dog Days Are Over' ascended to number nine on the iTunes singles chart. What's more, Flo was tweeted about a staggering 1,700 times per minute on Twitter, and she was the top search on Google for 10 minutes. So, a success, it's fair to say.

"Doing the MTV VMAS ceremony in 2010 changed everything overnight," said Mairead Nash. "We had such an insane response that we couldn't ignore it."

Florence + The Machine take the stage in incendiary style at the Rivoli Ballroom, south London, for the launch of *Lungs* on July 7, 2009. ANNABEL STAFF/REDFERNS

Florence's manager Mairead Nash—one half of the DJ duo Queens of Noize and founder of Luv Luv Luv Management—and Florence + The Machine drummer Chris Hayden get ready to party at W Hotel, Leicester Square, London after the NME Awards on February 29, 2012. DAVE M. BENETT/GETTY IMAGES

Florence and Mairead join the Flaming Lips onstage at the Electric Picnic, Sradbally, Ireland on September 6, 2009. DAVE MITCHELL/RETNA PICTURES

Florence and her sister Grace hit Primrose Hill with DJ pal Nick Grimshaw for his birthday party at Lemonia. Other guests included Sadie Frost, Henry Holland, singer Remi Nicole and Miquita Oliver. SPLASH NEWS

Florence and her boyfriend (the so-called 'posh boy from Hull') James Nesbitt stroll through central London on 22 March 2012. BERETTA/SIMS/REX FEATURES

Isabella 'Isa Machine' Summers, Florence's long-tim collaborator and friend. SPLASH NEWS

Florence appears on the set of *Gossip Girl* with the Machine at the invitation of her chum and *Gossip Girl* star **Blake Lively.** CW NETWORK/EVERETT/REX FEATURES

rence + The Machine guitarist Rob Ackroyd performing live onstage. CHRIS SCHWEGLER/RETNA LTD/CORBIS

rence performs a Halloween show in costume at the House Of Blues. KELVIN MA/ZUMA PRESS/CORBIS

Promoting her band's tour at the Sydney Intercontinental Hotel, Australia during August 2010.

Sarah Bernhardt, eat your... erm... 'hardt' out. Florence strikes a pose onstage behind drummer Chris Hayden at the Hammersmith Apollo, London on May 14, 2010. MARTYN FOSTER/LFI

Florence Welch, looking sharp, attends the Givenchy Ready to Wear Autumn/Winter 2011/2012 show at Paris Fashion Week. STEPHANE CARDINALE/PEOPLE AVENUE/CORBIS

Florence's attention-grabbing McQueen outfit certainly polarised the blogosphere at the 'Schiaparelli And Prada: Impossible Conversations' Costume Institute Gala at the Metropolitan Museum of Art. NANCY KASZERMAN/ZUMA PRESS/CORBIS

Florence Welch shows off those trademark lily-white ins at the Nylon Music Issue Launch Party on June 2011 in New York. HARRY PLUVIOSE/RETNA LTD/CORBIS

A romantic Florence at The 53rd Annual GRAMMY Awards held at Staples Center in Los Angeles on February 13, 2011. RD/ORCHON/RETNA LTD/CORBIS

Down Under: a contemplative moment for Flo in the Surry Hills, Sydney, Australia on January 25, 2010.
BRIANNE MAKIN/NEWSPIX/REX FEATURES

The host, Chelsea Handler, had fallen in love with Florence just as much as the rest of America had seemed to. Florence: "I passed her in the hall, and she went, '*You fuckin' rule!*' And I thought, 'Yes! Maybe it did go well.' Then I remember us all running down this corridor screaming.

"After the VMAs I felt like suddenly America took notice. Before that I had a fantastic and extremely supportive, but pretty underground, fanbase. America is so big that you kind of need an opportunity like that to make it."

The 2010 MTV VMAs was memorable for another reason: it was the event that Lady Gaga famously turned up wearing a meat dress made of real, raw flank steak. She even had a matching fascinator and bag, and the outfit, of course, caused quite a stir. It has since been preserved "as a kind of jerky", and put on display at the Rock 'n' Roll Hall Of Fame. However, Florence was mortified not by the idea of the dress itself so much as the fact that she had impulsively hugged Lady Gaga while wearing an eye-wateringly expensive borrowed Givenchy dress.

"I didn't notice that it was made of meat, I thought she just had some kind of body paint on or something," said Florence. "I did not notice until she got up onstage with Cher. I felt guilty because I was borrowing this Givenchy couture dress, and I just rubbed myself all over this meat." Look before you hug…

To add insult to injury, Florence's pale gold vision of a dress was criticised by mouthy bloggers for being just a little over the top for the VMAs. Florence brushed off comments from snipey critics. "Look," she said. "If Givenchy is going to lend you a dress, I'm not going to turn it down. I would wear that dress to just go out and buy a pint of *milk* if they would lend it to me."

So, meat-streaked, "too posh" gown aside (surely Givenchy would appreciate that these stains were a memory of a seminal pop moment?) Florence could do no wrong – and what a month October 2010 was turning out to be. A high-octane performance of 'Dog Days' on Ellen DeGeneres' chat show also helped to seal the deal – and after all, has Ellen ever been wrong yet? Her choice of musical guests is always cutting edge and she certainly has taste. Florence, clad in a peachy-pink mini-dress, wowed Ellen and audience alike, and charmed the presenter when she gauchely revealed how relieved she was not to have fallen over in her giant heels before apologising sweetly for hitting the microphone accidentally during her song.

Then there would be the appearance on *Saturday Night Live*, on which Florence and her band performed 'Dog Days' and a solemn arrangement of 'You Got The Love', presented by actress Anne Hathaway (who even gave Flo a standing ovation during the rehearsal). This appearance would win Florence another enchanted army of fans Stateside, all of whom were desperate to hear what goodies their new favourite star had in store on the next album, which promised to be an epic release. She wouldn't let them down.

Fan Alexandra Heap remembers that seeing Florence on *SNL* marked the first time she heard Florence + The Machine's music – but it certainly wouldn't be the last. "I was watching my favourite show, *Saturday Night Live*. It was late, around 12:00a.m. or so, and the musical guest was about to come on. Usually I use this time to get a couple minutes of much-needed sleep until the next comedy sketch, generally because I'm rarely in the mood to be serenaded at midnight.

"At this time I had never heard of Florence + The Machine. I had decided that the first few lines of the song would be the determining factor in which I would either stay awake, or drift off to sleep. But there was a moment, about halfway through the performance, in which my sister and I both turned to each other and simultaneously whispered: "Wow, she's amazing."

"I started watching *SNL* that night aspiring to be a comedienne, and emerged wanting to be a singer. There's something so refreshing about an artist who isn't afraid to step over societal boundaries to just be herself, and I think that's the reason why Florence has been such an inspirational role model to me. I hope that somehow they know that they are changing lives; one slightly awkward teenager at a time."

October, of course, means Hallowe'en... and again, Florence + The Machine found themselves in America for that time of year when the veil between the two worlds is at its thinnest. Florence and co were in New Orleans, Louisiana, to play the Voodoo Fest when October 31 swung around, and as the publication *Highbeam* observed, she was in the mood for mischief.

"She's driving through the crowded streets of New Orleans' French Quarter in a borrowed '94 Cadillac containing a gun that isn't registered to anyone currently in the car," they wrote. "Technically, the songstress' publicist is behind the wheel, though both the vehicle and the firearm belong to C.C. Adcock, a local swamp-rock fixture and *True Blood* soundtrack contributor who, just moments before, had been helping Welch and her band the Machine record a brassy version of Buddy Holly's 'Not Fade Away' for an upcoming album tribute to the late singer."

The tribute album, titled *Rave On Buddy Holly*, would be released the following June in honour of what would have been the bespectacled rockabilly star's 75th birthday, and featured contributions from the Black Keys, Paul McCartney, Lou Reed, Patti Smith and Modest Mouse amongst others. Good company.

"I'd instantly jumped at the chance as I've been a huge Buddy Holly fan ever since I was a kid," said Florence excitedly. "My grandmother took me to see *Buddy Holly The Musical*, which changed my life! I've had a crush on Buddy Holly ever since..." But back to N'Orleans...

Florence, appropriately, given her location, was playing Dr John on the car stereo, and as the music blasted and the characterful French Quarter flew by as they drove, members of the band jokingly wondered aloud whether tomorrow's headlines would be along the 'Florence Welch In Possession Of Illegal Firearm' lines. However, their glorious leader was more worried about something else she'd got up to that day. "What are the ramifications of breaking into a cemetery?" she asked plaintively. Well, it was Hallowe'en, after all. Florence fell in love with New Orleans on this trip, and on a future visit to the New Orleans Jazz Festival, she admitted that on this fateful All Hallows Eve, "New Orleans took a part of me, and I don't want it back."

While touring was often like a school trip with plenty of Famous Five-esque jolly japery, when it came to knuckling down, Florence ran a tight ship. Chris Hayden, Florence + The Machine's drummer and musical director, knew how seriously their commander in chief took the business of making music.

"She's a lot of fun to be around, but she's very serious about her music," he explained. "She wants the sound right, and she wants it deep and open."

"She has definite ideas about what she wants and she feels like she can trust us to deliver the goods," added Tom Monger. The Machine were an integral part of the sound, but the members also understood that part of their strength was that they melted into the background, providing a sparkling wall of sound that supported Florence's voice perfectly. As a result, they would rarely be involved in interviews, rarely appear in videos and, up to the time of writing, they have never appeared on an album cover.

Tom Monger: "It was always the idea that Florence + The Machine was Florence and an ever-changing collective, it just so happens that it's been a pretty stable line-up for the last few years. But, ultimately, it's Florence's baby and we all kind of knew that from day one, so we have come to accept that. Let's just say we do an awful lot of work as well!"

Hayden confirmed that *Ceremonials* would be "organised as an album, not a collection of singles". The release would be a journey that would need to be consumed in one sitting to be truly appreciated, not dipped into or listened to on shuffle amid the rest of your iTunes tracks. This would reflect the albums that Florence herself loved and appreciated, albums that were treated reverently and listened to with respect, often in the dark. Whilst lying on the floor. Possibly while drunk.

One thing was for sure, Florence was moving on from "hiding behind gothic imagery" and producing something more "heartfelt". The lyrics would, naturally, be more contemplative after having spent so much time away from her loved ones. The situation was very different. As Florence said: "The first one's like a scrapbook, this one I wanted it to be more like a story."

The title was inspired by, yet again, an art installation that Florence had spotted some years earlier. "It was this weird seventies Super-8 film of all these hippies in a procession in ceremonial robes, it was quite psychedelic. They were performing a strange ritual and it was all colour-based, there were balloons, kids in strange costumes… basically right up my street. It was called *Ceremonials* and then there was a roman numeral. This name is a bit more crystal and ethereal, the first album title was more bloody. I also wanted it to be one word that ended in an 's', like the first one."

The FATM look would change too – from the album artwork to the ensuing videos to Florence's own image, that slightly pagan, elemental vibe would change to something a little more sleek, elegant and art deco-inspired.

"We [she, Tom Beard and Tabitha Denholm] have moved on from being inspired by the Pre-Raphaelites to the New Romantics, looking at Klimt and Erte, art deco influences, it's moving on like an unfolding projection," she said.

So, we're talking glossy, velvety aesthetics and a cohesive, flowing sound. The sound of the harp had been such a prominent part of *Lungs* that the plan was now to give Tom something of a back seat, or rather, to drench his playing with effects and electronics, something Tom loved to do anyway.

"I think they decided that rather than make the same album twice, it would take a little more of a background role on this one," Tom explained. "In 'Shake It Out' you don't actually hear on there what you'd recognise as a harp, but it is on there. It's just under so many effects. If you listen very carefully, at the end of the record you'll hear a high-frequency twinkly sound, and that's actually the harp going through a crystal reverb thing. But you wouldn't know it's a harp."

Or as Isabella put it: "This time we're attacking it in a different way, let's make synth noises! Who cares about real instruments?"

Florence also revealed that they were experimenting with lots of new sounds for the album, such as Japanese drum samples and sound effects, sounds that hadn't even occurred to them for the first album.

"We recorded crows," Paul Epworth said. "Mutterings…"

"Like séance singing," Florence added enthusiastically. Another of Florence and Paul's favourite sound effects on the album was the sound of "a zombie head being smashed in…. They make good kick drums," dead-panned Paul, knowing that every time he cued the sound from his computer, Florence would screech and cringe with a mixture of delight and disgust.

The sound may have changed, but the dark, brooding themes remained. And they would, Florence assured us, continue to do so for some time, as no matter how successful she was becoming, she felt as if she was "still in the woods".

"I'm moving toward the intensity and passion of heaven and hell, revelation and retribution, that kind of battle. The first album was more about flesh. This is about light.

"Maybe in a few years time when I'm married and living in the country I'll be writing happy songs about bumble bees, but right now everything's still so up in the air and there's so much chaos."

Chaos was a presiding theme for Florence, and always had been, going right back to childhood. Maybe it always would be. However, an organised chaos, a constructive kind of chaos, often birthed a great deal of creativity, which was just as well as Island Records had apparently expressed that they had "high expectations" for Florence's new release. This will have no doubt been meant as a compliment; who didn't have high expectations for it? It's certainly better than saying they had low expectations. But this gave Florence something of an unwelcome jolt...

"I didn't read that!" she exclaimed. "They can have expectations, but they're not the ones doing it, are they? You should have high expectations for yourself and others should come second.

"Making a record is personal, and I really wanted to make something amazing, so I was putting that pressure on myself anyway. It would be fruitless and very counter-productive for the label to put pressure on me." So just watch it, basically.

Personal as *Ceremonials* would be, the idea of wearing her heart on her sleeve was "very frightening" to her, despite her emotional, free-flowing persona. She said: "Like a lot of British people, I prefer sarcasm and irreverence." However, the album would be rather more deep, sincere and emotionally charged than maybe even Florence could have imagined it would be. Aware of her young fans who would hang on her every lyric, Florence also consciously included "positive messages" in two of the songs: 'Heartlines' and 'Spectrum'.

"For someone so conflicted, who am I to give advice to anybody? It's such a funny, grandiose idea," she squirmed. "[But] I was thinking about positive messages on the record because I knew there would be kids listening. Like putting something in there that wasn't just for me, like 'Heartlines' and 'Spectrum', they're really earnest, saying don't be afraid of who you are and follow your heart."

And fans would indeed take Florence's lyrics to heart. No matter what you think of Florence and her music or concepts, there are a lot of people who feel their lives have been changed for the better because of it, or that they were spurred on to keep positive as a result of her well-chosen words and celestial sounds.

"Last year was very difficult for me," says fan Maria Soto, who has named her adoptive daughter Isabella. "This girl was my reason to keep going, to keep fighting; the 'Heartlines' song was in my mind all the time, 'keep it up, I know you can…' I will always be thankful to Florence for her music, for changing my life."

# CHAPTER THIRTEEN

*"I wanted to make my new album how I heard Madonna makes all of her albums: drum and bass first and then put in everything else."*

Christmas was coming, and Florence and her bandmates were looking forward to spending some time on home turf after completing a three-day residency at LA's Wiltern in early November, the results of which would be released as an album, *Live At The Wiltern*, on iTunes the following summer.

Once again, the ever-supportive Blake Lively popped up to cheer on her friend, and she brought along the Australian director Baz Luhrmann, the man responsible for the lavish movie *Moulin Rouge*. Instantly Baz knew he'd met someone special, not to mention someone he would love to work with.

"Our mutual friend, Blake, said, 'I'm going to see Florence + The Machine tonight. You should come.' And I couldn't go in New York, so I went to see you in Los Angeles at the Wiltern, and Blake had set up for us to meet," Baz remembers in *Interview Magazine*. "My crowd went and your mum and brother were there…"

"Were they?" Florence interjected. "No, it was Blake's mum and Blake's brother. Our mum wouldn't come."

"Wait, I am thinking to myself that you and Blake are so like twin sisters," Baz said. "It was *her* mum and brother. You came on stage, and there was this whirling drumbeat and this strange, whirling dervish choreography, and by the end of that night, all 2,000 people in the Wiltern were jumping up and down." This would not be the last Baz and Florence would see of each other – in fact they would be working on something remarkable together very soon.

After bidding their US friends a festive farewell, Florence + The Machine headed back home. There was one more big gig for Florence to honour before she could really kick back and catch up with family, friends and plenty of sleep. Yes, this would be no ordinary event – unless you count the Nobel Peace Prize Concert as ordinary.

The show, which took place in Oslo, Norway, on December 11, also included a diverse array of stars (something for everyone) such as AR Rahman, Barry Manilow, Jamiroquai, India.Arie, Herbie Hancock, Robyn, Elvis Costello and Colbie Caillat, and would be broadcast worldwide. Florence dazzled as always on the red carpet, wearing a shimmering seashell-coloured gown, and she won over a raft of new hearts with her transcendent renditions of 'Dog Days' and 'Cosmic Love'. Make no mistake, Florence might have been getting used to a whole new strata of venues and engagements, but the Nobel Peace Prize was an altogether new and daunting experience.

"That was one of the ones I enjoyed most," Florence remembers. "It's an amazing thing to look down at in my itinerary. 'Things to do.. Nobel Peace Prize!'" Florence enthused. "They just asked me if I'd like to perform. It's one of those things you wouldn't think you'd even be near. The King and Queen of Norway were there…"

Yes, the honour was great, but Florence soon realised that this extraordinary experience would also inform her musical ambitions from here on in. "It was a real moment, I got to perform with a 60-piece orchestra and 20-piece choir, no drums or percussion. It made me think about music I'd like to do in the future, orchestral… It was interesting taking songs that use a lot of percussion and then strip them back."

For Florence, the drums had been such a hugely important part of her music since day one – but now, perhaps, a subtle change had been set in motion that would be reflected in her next album and subsequent performances (at least, the ones with space for strings and extra voices).

Once she returned to England, one of Florence's guilty pleasures would be truly fulfilled: she'd previously admitted that she would be thrilled if someone performed one of her songs on *The X Factor*. Well, now someone would: Florence herself, and the result would be phenomenal, adding thousands of new enthusiasts to her already impressive fanbase.

"I like all aspects of culture, to me the most commercial pop song and the most obscure classical thing are equally important," said Florence, in defence of her decision to be part of *The X Factor*. "I might be an anomaly in that world but you can get experience from anywhere so I'm quite open in that way. It's good to mix them up, you can gain so much from being open and not closing yourself off. You have to keep involved in what's going on."

Finally she would have a well-earned opportunity to wind down, although not in normal lay-person's terms, of course. There would be other one-off pre-Christmas engagements abroad that Flo would hop on a plane for – such as *Spin* magazine's Year In Music party in New York, just days before Christmas – but as far as touring *Lungs* was concerned, it was time for a break. However, on December 1 some amazing news was announced: Florence + The Machine were up for a Grammy award, as 'Best New Artist' to be precise. Her competitors for the award included jazz artist Esperanza Spalding, pop star Justin Bieber, Drake (of whom Florence is a huge fan) and fellow Brits Mumford and Sons.

The news reached Florence as she was relaxing at home with her family in Camberwell, wearing "this vintage bright pink Christian Lacroix dressing gown, which was kind of ideal to receive news like that". Naturally.

"It has these incredible shoulder pads, and I sometimes wear it with this feather headdress – it's like the cowboys and Indians flimsy kind – that my sister made. It makes me feel like I'm in *Gone With The Wind*."

Obviously she was thrilled by the incredible news, which was very much deserved by all of the band who'd put so much energy and love into the music and performances. Awards season was just a few months away... but as always, Florence remained realistic and down to earth, outwardly at least. But the reality was that, while all of this frenzied attention was fantastic and flattering, for Florence, nothing mattered more than the music. Back in 2009, she had stated clearly that it wasn't about winning awards for her. On the brink of 2011, well, so much had changed, but Florence's *raison d'etre* stood firm.

"There are times I just feel a bit shell-shocked and very tired. This year's been crazy," she said. "Singing is my greatest pleasure. I retreat into another world. No two performances are the same. When it's great, it's amazing. You have to think of that when you go through the lows."

In the meantime, Florence and Paul planned to knuckle down in the studio in January and grab a chance to work on *Ceremonials* in earnest, while the various Machine-members had their own projects to pour their energy into after being on the road for so long: Tom had his group Lunamoth, for example, which he had been working on remotely on the tour bus on his laptop studio. But there were other things too that required his attention.

"The main drawback is not being able to plan anything because you never know what might be coming up gigwise," he admitted. "I still haven't been able to go on honeymoon; but that's the way it goes, you have to be able to become accustomed to that."

Meanwhile, guitarist Rob Ackroyd was planning to work with Pixie Geldof and her band Violet. "Pixie and I have been friends for years," he explained. "She has always been a writer and a singer behind closed doors and when she told me she was ready to make a go of music, I leapt at the chance to play with her. After years of promoting *Lungs* we [Florence + The Machine] were due a year off. By 'off' I mean back home in London writing and recording the new album, but nevertheless a much more consistent and anchored year. So I thought whilst Florence is quiet I could spend six months playing and writing with Pixie."

Once they had developed some demos, the pair would head out later in 2011 to LA to see TV On The Radio's Dave Sitek, one of Florence's initial possible choices of producer for *Ceremonials*.

"I'm a huge fan of TV On The Radio and the work he's done with the Yeah Yeah Yeahs. He lives in James Dean's old house up in the hills and has filled the place with amps, guitars, pedals and gadgets. We literally spent three days with our heads against amps blowing our ears out with reverb and delay units, really indulging ourselves. There are about 38 guitar tracks on each demo!"

Isabella had a couple of extra-curricular projects up her sleeve too, one being the "prog" side project The Life The Love And The Grateful − featuring three guitarists, no less − and the other being a fulfilling musical collaboration with the singer-songwriter Ivan Ink + Pen (Oliver Briggs to his mother). The pair had known each other for years, having met in a '!WOWOW!' squat presided over by the artist and DJ Matthew Stone. This artists' collective in Peckham started off at the back of the Joiners' Arms pub in Florence's home borough of Camberwell. As singer Dia Frampton, who would later work with Isabella, observed, she is "a mad-scientist writer", and her skills were respected long before she ever became a well-known name.

"We were all living in a house on Lordship Lane," Isabella remembers. "And [Matthew] started this !WOWOW! thing, and then we ended up having a massive squat in Peckham which has since been torn down. It was amazing − because it was so huge it had a nightclub on one floor, a gym on one floor (complete with eighties gym photos and pictures of people on steroids) and a sunbed that actually worked if you kept feeding it 50ps. I got properly hooked on the running machine for a bit…"

!WOWOW! parties were something to behold: one winter the squatting artists scoured the neighbouring streets for unwanted Christmas trees and created a forest inside the gallery, something Florence later wanted to create when they were recording in an old gym for *Ceremonials*. Perfect for sneaking about pretending to run away from werewolves in the moonlight. The studio even had a moon gobo projected onto the wall. ("We turned all the lights off and we were doing a song about dreams, and made a movie of it," Florence gushed. "I was lying on a bed and had to just sort of mutter and think about dreaming… there were all these old Christmas trees and we were going to make a wood where the wolves can roam. Do I believe in them? I've yet to meet one.") Anyway, back to !WOWOW!...

"When the police tried to shut the party down the main thing they were concerned about was the inside forest catching on fire," recalls Isabella. "But they couldn't stop the party because the nightclub was so massive, so it ended up with a long line of us passing Christmas trees out of the door." Health and safety and creativity don't always mix.

Ollie and Isa hung out at Antenna Studios, Ollie bringing song ideas to the table and Isa creating beats and sounds that would fit. Together they would form Ivan Ink'n' Isa.

Ivan: "I'd send an idea to Isa and it would come back all cinematic with strings and beats, from sitting in your bedroom with a little song to a big production, it was exciting."

"He had a guitar which he could make lots of cool sounds on and I had my MPC with my beats," Isabella explained. "We both shared the like for the dark and macabre sounds, so we came together and it was like, 'You've got some bits of songs, I've got some bits of beats, let's put them together, and it kind of worked. It's split between light and dark. I go from feeling moody about things and wanting to make James Bond soundtracks to doing really over-the-top happy things!"

Ivan Ink'n'Isa spent the whole of Christmas 2010 beavering away on material at the studio. This was an opportunity for Isabella to spread her wings musically and develop her own concepts, although she had to admit it was strange playing the Barfly in Camden after having played huge shows around the world with Florence.

"It's so much scarier when it's a new thing," she said. "Florence is such a support mechanism so it's weird being on stage with other people, but I think this thing with Ollie is going to be really cool. Florence always brings me with her around the world and she often talks about me in interviews, so I guess as well as being not the main focus, it's nice because I'm still a major part of it. But it's nice to do something that's slightly smaller and maybe a bit more true to me. My beats from my MPC, which is for me how it all began, I can play with all my dark sounds."

Anyone else would think that a break from touring with Florence would be an opportunity to have a rest. Not Isabella. She was feeling more creatively charged than ever. "I do want to get in to the studio and get a bit of writing under way – I've got two songs to finish with Florence, and me and Ollie have worked out a cover I'd like to completely produce. We're doing 'Frances Farmer Will Have Her Revenge On Seattle' by Nirvana."

Ivan Ink 'n' Isa were preparing to release their self-titled debut EP on Ollie's label Brink in February 2011 with a launch at the Barfly, complete with cellist and bassist, not to mention "unicorns, lizards, glass boxes…", Isabella added. "It will be magical." So, with Ivan Ink 'n' Isa and further work with Florence on album two, that was Christmas and January pretty much sewn up for Isabella – with a quick break at New Year itself to fly over to Las Vegas with Flo for Jay-Z's New Year party at the swanky new Cosmopolitan hotel on the world-famous Strip, of course.

This, naturally, wasn't just any New Year bash; it was labelled "the most A-list party ever", with Rihanna, Beyoncé, Gwyneth Paltrow and Chris Martin, 50 Cent, Jennifer Lopez and Florence's buddy Blake Lively on the guest list to name a few. They sang, they danced, they drank Armand de Brignac champagne in £250 gold-plated bottles. "That was pretty rad…" Isabella mused, as well she might. Florence braved the cold January air and showed off her lily-white pins in a pair of bejewelled hotpants, much to the photographers' delight.

This was Florence's first time in Vegas, but she was among friends, not least her Stateside BFF Blake Lively. Florence was thrilled to see her, and the pair of them certainly dressed for the occasion. "I brought everything sequined that I could think of," Florence told the press before trotting into the party with Blake (also in sequined trousers) at her side. Florence was also sporting a black and gold L'Wren Scott kimono and earrings bought from the vintage shop next to Isa's studio: "A little bit of Crystal Palace in Las Vegas," chuckled Florence.

"It's a strange town," she mused of Vegas. "It's like nowhere else, you can see the desert sky but you're in this hub of energy where anything could happen, especially on New Year's…" And especially with hard-partying Isabella and Blake in tow.

Isabella, like Florence, had catholic tastes when it came to music – she embraced everything from Nicki Minaj to Led Zeppelin to hip-hop artist (and Grammy rival) Drake, and it was this young fellow who Florence decided to work with in January on some new material for his upcoming album – or that was the idea. Because, let's face it, it's not like she had that much on her plate…

The pair had met at the VMAs the previous October, and ever since Drake saw Florence's fiery performance that captured America's heart, he had been determined to get in the studio with her. Sadly it wasn't quite that easy. The pair loved each other's company, so much so that whenever they got together with the intention to record, they ended up just "hanging out", according to Flo. The reality was that both Florence and Drake had albums to work on that would be released around the same time, later in 2011. Maybe their focus and energies were too polarised, who can say, but as it turned out, the time simply wasn't right.

"I think we're both big fans of each other's work," said Florence. "If we would have the time it is something I would definitely like to do, but we're both really busy."

February arrived, bringing awards season with it. As guitarist Rob Ackroyd observed, "Our live schedule is still keeping us busy long after it was supposed to have gone into hibernation at the close of summer 2010." Recording sessions for *Ceremonials* had been booked in at Abbey Road for April, which everyone was seriously excited about, but now it was off to LA for the 53rd Grammys on February 13.

Well, 13 might be lucky for some, but from the point of view of winning the gong, it wasn't for Florence, as she'd lose out to jazz artist Esperanza Spalding in the Best New Artist category. However, as always, much of the media seemed as much if not more interested in what she'd wear than whether she'd win, and she didn't disappoint, taking to the red carpet in "Givenchy haute couture", she informed reporters in her best French accent.

Florence certainly had her choice of designer gear to choose from. Her stylist, *Vice* fashion editor Aldene Johnson, who had been working with Florence since 2009, had hinted that they were working with Yves

Saint Laurent on a custom-designed outfit for the night. "But we always have last-minute options," Johnson had added. "A wonderful part of this is that designers are creating specific pieces for Flo now."

Indeed, Florence's turn at the Grammys would make some seriously powerful people aware of her. One of these VIPs was Gucci's creative director Frida Giannini, who was so enchanted by Florence's look and persona – that of the "mysterious muse" – that her subsequent autumn/winter collection would be created with the dreamy Camberwell girl in mind.

"She has a powerful personality and an entrancing quality to her performances," said Giannini. "She also has that confident and self-assured look that goes hand in hand with the Gucci woman." Well, they say that 80 per cent of success is showing up – but show up at the Grammys and end up having an entire Gucci season designed in your honour? That's quite a result. Giannini would also design Florence's own costumes for the subsequent US tour. It's certainly a long way from the thrift shop – although Florence's obsession with vintage stores and flea markets would never fade.

Despite the assumption that everyone present had been partying down, Florence was upholding her self-imposed drinking ban, and insisted that she and the group were feeling "pretty mellow. We've pretty much stayed in every night. I've been trying to conserve my energy." With good reason: she was to take to the stage that evening as part of a huge-lunged, seven-song tribute to soul queen Aretha Franklin with Yolanda Adams, Christina Aguilera, Jennifer Hudson and Martina McBride – a bevy of big voices if ever there was one. Flo sang the super-funky 'Think', as the other ladies sang back-up; surely the most star-studded bunch of backing singers anyone could dream up.

Bloggers might have liked to speculate that the atmosphere in rehearsals for the Aretha tribute was awash with tension and diva rivalry, but the truth was they were as relaxed as they could allow themselves to be. Yes, everyone must have been just a tad nervous, but the ice was broken when Jennifer Hudson's toddler charmed everyone by doing his Michael Jackson impression, which made everyone dissolve.

Florence, meanwhile, deliberately played the part of the 'crazy English girl', dancing about backstage and making them laugh.

"There was a real warmth and it was quite celebratory," she insisted. "But the actual performance was really frightening. You're singing in a line in a tribute to the Queen of Soul, and you're like, 'Oh my God, my turn's coming.' I had to hold the 'Freedom!' line for about five minutes."

One of Florence's favourite memories of the night was the fact that she could wear three fabulous couture gowns throughout the course of the evening: an Elie Saab "pink sequined thing" to the show itself, a Riccardo Tisci for Givenchy swan-inspired dress to the entrance, and then for the ceremony itself, a custom-made YSL lavender gown.

"You don't get to keep most of them, though," lamented Flo. "I still have the YSL one because it was custom-made. But the others had to go back. It is Cinderella: you do get to wear it, and love it, but for only one night."

Two weeks later, stepping in for the heavily pregnant singer Dido, Florence + The Machine would be whisked to Hollywood once more, this time to perform the song 'If I Rise' (from the movie *127 Hours*) with AR Rahman (complete with electric sitar) at the Oscars Ceremony before Hollywood royalty, before popping up again to sing at fellow Brit Elton John's post-Oscar party.

Of course, appearing at the Oscars was a strange and unique experience, not least because during rehearsals they had what Florence describes as "those Guess Who?-style face cards that go on all the chairs" to perform to. "That was weird," she said. "Brad and Ange, Celine Dion, Justin Timberlake, Robert de Niro…

"The thing AR Rahman said to me was that he wanted the audience to levitate. It was to be a very serene performance, light years from the Grammys performance."

Elton's party would be a little less serene, unsurprisingly. Florence's diary entry for this night must have been quite amazing – if she had time to keep a diary, that is. She would perform a duet with Elton John, singing 'Tiny Dancer', while he belted out 'You Got The Love,' much to her delight. That party certainly meant some "big hob-nobbing" as Florence put it.

So Florence + The Machine were officially hot in America (they would even make it onto Barack Obama's Spotify playlist), and their reputation was growing internationally. *Lungs* had gone multi-platinum and the single 'Dog Days Are Over' was now familiar all over the planet. World domination? Not out of the question.

Irish megaband U2 could give them a few tips on that, as they had invited Florence and co to support them on their intergalactic-themed 'U2 360°' tour at the end of June in support of their album *No Line On The Horizon*. This tour was, needless to say, a huge deal for all concerned. Concerts would include a live video link-up to the International Space Station and would be announced as the highest-grossing tour in history. IN HISTORY. And Florence + The Machine would be getting a big slice of the action.

2011 was still young, but Florence was going to need to stabilise her emotional foundations if she was going to get through the thrills and spills of the year ahead unscathed by fatigue and burn-out, because let's not forget, while Flo was spending time in America, she was still working hard on *Ceremonials*, recording vocal takes in studios wherever and whenever she could.

Fashion might have seemed to be taking something of a precedence in Florence's life, but of course, nothing would come before the music. However, Chanel's maverick designer Karl Lagerfeld was one of the many designers who, when he met her that March, was impressed with Florence's look, fashion sense and general vibe, not to mention the way in which she had gauchely managed to become a pop queen to be reckoned with.

"When she sings in public, her voice goes much higher than on CD," Lagerfeld mused. "I think she's a genius. She looks like a great English lady, but in fact is a very funny young girl. She's my favourite singer for the moment." Just for the moment, mind... Just like a fashionista to accept even at this point that his affection will probably be transient. (But at the time of writing, he certainly doesn't seem to have gone off her.)

Lagerfeld wanted to get his hands on some of that Welch magic for himself. She'd turned up at Paris Fashion Week in March, looking fabulous and rocking a gorgeous Chanel bouclé jacket – a perfect choice of garment for when one is about to meet the king of the label himself.

Florence remembers the moment they met. She admits she didn't feel quite on top form, but that didn't bother her new number one fan. "I was at the Chanel show at the Grand Palais that had the fountains and the pink feathered dress that looked like it was floating on air. I was so hung over and had a cold.

"I got papped leaving the show and the papers were like, 'Florence wears no trousers.' And I was like, 'I was wearing a skirt!' But I met Karl, who was very nice and was like, 'Your skin is like porcelain.' I certainly didn't feel porcelain. I felt very rough. But he was really nice and attentive."

Florence was also seen rocking a billowing purple dress and matching boots, something the fashion bloggers weren't too sure about, but what did she care? Those bloggers weren't about to get invited to perform at Chanel's catwalk show later that year, as the spring/summer 2012 Paris Fashion Week swung around in October 2011. (If you always have to think twice about the dates of these things, you're not alone. And if you don't, then you're clearly very trendy.) It was no surprise that Lagerfeld wanted to get her involved, but it would be even more magical than anyone could have imagined. OK, so there weren't fairies or unicorns, but it *would* be an exceptional performance that would have columnists gibbering with glee. But that was a whole seven months away yet. Plenty would happen to Flo between now and then.

As always, the demands on her time and energy would be great, and ever-increasing, but at least the engagements Florence was invited to sprinkle some of her magic dust over were varied and often fired up her creative side. She had been contacted by the Teenage Cancer Trust, which was keen for Flo to design the packaging for a special charity edition of Kiehl's Crème de Corps moisturising cream in a bid to raise funds for young people suffering from cancer. The invitation appealed to Florence, who still spent so much time drawing anyway, on so many levels. She immediately tuned in to how an adolescent cancer-sufferer must feel, and while she was careful not to disclose the personal reasons as to why the TCT was close to her heart, Florence felt strongly about being involved.

"If you asked me to go back to being 14 or 15, I couldn't – it was a terrifying time," she said. "I was so awkward in my own skin. I used to hide behind my hair because I was so ridiculously self-conscious. It's impossible to imagine how it would be to go through that period in your life – when everything is changing and you have these intense emotions – and also have to deal with something as terrible as cancer.

"The Teenage Cancer Trust does incredible work supporting and caring for teenagers and young adults with cancer, and it's a cause that is really close to me and my family."

"It was fun to work on the design,' she says. 'I wanted to create something bold that wasn't too fussy and fitted the Kiehl's aesthetic, which I love. I simplified the first logo I designed for Florence + The Machine when I was at Camberwell – I think it looks great." The design, which would hit shelves that May, featured a very Florence bright red heart with an arrow through it against a background of wide pink and white candy stripes. The finishing touch? A felt-tip-style signature: 'Love Florence xx'.

Florence + The Machine would have to get back in shape for their tour with U2 throughout July, and not only were they practising hard, they were developing their new songs and, for four weeks before heading to the States, they were hidden away inside Abbey Road Studios, where work could continue apace on *Ceremonials*. Paul Epworth had co-written seven tracks with Florence, and Isabella's writing skills were also featured as were James Ford's, the composer and producer Eg White's and Florence's old Nambucca comrade Kid Harpoon's. The results were so powerful and exciting that it was difficult to choose what could stay and what should go.

Epworth: "I feel for the A&R department having to try and whittle these tracks down to 10 or 12 because there really are no weak ones. It's a weird record that sounds live in ways and like a machine in others, with sensitivity and power from both the music and Flo's voice."

The historic studio two at Abbey Road was the dream place to record, pregnant as it was with atmosphere and magic; its church-like environs fitted the devout theme of the album perfectly. It was also the ideal place for the band to have a sense of celebration for everything they had achieved so far. What better place to enjoy that sense of 'we've made it!' than here?

"A lot of it was about choosing Abbey Road," Florence told Radio 1's Zane Lowe. "I wanted it to be special for all of us and it was kind of a dream, it was something we could all share and a dream come true for all of us.

"I was supposed to be having some time off because I'd been working solidly for nearly three years but I didn't really go anyway, I just sat at home and wrote for a while, but they couldn't really keep me out of the studio, which was a problem!

"It's been really amazing, the process, especially Abbey Road. It's been great working more with the band, we've become friends, like a family, travelling and touring together. You'd think we'd get annoyed with each other but we really like hanging out. It's fun making music together and see the album develop together, which was really wonderful."

It was a space in which Florence could experiment with her voice and lay down tracks with her new vocal skills after several years of playing gigs on the road. Performing live for such a long period of time had certainly brought new qualities out vocally. For one thing, she had the confidence to use restraint on this second album. There would be plenty of hollering too, of course, but she was more measured with her use of volume, the dynamics were more clearly defined and her music would display a greater sensitivity as a result. As Zane Lowe would observe when in conversation with Florence on Radio 1: "You've learned a few things over the years being in the music business, and discretion is one of them."

"Through performing and singing, I'm still learning how to sing, how to learn restraint," explained Florence. "When I first started singing I used to just scream! It worked when I was playing in clubs and pubs, just me and an electric guitar, it was almost like a battle to be heard and to make people pay attention to you."

Fans of Florence's high-powered yell had no need to fear, however – it would be present and correct on the album. "There was a lot of screaming at Abbey Road, I really like using the voice as an instrument and layering it up."

Epworth too was in his element, and here he could do what he did best in the most significant of locations. And one of the things that he felt was truly important was getting a good live take, in which the band played as if it were a performance, rather than in layers, with people coming in and out of the studio over-dubbing their parts. It seemed right that, as Florence + The Machine was such a collective effort, the final takes should display as cohesive a sound as possible.

"I'm a real sucker for getting a really good live take," said Paul. "Even if you replace everything, I'll still always work to get that live take that's really exciting, because it's the way I always worked in the past. I never had the luxury of time, I had to try and capture as much as I could in one sitting, I feel like if you capture that energy on a drum track, you can overdub the guitars and everything else to slot in, because you've got four people in the room and their energy's in the drum ambience.

"If you do everything separately, the musicians are too busy thinking about playing to the click or playing to the parts, rather than just letting themselves go and playing 'above what they know'."

One of Paul's roles, he felt, was to ensure he got the best out of the people he was recording, whatever it took (within reason). "Sometimes artists respond to being out of their comfort zone as well. If you're after a take that's got tension to it, there's certain things psychologically you can do to an artist... I guess you have to be a little bit manipulative, really, if you can. You have to get them into a space where you think that they're more likely to perform in a way that suits the song."

Who knows what's inside his box of tricks... we can only assume it can't be *too* bad if singer-songwriters (Adele being one – she wrote her 2011 hit 'Rolling In The Deep' with him) keep going back to him.

There was just one moment that no doubt would have made Epworth cringe. The band was honoured with a visit from the legendary George Martin, who famously produced and arranged for the Beatles at the very same studio where Florence was recording. But, as Florence breezily admitted: "George Martin came, I didn't know who he was!" Oops.

As they had booked out Abbey Road, Florence had time to spread out and relax and make it homely – or rather "like a mad person's den", as she put it. The process of making the record would be so different from the making of *Lungs*, not least because Florence had more experience and therefore more confidence. "The first album feels almost desperate. Being really desperate for someone. I was definitely in a more settled place for the second, which was helpful for my concentration because I wasn't, like, crying all the time.

"This time round I was calmer and I knew what I wanted to do, I had more of a plan, I wanted to do it all in one place with one producer, so in that way it felt like a slightly smoother process. There were definitely times when I was sitting on the floor of the studio surrounded by sheets of paper covered in black marker pen and you can't find that one word... The floor was covered in these massive pieces of paper I'd written words on – words, words, words and endless crossings out, and I'm on the floor, in a ball, clutching my skull."

OK, so maybe she wasn't always that calm, but Florence's focus for *Ceremonials* would prove more honed and at the same time would give her the space to explore the many different kinds of music she loved listening to and put her own stamp on it. The album would be, as Florence insisted: "a reflection of, like, having an iPod. I think the album is almost like a reflection of that, of being a part of that generation. Just picking bits from soul, bits from even, like, hip-hop influences, and it's that mix of styles that really influences me."

It's always hard for an artist to feel entirely happy with their work, but what would result from these sessions, and the years spent writing and accumulating material for *Ceremonials,* would be an album that Florence felt "more satisfied with", although she admitted she was still nervous about it too.

"You're never completely happy, otherwise you wouldn't ever make the next one," said Florence. She admitted that she was frightened that, having been given so many incredible opportunities artistically, she would "fuck it up". But the whole process was about growing, maturing and moving forward.

"It's partly what the new album's about. Do I want to be stuck in teenage-land, where everything's free and easy, or do I want to become more responsible? You know, is it time to grow up?"

One of the many benefits of hanging around in Abbey Road Studios was the sheer number of interesting people who would come and go, and Florence and Isabella were always ready to make new friends – it's just that these 'friends' would often be huge stars themselves. One of the people Florence would get to know at the studio was the American pop singer Katy Perry, and their impromptu meeting sparked a typically dramatic response from Florence. "She was coming out of the toilet," Florence recalled to *USA Today*. "I was so excited, I screamed and fell on the floor. She was lovely to me. There's something about her music that feels really honest.

"She totally wears her heart on her sleeve, and she really wants to reach out and make people feel good. She's a born entertainer. I had *Firework* on repeat and listened to it over and over. It's chemical, it's undeniable. It's irresistible pop, no matter what your taste is."

Their period at Abbey Road would be broken up into two main chunks, either side of their first major stint on the road that year. The U2 tour would be preceded, thankfully, by a run of US dates of their own, from a date at the Greek Theatre in Berkeley, California, on June 12 to the Sun Life Stadium in Miami, taking in LA, Chicago, Philadelphia, Baltimore, Boston, New York and East Lansing in between – so they had plenty of opportunity to warm up. Not that a Florence + The Machine gig could ever be treated as a 'warm-up' or a rehearsal; every concert was given full energy and commitment from those onstage.

So, once again, the old stand-up trunk would be packed, the passport located and Florence was off on the road. She had been so busy over the past two years, she'd not had time to spend much of the money she was earning. Her dream purchase? A castle. Why are we not surprised?

"I really want a gothic castle, or a church… but I haven't had time," she huffed. "I've only been home for about two weeks in the last two years."

Well, if time is the only thing preventing the purchase of a castle, then you're probably not in a bad position. And the time for turrets and moats would come later; after all, Florence hardly would have been able to spend much time in one at this stage in her career – but the excitement of getting back on stage and the whole jamboree of the touring show was building.

Florence had some special guests joining her entourage (and, in one case, one who would ultimately act as an assistant alongside Mairead and co-manager Hannah to ensure Florence didn't forget her head). Yes, as well as Tabitha Denholm, who would be capturing Flo on her American travels as a series of short films – nothing if not productive, this lot – Florence's sister, Grace, would come out to the States to be with her once she had completed her term at Sussex University. Fun times were most certainly ahead, and not only at concerts or on TV sets. Even going to the gym would prove an opportunity for mischief for these two siblings.

"We can't take ourselves seriously because we don't really look right in the gym," Florence laughed. "We're always trying to make each other laugh; I was on the running machine and I pulled my T-shirt over my head but she wasn't looking and I just fell off really hard. She didn't even see. We're not very committed. The times we go to the gym normally end up just like that." Gym = bad for you. It's official.

Once the cusp of the next leg of Florence's tour had kicked off in the US, team Flo would be whisked to New York's Metropolitan Museum Of Art for one of the most glamorous dates on the fashion world's calendar – the Met Ball. This year's event would be in honour of the late designer Alexander McQueen, who had tragically taken his own life the previous year at just 40 years old. Florence loved McQueen's designs, and was honoured to be part of the celebration, at which Florence and co would be performing.

Everywhere you looked, the gowns were flowing, the make-up was perfect, the hair was lacquered and amazing… Florence looked gorgeous too, although she always felt somewhat cowed by the presence of so many fashionistas looking perfect and preened. And who wouldn't, at the Met Ball?

"I don't think I'll ever be polished. I'm just integrally slightly scruffy," she pondered. "You know you meet those women who are so cool? I'm striving for that so much. And I'm always too flustered."

Nobody would have known, as Florence was poised as ever, graceful and flowing in an orange-gold Alexander McQueen dress. Appropriately, the decadent Baz Luhrmann was in charge of directing the evening's stage performance at this glittering event. His wish to work with Florence Welch was granted, as they would indeed work together, as he had predicted previously after meeting her at the Wiltern with Blake Lively.

After a day of interviews (with boyfriend Stuart killing time by meeting some skater friends in New York's Bowery) and a brief chance grabbed for a family meal, Florence would sing at the Met Ball before a star-studded audience, something one would think she would be quite used to by now. It still felt "weird" though, not least because she was "dressed as David Bowie" and had bleached her eyebrows to invisibility.

She sang a selection from *Lungs* before launching into Bowie's 'Rebel Rebel', dedicated to the maverick McQueen. This fiery, sexy swansong saw her prancing around and skipping into the audience, dancing in front of Paul McCartney, Madonna and her old chums Jay-Z and Karl Lagerfeld. In a moment of super-confidence, she sang the line "Hot tramp, I love you so" whilst staring closely into Macca's eyes. All in a day's work.

"I'd run offstage into the audience like out of the Temple of Dendar in this cape looking like David Bowie's younger sister, and was dancing through the tables and Paul McCartney was doing this dance with me and I was thinking, 'My life has become irrevocably weird! I can never go back from here now!'

"I remember thinking to myself, 'Oh my god. This is actually happening...' At the same time, I remember thinking, 'I have to get back to the stage somehow. I have to turn around'... It was just one of those moments where I realised that my life had become a very strange place."

"She had never met McCartney," reported *Interview Magazine*. "But he, like most everyone else in attendance, was up and dancing... The

Met gig marked a culmination of a season of high-profile command performances for Welch – she'd also been summoned earlier this year to sing at both the Grammys and the Oscars... Aretha Franklin funnelled through Carly Simon and dressed up like Kate Bush; her lyrics read like extended journal entries; live, she seems like she's leading a rapturous spiritual gathering that's also a clubby performance-art piece."

As Baz Luhrmann observed, while in conversation with Florence for *Interview*, "It was a situation that could have been very intimidating, but you made us all forget our fears for a few brief moments and feel free and exultant. Do you recall that moment?"

"No," Florence responded, "because I think I was so busy fighting through my own fear and conquering the absolute terror I was feeling..."

Thanks to the smoke and mirrors of showbiz, the enforced confidence, the swirl of the garments and the toss of her crimson locks, no one noticed. One thing that Florence was certainly succeeding in doing was whipping up an almost magical atmosphere, but a very potent, strong and earthy one, rather than conjuring a soft, ethereal, 'fairyland' vibe.

"When I would see live bands, I wanted to do it like they did it. I was drawn to male performers and that aggression and how debauched it was," Florence observed. "I always thought I would love to do something so powerful."

The leg of the tour that followed this stunning evening was another sartorially stunning affair for Florence, who would be dressed by Gucci, and at last, another new song would be debuted: the glorious 'What The Water Gave Me'. They offered this up to the audience at the Greek Theatre, Berkeley, and were rewarded with a tidal wave of love – and also some pretty Flo-style flower garlands. One fan, who created flowery headbands for herself, her friend and Florence, was thrilled to see that, after throwing her offering up to Florence on stage, the garland would not only be kept by Florence, but it would take pride of place at future gigs too.

Fan Teejay Hallett remembers: "At the Greek Theatre, Florence saw that me and my best mate were in the front row wearing handmade flower headbands. We had made one for Florence hoping that we would get a chance to throw it up on stage. We got to toss it to her directly and she put it on her head and continued to wear it. The second time I saw her in Philadelphia, I saw that she had kept my flower headband and it was a part of her set, hanging on a bird cage.

"The third time I saw her, I was wearing my flower headband again and this time she saw me and ran back to the bird cage where it hangs and said, 'I see some girls in flower headbands so I thought we should wear them together.' I guess she heard me yelling that I made it for her! She got a spark of recognition on her face and was like, 'You did make this for me, I thought that was you! Well, you look so beautiful in yours I shall wear mine!' I almost died!"

It wasn't just Florence who remembered how important it was to honour the fans, the ones who'd bought the records, the concert tickets and had basically propelled them to the top. Florence + The Machine Army member Libby Williams was stunned to find herself getting up close and personal – briefly – with guitarist Rob Ackroyd after a particularly successful gig.

"He ran towards me and gave me a hug and said 'We did it!' and gave me a high five," says Libby. "I will forever remember it because it was pure and it was heartfelt. The whole band are lovely, they all have a sense of appreciation towards us."

Not for Florence + The Machine the sense of chilly distance that many stars like to maintain; and their fans loved them all the more for it. Even the birds seemed to love Florence and co, adding to an open air set in New York City's Central Park by flapping about sweetly above them, singing.

"Central Park Summerstage was amazing," said Florence. "There were birds' nests in the top of the stage! There was literally a nest above where my microphone stand was, and all of these birds were flying in and out of it and twittering." Hopefully the birds restrained themselves from adding their own decorations to the stage during the performance. Their contribution to the gig might not have been deemed quite so charming then…

It was at Florence's glorious summer gig in New York City that Atlanta Cobb, the co-director of the fan club the Florence + The Machine Army, first met Florence and the band in the flesh. She was far from disappointed, not least because they showered her and her friend with gifts.

"People always say 'never meet your idols' as they will always fail to meet your expectations of the idea you have created as to what your idol is like," Atlanta said. "Florence definitely exceeded mine."

After being met by Dana Erickson, part of Flo's US management team, Atlanta chatted with Tom, had a drink with Flo (whilst chewing the fat about *The Rocky Horror Picture Show*, Florence's favourite film) and hung out with Isabella, who pounced gratefully on the nail polish Atlanta and her friend Carina had brought as a gift, and started painting her nails immediately. Isabella told them she was considering dying her hair red for the Summerstage show but, as Atlanta recalls, "Florence wouldn't let her as that was 'her thing' so Isa ended up dying it pink, but it didn't work as she washed the dye off too quickly.

"She asked us what we thought of it, and as we hesitated she laughed: 'It looks crap, doesn't it?'" Like Marilyn Monroe insisting she should be the only platinum blonde on screen in her movies, Florence had the monopoly on red. "Sometimes I get jealous when I see fans with amazing red hair," she confessed. "I want to ask them where they got their hair done, but that would be a bit weird."

Evelyn and Grace were in attendance, which caused a little awkwardness when Evelyn spotted Florence's bird-cage tattoo. "Evelyn hadn't seen Florence for a few months and had only just noticed the tattoo on her finger. She said, 'Florence... what's that on your finger?' Florence looked like a child that's just been caught eating all the biscuits out of the tin. 'Erm... nothing Mum... just a drawing'. She tried to hide it and then went on to tell us that she'd finally managed to convince her mum that her other tattoo ('Sadsack') is 'just a stick on'."

The day ended perfectly – with Atlanta, Carina and Atlanta's mum watching the show with Florence's family and Stuart, while Flo dedicated 'You Got The Love' to the girls. To say their day, year, decade was made is putting it mildly.

The contemplative song 'What The Water Gave Me', while a new track, was still in the Florence Welch songwriting mould in the sense that it built and built to a rapturous climax, but there was a new maturity to her writing, which was evident in this sparkling track. It was mysterious, elemental, of course, and sensual. And, surprise surprise, it was inspired by a work of art, which then sparked a stream of consciousness swirling around the concept of the "bloodlust" of the rivers and seas. It certainly spoke to the imagination and had a magnetic effect on listeners. As soon as they could get their hands on a promo, respected US stations including Los Angeles' KROQ gave it heavy radio-play.

"The title is about a Frida Kahlo painting," said Florence. "That one where her feet are in the bath and all of her nightmares and dreams are in the bath with her. It got me thinking about the water and the sea.

"When I was growing up, there were these news stories that kept popping up in my life about children who would get swept out to sea, and the parents would dive in after them. I'd seen these news stories crop up again and again, and it made me think of this idea of the sea being this entity that needs a sacrifice, like, if it's going to take your children, then you have to give yourself.

"It got me thinking about the power of water, like in Virginia Woolf, and that sense of really being overwhelmed by something. I also remembered this idea, I think from a childhood story, about a river that has to have someone drowned in it before you can cross it – like, if you see a river running smoothly, it's because someone has drowned in it, and if it's raging, it means that it's still got bloodlust... It's all very morbid. My dad always gets asked at parties, 'What did you do to her?'"

It was then time to get visual and plan a suitably dreamy, drifty music video to accompany 'What The Water Gave Me', which would debut in August on the band's website. This video even featured other members of the band too, which didn't happen very often, and it cut between studio shots and footage of Florence in a high-necked, sheer white gown, arms aloft or flapping wildly as the song crescendoed.

"We bought quite a lot of stuff for it from Merchant Archive," Florence said. "It's a vintage place run by Sophie Merchant. That white chiffon thing, and on the album sleeve the pink kimono is from there. They used to be right next to the studio where we recorded the album, so I used to pop in there quite often!"

The video, when unveiled later that summer, would garner an incredible 1.5 million views in just two days – and no doubt that rather personal take in the promo, showing Florence + The Machine in the studio, was a master-stroke. For all the magic of her previous videos, fans would revel in seeing some rare 'behind-the-scenes' footage.

But first, Florence and her comrades had a tour with U2 to complete, and it would be an experience that would propel Florence further into the big league – while also giving her the refreshing experience of not being the headliner for once. "It's funny, in a way, I almost prefer being the support band. There's just less expectation."

Working with U2 was a learning curve and would change how she acted while on the road – not only did frontman Bono have some pearls of wisdom that he was happy to share after so many years of rock stardom, but Florence soon realised that if this tough new level of touring was going to be the norm, she had to clean up her act.

It was on this tour that Florence decided to stop drinking when she was working. She could still enjoy alcohol when she wasn't on duty, but she owed it to her band, the fans and, most importantly, her voice and her performance, to cut down. Apart from anything else, not drinking helped allay the "waves of guilt" she still suffered from, the demons that came to plague her at the dead of night and in the lonesome hotel-room mornings…

"When we toured with U2 it was such a gruelling schedule. I had shows every day and I can't do that with a hangover. So I've been good to myself," she explained. "I feel a bit more responsibility for my body and for the fans who come to see us."

This would mean that, when Florence did have a day off and could allow herself a drink, she went all out and tried as many unusual cocktails as she could. Salmon bloody mary, anyone?

"When I'm living in London or out with friends it's quite easy to let your hair down and go out partying but when it came to the tour, I thought, 'I've had my fun.' This is the best job in the world and I don't want to spoil it." Florence also realised that if she wanted the kind of career longevity enjoyed by the likes of Björk or PJ Harvey, she'd do well to "temper the indulgences".

Florence + The Machine open for U2 at the Sun Life Stadium in Miami, Florida. Bono gave
Florence some tips about swaggering about onstage in high heels... SAYRE BERMAN/CORBIS

Florence and her then-boyfriend Stuart Hammond are snapped at the 53rd Annual GRAMMY Awards at the Staples Center on February 13, 2011 in Los Angeles. LARRY BUSACCA/GETTY IMAGES FOR THE RECORDING ACADEMY

Florence Welch, Jennifer Hudson, Christina Aguilera, Martina McBride and Yolanda Adams prepare to perform at the 53rd Annual GRAMMY Awards in tribute to soul queen Aretha Franklin. KEVIN MAZUR/GETTY IMAGES

Florence + The Machine do 'the voodoo that they do so well' at the New Orleans Voodoo Festival on October 30, 2010. AMY HARRIS/CORBIS

Florence performs with Nathan Willett of Cold War Kids live during day three of the 2010 Coachella in California during April 2010. Florence had long been a fan of CWKs, covering their song 'Hospital Beds' early in her career. DAVID ATLAS/RETNA LTD/CORBIS

Florence and Tabitha Denholm—Mairead Nash's fellow Queen of Noize and director behind many of Florence's videos—enjoy a night at Hollywood's Madame Tussaud's. AXEL KOESTER/CORBIS

Flo joins Sir Elton John onstage at the 19th Annual Elton John AIDS Foundation Academy Awards Viewing Party on February 27, 2011 in West Hollywood. They sang 'Tiny Dancer' together, amongst other numbers.
MICHAEL KOVAC/WIREIMAGE

Florence, clad in Chanel, braves the cold with guitarist Rob Ackroyd to open the Harrods sale on December 2, 2011. ANDREW PARSONS/ZUMA PRESS/CORBIS

Florence posing in triumph with her precious awards at the NME Awards at the
Brixton Academy on February 29, 2012 in London. DAVE M. BENETT/GETTY IMAGES

'The Voice Of Germany' contestant Ivy Quainoo sings onstage with Florence during the final of the TV talent show in Berlin. JOERG CARSTENSEN/EPA/CORBIS

Florence and little sister (and PA) Grace let it all hang out at the Universal Music Brits party hosted by Bacardi a the Soho House Pop Up in the Tate Modern on February 21, 2012. DAVE M. BENETT/GETTY IMAGES FOR SOHO HOUSE

lorence + The Machine and an army of dancers go Grecian during their performance of 'No Light, No Light' uring the Mastercard Brit Awards at the O2 Arena in Greenwich, London, on 21, February 2012. RETNA PICTURES

lorence and The Horrors' Faris Badwan duet onstage at Alexandra Palace on March 10, 2012. Two perfect stars the 'doom-pop generation'. RETNA PICTURES

True romance. An elegant, dazzling Florence sings at the Royal Albert Hall during
Not a brogue or 'Blossom' hat in sight. CHRISTIE GOODWIN

Hard as it might be after a show to resist the urge for a drink, particularly with the rest of the band around her, adding to the party atmosphere, Florence stayed firm. The amount of work they had to do whilst on tour — interviews, TV and radio appearances and the rest — meant that she could no longer try to scrape by with a crashing headache. Florence admits it "used to be like drinking competitions before we went onstage". Now her pre-show ritual of downing tequila shots and pineapple juice would be pushed aside in favour of vocal warm-ups.

"Before, part of it was just the energy and it didn't really matter if you were hitting the notes. But now I can have both," she smiled, before recalling: "Some of the shows were completely unhinged. I'd be up a wall in an Irish theatre, I'd climb up onto a balcony and be in someone's box, doing a shot of whisky with them and then back down to the stage.

"I used to think it was all part of the performance to go out there, go on tour, and get as drunk as possible. Like, oblivion. Living almost out of control. We nicknamed this 'the temperance tour'. I'll try it this way, and if it doesn't work I might go back to the shots of tequila. I love that kind of euphoria. I like that feeling of abandon. I like to dance. I like parties. I love shots. I love them."

It would certainly be easier to eschew the booze when the band didn't have brass sections or classical musicians playing with them, as, she would soon discover, they could be the most determined drinkers of the lot.

"They're always the hardest-partying guys," she observed. "We don't have a brass section, but I wish we did. They're the rock 'n' rollest of the bunch. It's always the cellists and violinists who are hitting it the hardest in the hotel bar." It didn't help Florence that the rest of her band did not join her in her abstinence. She laughingly called it "annoying" but stuck to her guns.

As Florence was discovering, not just from her own point of view, but clearly from the perspective of her contemporaries too, the music industry was no longer all about drugs and alcohol, or rather, if you were an artist, it couldn't be if you wanted to survive. She soon found that, while working at least, being in a state of clarity worked for her.

"You need to be so bloody healthy to keep up with the pace of work. I couldn't do it if I wasn't totally straight all the time and focused," she said. "I can't think of anything more terrifying than turning up to a photo shoot or a TV appearance or a gig with a hangover from hell, and having to get up the next day, and the next. If anything, I'm healthier than I've ever been. I'm focused on doing my next album and I don't want to lose myself. What works best for me is to keep a clear head when all around is mad."

Responding to news of yet another FATM-related success with a groan and a request for painkillers would be a thing of the past, even if sobriety could be daunting, especially when you've hidden behind a haze of alcohol in order to get through a nerve-racking stage performance.

Once Florence saw the venues she and the Machine would be playing with U2, she realised that her instinct was right too: she would certainly have to be on top of her game playing in such huge venues. "It was like performing in a coliseum, I felt like I was going into gladiatorial combat. It was in the round and you were exposed to the elements and the open air. [It felt] like slaying lions in yards of chiffon."

However, the band they were supporting couldn't have been sweeter to this bunch of young bucks. Bono even gave Flo some advice on how to perform in high heels. (Most curious…)

"Bono was great. He told me how to keep my feet on the spot and use my arms. He also told me about U2's Glastonbury performance and how everything that could have possibly gone wrong went wrong – including him ripping his trousers on stage. I think he was lunging and his trousers ripped! He was telling me how he had to find a new way of performing that didn't involve moving." Necessity is the mother of invention.

Bono is apparently well known for imparting advice to his support groups, and while Florence wasn't particularly aware of being given 'the talk', she appreciated how welcoming he and the rest of U2 were. After all, they were conquering the world before most of Florence + The Machine were even born.

Thankfully not much would go wrong during this exciting stint on the road – although Florence, queen of the elements that she is, did nearly set fire to the stage when they played Indianapolis on Independence Day. That's certainly one way to celebrate it…

Abby Hillock was in the audience – and thankfully still has her eyebrows. "Florence commented on how even though her mother was American that she had never celebrated the 4th of July before. She came out with a sparkler and told us that she never had held one before either. She was so cute and wrote her name in the air (but) she had no idea about how to put it out, and she tried to set it down on the ground.

"We were all like 'No! Don't put it on the ground!' Thankfully, one of the stagehands came out and grabbed it from her so she wouldn't set the stage on fire. It was so funny!" Bono was right there with the 'dancing in heels' advice – where was he when it came to sparklers?

Celebrations aside, this July would also be etched on many people's memories as the month that saw the tragic death of Amy Winehouse, one of Florence's British contemporaries and Island label-mates, and one of British pop's most troubled icons. The singer, who'd had a long history of battling drugs and alcohol, was found dead in her flat in Camden, North London, aged just 27. She basically drank herself to death, and was reportedly found to be five times over the drink-drive limit. The news sent shockwaves through the music world.

"I was devastated when Amy died," said Florence. "It was such a shock, it shouldn't have happened. We weren't close but I thought she was an incredible performer. The first time I saw her was the first time I'd performed at Glastonbury. We had some time off so my friends and I went to watch her and she was incredible."

While Florence was in the US, tributes were pouring in for Winehouse, and Camden Square, where the late singer lived, quickly turned into a giant flower-strewn memorial. Plans were made to pay tribute to the star, including a concert that would take place featuring the biggest stars in pop, organised by Amy's father, Mitch, who came up with the idea not long after his daughter's death. Florence was on his early wish-list for the event, which would be planned for July 2012, a year after Amy's demise. Florence would also lead tributes alongside artists including Nas, Wanda Jackson and the Dap Kings, who had worked with Winehouse, in a cable broadcast concert (VH1 Divas), singing the poignant 'Back To Black'.

In September, just after the release of 'What The Water Gave Me', Island put out the lead single from *Ceremonials* – 'Shake It Out' – as a digital download, with standard release set for October 11. Florence was amused to hear that the track was being pumped through the sound systems of gyms the world over. Sports centres weren't exactly Florence's natural habitat, as we know from her comical gym-based escapades with her sister, Grace, but, as she observed, "If a song makes you want to move and run, that's good. But running outdoors. I'm not very big on the treadmill because it freaks me out. I don't like running when I'm not going anywhere. I'm kind of like Phoebe from *Friends* when I run. Lots of flailing."

As we know, trainers and tracksuits are not exactly synonymous with Florence Welch, but there'd be plenty of flailing in the video of 'Shake It Out'. It was shot in the ornate Eltham Palace (where Cheryl Cole shot her video for 'Parachutes'), a place that practically dripped with atmosphere – and also wasn't too far from her home turf in South London. "Dawn Shedforth, who directed the video, sent me pictures of it; I'd never seen it before but I just fell in love with the place," Florence said.

In tune with the new art deco aesthetic that Florence + The Machine were embracing, the ensuing promo would be splendidly over the top, wild and radiant with dark glamour and sophistication, with more than a little occult dabbling thrown in.

As BBC DJ Steve Lamacq told Florence, "You'd certainly get the part in *Poirot*."

"We were kind of going for a sort of 'Gatsby at West Egg'-style house party but with maybe slightly ritualistic and sort of satanic undertones and séances," Flo revealed mischievously. The conclusion of the video would see Florence in an angelic white dress, drifting up into the embracing branches of a tree after thrashing about joyfully like a lunatic at the 'party'. All very symbolic…

"That was such a fun video to shoot, for me especially, because I had all my friends down there, and they all came and we all got to dress up and do a casual séance in this beautiful art-deco mansion. It's basically a party house; there's one room which was purely just for cutting flowers. My best friend is sitting with me in the tree at the end of the video, and we just got to hang out in a tree for a while. It was really fun."

Appropriately, given Florence's recent turnaround on boozing, 'Shake It Out' was written about obliterating the world's worst hangover, and the dark feelings that come up after a drinking binge, emerging from the murkier corners of the soul when you're feeling at your most raw.

"It's about those creeping regrets behind your eyeballs, the ones you can't quite get away from that you just wish you could put in the past or finally let go of. The chords at the beginning of 'Shake It Out' brought up these strange images of reverent, almost church-like things, heaven and hell, demons and whatnot! So I think you're almost a translator for it, the music will always tell you where to go, in a way.

"I came to the studio with a bit of a hangover, and it was one of those strange days where you're not really sure where a song comes from. Paul just had these chords on the organ, and they sounded optimistic and sad at the same time, and I was thinking of regrets, like, you know when you feel like you're stuck in yourself, you keep repeating certain patterns of behavior, and you kind of want to cut out that part of you and restart yourself.

"I can be a bit hard on myself, I think everyone can," Florence continued, "You can get stuck in these destructive thought patterns and be like, 'Why am I still doing this?' So it was literally like wanting to shake this stuff out. Like 'Shake yourself out of it, things will be OK.' Sometimes I have to write songs for myself, reminding me to let it go. Music or dancing, I can get away from the [dark thoughts], I think that's why I'm a real pacer as well, I'm constantly trying to walk away from my regrets... maybe that won't catch up with me if I keep pacing!"

But however healthy the intention behind 'Shake It Out' might be, Florence was nothing if not realistic. "The refrain of 'what the hell?' at the end is quite important, because whatever dark forces have been enticing you, you'll probably find them again. You'll dance with the devil again at some point," she said wryly.

"And maybe it will be fun... I've heard he does a really good foxtrot."

# CHAPTER FOURTEEN

*"It's amazing how it's turned out considering none of us had a clue what we were doing. She's become a woman suddenly, she's grown into her own skin."*

Mairead Nash to Q magazine.

It's September 2011, a month before the highly anticipated release of *Ceremonials*, and Mairead is getting ready to officially launch a beloved project of her own – her management company and label Luv Luv Luv. Since working with Florence, her own name in the field of music management had grown and become more established, and now it was time to throw some gold dust on it, have a party and wet its head. The huge success of *Lungs* had meant that Mairead had had to work for a year longer on the campaign than she'd thought, *and* bring the release of *Ceremonials* forward. Between the two campaigns, Nash had had a mere few weeks to clear her head, although she called it "more of a handover than a break".

London's favourite party girl had had her nose to the grindstone for too long. It was time to create a night to remember – OK, so there'd been plenty of those over the past few years, but this time it was about her, the work she'd done so successfully with Florence, and the work she would be doing with other artists, including Jamie N Commons, Theme Parks and Florence's old friend Dev Hynes and his new project Blood Orange.

As the sun went down on September 29, a white-washed, vintage-decorated office in an old MC Motors building in Dalston, East London, was filled with cocktails, lamb burritos, music (supplied by Jamie N Commons and celebrity DJs including Nick Grimshaw) and hipsters who had come to celebrate Luv Luv Luv. It had been an unusually hot day, and the heat continued long into the evening, mingling with the sweaty excitement that was crackling through the crowd like a seam of electricity. There would also be a secret guest appearing that night, although you didn't have to be Columbo to work out who that would be.

"Causing an almost tidal wave of people surging towards the stage, for clambering onto the stage complete with new material, and not to mention an awesome new hairdo, was Mairead's biggest client, Florence!" wrote *Planet Notion* excitedly. "Performing an emotion-inducing set bursting full of classics coupled with tempting new tracks, the mood can only be described as one of glorious happiness. Altering the style of her sound just a fraction, Florence still stayed true to her devoted fans. Everyone left feeling fulfilled and happy."

It's fair to say, the launch of Luv Luv Luv was a great success, and the euphoric mood lasted long after the last guest had departed into the Dalston night (or morning, rather).

Excitement was building for the release of *Ceremonials*, which would be unveiled to the world on October 31 – Hallowe'en, appropriately, for this queen of "the spook generation", as Florence herself put it. Because there was such a proliferation of material, the album was released in a standard 12-song version, and also a deluxe 20-track version with additional songs, demos and acoustic tracks.

Posters bearing a sleek, art deco-inspired Florence mirrored against a moody black background could be seen in every Underground station and on every billboard and bus stop. Channel 4 was poised to stream the album, which the critics were already going wild over, on October 27. Nick Grimshaw – close friend of Mairead and Florence herself – was lined up to present a T4 special on the release, and the official album launch gig was taking place at London's theatrical palace of Victoriana, Hackney Empire, tickets for which were selling fast. The game was afoot.

Naturally, Florence's diary was getting more and more packed during the countdown to the launch – she was already hot property, but right now it seemed that absolutely everybody wanted a piece of her. She was still a big favourite with Chanel's Karl Lagerfeld, so much so that not only did he want his models to trot down the catwalk to the sound of her transcendent music at his spring/summer show at Paris Fashion Week that month, he wanted her to be right there on the runway herself to sing her soaring track 'What The Water Gave Me'. In fact, she wouldn't just be singing, she'd be emerging, Venus de Milo–like, from a giant clam-shell in the watery paradise he had created for the show.

"It was funny because Karl and I were doing a shoot for Japanese *Vogue* and I was talking about the underwater themes in my record, and he was saying how he wanted to do an underwater theme for his show. Then he said: 'Wouldn't it be nice if you came down on a big wire like you were floating?' and I was like: 'What?' And he said: 'We can get all these harps together…'

"All these ideas were coming to him just really off the cuff… so I thought he was joking and then he put his hand on mine and said: 'OK, so we'll do it, I'm glad we talked.' It was all really spontaneous!"

The clam-shell idea couldn't have been more Florence – she'd always wanted to be a mermaid, after all, and thankfully on this occasion she wouldn't have to master breathing under water, she'd just have to look fabulous, and let's face it, she already had that nailed.

"I was crouched inside waiting to come out and they were playing this amazing techno-Wagner! I was wearing this Chanel scale costume, and opened up into this beautiful under-sea landscape in the Grand Palais… my mermaid dream came true." As Florence emerged to the sound of Tom playing a beautiful white harp, the audience gasped and "wowed".

"It was great to be a part of the spectacle, it wasn't purely just my performance. It was about the clothes and the models, and this whole set as well so it was quite nice being a part of something so exquisite and exciting. The clothes were wonderful, they all looked like beautiful, pastel-coloured fish in this underwater landscape with the pearls all over them.

"There was a moment when I was walking out hand-in-hand with Karl and I was like, 'What am I doing here?' I don't know how to walk," she said. "But it was a beautiful experience."

Just one problem: being next to a bevy of skinny, strutting models made even the slender and willowy Ms Welch feel just a little self-conscious.

"Did you see the way I walked out with Karl?" she cringed. "All the models were like these beautiful sea anemones and seahorses and there I was like a big jellyfish going bloob bloob bloob." It just goes to show that how we see ourselves is often nothing like how we appear in the eyes of others. It also goes to show that Florence is just like every other woman when it comes to self-image. Fans might see her as a goddess, but Florence simply sees herself as an average woman with wobbly bits.

Next up was a trip to New York for an acoustic showcase at the glamorous Standard Hotel, but it wasn't the performance, for Florence + The Machine, that would be the most memorable part of this trip. After the show, Florence allowed herself a drink. "About 17 dirty martinis," to be more precise. A night of decadent destruction would follow, and incidents included Florence losing her phone, tearing her dress, chipping a tooth and, ultimately, setting her room in the Bowery Hotel alight. The story ripped through the media, but the reality of the incident wasn't quite as rock 'n' roll or Keith Moon-esque as it might have initially sounded, involving, as it did, a cinnamon tea light.

"We had this room at the top of the building and it was supposed to be just us getting changed in our hotel room having a drink," Florence explained. "But all these other people were in there too. Kanye West, Lykke Li. A couple of the doormen from the Bowery Hotel... and I was in the bathtub fully clothed. This is the craziest thing that happened throughout a fairly crazy year of touring – I set fire to my hotel room.

"I'd left a cinnamon tea light burning. I passed out in my ripped dress, no phone, chipped tooth, came round and there was black stuff all over the wall, my book had melted on the bedside table and there was a bucket of water on the floor. The last scene you want to wake up to with a hangover."

A lucky escape for Florence – no more tea lights for her (easier than saying 'no more dirty martinis'). But the biggest bill to pay would not be the fire damage, but the drinks bill after her impromptu star-studded hotel room party. Florence admitted that this "really hemmed in my vintage clothes buying". Which, in New York, can't be an easy thing to resist.

Florence (and the band account) had barely had time to recover from this drama before she and the band were back in London preparing for the sold-out launch gig at the "very baroque" Hackney Empire. Looking gorgeous and regal in a gold dress, Florence held the audience spell-bound as they lifted the lid on the entire album before a thrilled audience of fans and critics.

As always, it mattered to Florence that her fans were happy, and she was overjoyed to see their reaction and spot some of the people who had supported her from the off. "People were listening intently," she said. "Every time it was quiet it was dead quiet, and I could see some of the fans who'd been there from the beginning. It was a really nice atmosphere. When we did 'Shake It Out', there was such enthusiasm in the crowd and it really did feel like we were all exorcising something together."

"I was so nervous," she said after coming off stage. "I don't really suffer from stage fright unless I'm doing live TV – and this was a live broadcast, the whole thing! So I had that TV anticipation, you don't know how many people are watching and it's up there forever, my heart was going crazy. I didn't consciously think about it once I started but the thing I try to do is lose myself, almost imagining you're alone in your bedroom, to feel uninhibited."

It was vindicating for everyone in the band, Paul Epworth and Mairead, that the album was so heartily received that night. The sound that they had settled on was certainly the right decision. "I'd wanted to go big," reflected Florence. "And now it's so big that I don't know what I'm going to do for the third album, I'll have to go completely the other way!"

One die-hard fan, Daniel Willimott, travelled an impressive 252 miles from his home in the North-East of England to see Florence perform *Ceremonials* at Hackney Empire. The album had leaked a week before the concert and many fans, unable to wait, listened to it online. But Daniel steeled himself for the live experience, which he knew would be worth waiting for.

"I had the willpower because I wanted to hear it live, as that's when the music comes alive," he said. "I knew I didn't have to wait long before I heard it. Once we got there, I was standing at the back of the Empire with the hopes of meeting Florence. We had been there for at least two hours chatting to other fans that later disappeared. I heard a knock on a window, me and my friend both looked around, and we saw Florence standing at the window – unable to open it, she mouthed the words, 'I love you!' and blew us a kiss. My legs went to jelly and I almost fainted."

The critics too were highly taken with Florence's new output. Difficult second album? Apparently not. Zane Lowe simply exclaimed: "What a record! What a return!" on his Radio 1 show, while *GQ* praised the "incredibly well written" songs on the release, even if 'Only If For A Night' was a "dead ringer for Kate Bush's 'Cloudbusting'. "Behind all that rococo musical scenery and kooky affectations lurks a pop craftswoman."

Florence's contemporaries were impressed too. Rapper Professor Green, who first shot to fame when he collaborated with Lily Allen on their cover of Beats International's 'Dub Be Good To Me', admitted that while he was "pissed off" that his own album *At Your Inconvenience* was released on the same day as *Ceremonials* – which would beat him to the top of the album chart – he was keen to collaborate with Flo. Also, despite his initial irritation regarding the timing, he "still bought her record". What a gent.

"I didn't mind the battle. It was wicked just being a part of that race to be number one," he told *NME*, which was possibly hoping for a bit more bile from the MC. "Florence has got a great voice. I'd love to work with her. She's got such a different outlook on music to anyone else out there. Together we'd be able to come up with something great."

The USA wanted a slice of Florence circa *Ceremonials* too, naturally, and another appearance on *Saturday Night Live* beckoned – this time Flo would be part of one of the show's famous skits, this one being titled 'New Jack Thanksgiving', during which she sang, mock-sultry-style, a turkey-themed R&B tune, as well as treating viewers to a performance of 'Shake It Out'.

"Everyone [on *SNL*] is so nice," she said. "I sat in the writers' room with everybody and just kind of seeing how everyone gets crowded into this tiny room and sits on the floor, and being there with all the writers and the actors, it was kind of really amazing."

The following month, Florence fans had to look twice when watching the show, as it appeared that she was making a second cameo. Close but no cigar. This was Katy Perry in disguise as Flo performing a pastiche of a Florence track 'The Dog Trial Is Over' (bet you can't guess which track she was affectionately sending up...). Florence was thrilled by the sheer idea of the 'tribute'.

"I haven't seen it yet! I've seen pictures!" she said. "She looks amazing! I was like, 'Yeah, that's it! You've got the hair, the dress, everything.' ... I feel very honoured to be part of a skit without actually being there!"

While in New York, Florence made another contribution to Tabitha's short film series about the Florence + The Machine touring experience. 'Return To The US', a two-minute video, saw Florence tap-dancing through Times Square and rifling through flea markets, revelling in feeling anonymous in places that were buzzing with so much life and activity that no one really took much notice of the pale girl in the burgundy jacket. These short films are revealing, frank vignettes of life on the road with Florence.

While the world inhaled *Ceremonials* like some kind of magical vapour, Florence, on the other hand, "hid" from it. She'd been afraid to listen to it in its entirety, but the spell had to be broken. "We were driving somewhere and I was like, 'OK, let's do it today.' We put it on and I had a little bit of a tear, because I was so happy with the sound! It was quite an emotional moment, it sounded like I wanted it to sound in my head."

Florence was not the only one to respond emotionally to the record – when her mother Evelyn listened to it in the car, she wept – the intense emotions and heartrending lyrics made her fearful for her child. "My mum cried," sighed Florence. "I feel really bad. Grace wrote out all the lyrics and said, your lyrics make me feel sad. And they're right, at the core it is a very sad record. Bit I am not an integrally sad person."

Brave as she was, however, Florence had been under increasing strain emotionally and physically, to the point that she had considered medication. Grace talked her out of it. Apart from anything else, Grace argued, it's the sadness and raw emotion that makes the music so unique and heartfelt. "I was talking to my other sister about anti-anxiety medication and she said, 'Oh no, part of the reason that you make stuff is the anxiety.' Being content feels like betraying what is at the heart of the record."

Typically, Florence was now looking ahead, projecting into the future, and thinking about what was to come in rather gloomy – or maybe realistic – terms. She was bigger, more successful, more famous than ever, and with that came increased pressures and fewer moments to herself. Sadly, one of the precious elements in her life to take the strain would be her relationship with Stuart. After two years of intense touring, absences and having to stay out of Florence's way when he joined her on the road when interviews and appearances beckoned, anyone would have felt a little conflicted, and Florence couldn't have felt entirely comfortable with this either.

Both of their respective careers were blossoming in different ways too, and their focus was understandably split. Trouble was once more in the air, hovering above their romance like a dark, swollen cloud. She felt it was unfair being on the road with a partner in her life, and it was clear that the situation was coming to a head. Florence had certainly been giving it a lot of thought during those long, solitary mornings spent in hotel rooms.

"You have this intense connection with a few thousand people and it feels real," she explained. "Then you come off tour and it's hard to slip back into the mode of having that intense connection one to one. That was always difficult, the at-home-you-away situation.

206

"I wonder if having a connection with that many people makes it impossible to have a meaningful connection alone with one person. I'll have to wait and see. But I looked at my band when we were on this tiny plane a few days ago and they were all curled up asleep on each other. And I felt huge maternal love for them all. Playing music together is the best job in the world, it really is."

There was still a keen sense of dread, however, for Florence. She felt sincerely that her opportunities for joy on a personal level were narrowing. "I felt really happy today," she mused. "I've had 45 minutes to myself and became aware that I've been walking with my arms out and doing the occasional spin. I feel like that's going to be happening less. But you take those moments when you can."

It was sad to think that Florence was so keenly aware that her time would be even less her own, and that moments of private happiness would, in her eyes, be fewer as the demands on her increased – although at least some of these demands would often be fulfilling and rewarding. One thing was still for sure: Florence remained at her happiest onstage, baring her soul to thousands of people as the music thumped and soared along with the wild movements of her flowing hair and diaphanous stage clothes.

"My brain moves too quickly between things," she said. "I think onstage I have the clearest head, it's like breathing space for my brain."

No matter how busy Florence became, no matter how packed her schedule was, there was never any danger that she would hanker for early retirement or extended sabbaticals. Music was her life; it wasn't about achievements or money for Florence. She only truly felt happy and free when succumbing to the escapist call of the stage and the live performance. And yet, conversely, there was an inner yearning for something more.

"Touring, and being in a band, it's almost like the other stuff, the other parts of life, get put on hold. And I'm kind of waiting, really longing, for that part of my life to start."

# CHAPTER FIFTEEN

*"After all that intensity to suddenly be alone, it's … my God! The demons are encroaching! Singing is the only time I feel truly happy."*

"The dog days are most definitely over – and Florence Welch is poised to have a stellar 2012!" shrieked celebrity blogger Perez Hilton on the cusp of the New Year, but this was a contemplative time for Florence. The beginning of a new year is often a thoughtful time: what would we do differently? What do we want to change? And where do we see ourselves *next* year? Or in 10 years?

We are the things we do every day, and Florence was all too aware that while one side of her life was shooting into the stratosphere, glowing with success and recognition, the other, more personal side, was in stasis. Florence knew in her heart what she wanted – her own home, her own family even – if she allowed herself to admit it, but she would just as quickly talk herself out of it, justifying why it wasn't happening and protecting herself from disappointment.

She also was starting to harbour dreams of going back to university, this time to study English and learn Italian. "I think I'll spend some time living in Rome when all this calms down – maybe in the next two years or so. I'll go to Rome, learn Italian, read some books and see some art."

Cue a million news stories screaming that "Florence is moving to Rome!" It might be a little far from the nest, but Evelyn for one had always thought her daughter was not making the most of her natural intellect by rejecting university in favour of life as a musician. "I think 'waste of your brain' is something that my mother would say to me occasionally... I think it's usually when I'm telling her something like I can remember every outfit I've ever worn."

But, as Florence admitted, maybe it wasn't such a bad thing that a move wasn't actually on the cards just yet. She wasn't exactly the most practical person in the family. "Mum still worries constantly about me coming home without any keys. We're still in that stage. One day I'll fly the nest. I'd love a sprawling country mansion where nobody wears shoes and love is everywhere."

As 2011 had drawn to a close, two dramas were at hand for Florence: first, it became very clear to both herself and her partner, literary editor Stuart Hammond, that they had come to the end of the line. In October it was confirmed publicly that the pair had split mutually as their careers were taking them further away from each other.

Florence smiled bravely through the tears. Before Christmas was barely over, she and her Machine would be opening the glittering Harrods Sale with an acoustic set on December 27, the first band ever to open the sale. Looking stunning in a sheer black Chanel gown and a Karl Lagerfeld (naturally) wool cape, she arrived in a Harrods Routemaster bus, waving gleefully at the banks of fans and photographers (although she apparently had to be "coaxed off" after a sudden attack of nerves).

Florence cheerfully told reporters how much fun it was arriving on the old-fashioned bus, her delight at seeing the chequered seats. "I haven't been on one since I was a kid..." she chuckled.

Her performance brought sparkle to that dark London day, and her polished glamour was the exact look and feel that Harrods felt was synonymous with its classic British brand. No one could have known what a struggle this appearance must have been for Florence, who just hours previously was still in her pyjamas at home, feeling decidedly bruised emotionally. She didn't dare even look in her diary – she was already booked up for the whole year: "I could probably tell you exactly what I'm doing for every single day!" she joked to XFM. A big moment for fashion-lovers was seeing Florence's gorgeous Mario Testino *Vogue* cover shoot that rang in 2012, one of her biggest shoots to date. The glossy, fresh and bright-eyed public image displayed here was directly at odds with how she must have been feeling.

Florence wasn't the only high-profile girl who was suffering from heartbreak, however. Her friend Katy Perry had also split up with her husband, the British comedian and notorious lothario Russell Brand. Not that we can ever know what goes on behind closed doors, but apparently one sticking point that dogged this 14-month marriage was that Brand, a former addict, was enjoying living a healthier life and had difficulty coping with Perry's party-loving streak. Florence was friends with both Brand and Perry, and it was hard to see them go their separate ways.

Florence had spent her New Year in Suffolk at Isabella's reliably crazy futuristic New Year party – Summers had built a time tunnel so everybody could enjoy multiple New Year countdowns, but the friend in charge of the tunnel became somewhat confused at the crucial moment and forgot how to count down from 10. ("I was confused too," admitted Florence. "I was lying on the floor with Isa who was dressed up as a moon unit.") Soon after returning to town, Florence was spotted with Russell and friends coming out of the Savoy Hotel in central London, none of whom looked particularly celebratory. New Year distractions aside, Florence was feeling low.

"I've been weeping for the past week," Florence told an interviewer. "January is making me feel weird. It's horrible being back in London, you put everything on pause and suddenly it's feelings!"

Christmas had been spent in her pyjamas at the family home, snuggling up with Mao, her cat, drinking tea and catching up with box-sets (not to mention her secret TV obsession, *Country House Rescue*) as she worked through the sheer exhaustion bearing down on her after the whirlwind year she'd just had. Florence admitted, with a twinkle in her eye, that the so-called 'most wonderful time of the year' had been spent in a "semi-coma, jet-lagged after spending three weeks in America," she told *Boy Meets Fashion*. "So I slept through the whole thing, and I had to convince my mother that putting on lots of costume jewellery with pyjamas *is* the same as getting dressed… and as long as you've got a paper crown on, then you're dressed."

A brave face, costume jewellery and a crown are all very well, but Florence opened up to *Q* magazine in an interview about how she was really feeling: "I feel pretty terrible. I was saying to Grace last night I've never felt so lonely. I am kind of dreading what lies ahead but I suppose that's because I'm only a few weeks into a very long journey," she said of the break-up, which she described as "very traumatic". It was less of a shock, more of a heartbreaking inevitability. And having to perform songs like 'Breaking Down' was partly upsetting, and partly uplifting during this period.

"Music [is] a catharsis, something to take you out of yourself and something that can maybe absolve you," she said. "I had that moment of just being so tired of myself and these patterns of behaviour I've fallen into, and I think everyone can be quite hard on themselves, and music takes that out of you. It's that moment of clarity that everyone is looking for, where you don't have a future or past. If I feel something, be it love, be it panic, be it joy, be it fear, I feel it in a really intense way. It takes over me, and I can't control it.

"I really did feel like I was breaking down several times, it's true. Felt totally mad. But things are getting a little better. I haven't done the walking weep for a while, when you're walking down the road and you're trying to carry on as normal but you just keep bawling. I seem to have that under control," she mused, before adding poignantly, "Although I almost did just burst into tears a minute ago, so you never know. I could blow at any minute!"

At least Florence had Grace (described by *Q* as a "royal aide", making sure Florence didn't throw away her phone or get lost) and Isabella on hand to lift her spirits, dragging her to markets and vintage emporiums in a bid to distract her. One trip to such a store was interrupted by a phone call from Queens Of The Stone Age singer Josh Homme, calling about a collaboration that was on the cards between himself and

Florence on her MTV *Unplugged* show that was coming up, and that would later be released as a live album.

There was certainly plenty to concentrate on (she even developed a crush on Ryan Gosling after seeing him in the film *Drive*, which took her mind off things) but the lingering feeling of sadness remained in the pit of Florence's stomach. The break-up was not the only issue hanging over Florence's head, however. Drama number two, of course, was the controversy that had surrounded the video to the *Ceremonials* track 'No Light, No Light'.

The promo, directed by Icelandic duo Arni & Kinski, features Florence being pursued by a man in black body paint who jabs needles into a voodoo doll (there were also candles, angelic dog-collared choir boys, crystal skulls, they'd thrown everything in) before Florence ends up falling to her apparent doom through the New York skyline, through a stained glass window and into the arms of a group of choir-boys.

This imagery led to Florence being confronted by a furious race row, with bloggers angrily declaring the video was crammed with "white supremacist views". From Florence's point of view, this was not where she was coming from at all. In fact the ideas that truly impressed her in the pitch stage were the ones that involved falling from a great height, and the use of New York as a backdrop.

"When Arni and Kinski pitched it to me, I loved the idea of the stained glass ... and this falling thing, to do it on a New York skyline was really important to me, and there's some weird stuff with my grandmother about New York that's kind of too dark to go into," she explained. "The idea of falling from a great height in New York is intense... because my grandmother, she died in New York, and I literally didn't think about it until we were filming and I was like, 'This is kind of insane.'"

The decision to go ahead with the 'light' and 'dark' theme of the video in the way that it was depicted will have likely been a naïve one, rather than a racist one. Nonetheless, the furore will have shocked her and her team to the core, although the result was, inevitably, more hits on the video than if it wasn't shot through with a seam of controversy.

The website Racialicious picked the video apart, stating: "Discussions about whether or not Welch is personally responsible for this racist music video have cropped up. When you break it down and imagine the number of people who were behind the storyboarding, choreographing, casting and creative direction around this video, it is slightly astounding that not one person raised concerns about how problematic this video is."

An industry insider ponders: "I don't know at what point anyone said, 'Hang on, this is a little bit dodgy, don't you think?' I think the idea was accepted innocently, for purely creative reasons, and then a few people at the label who perhaps should have known better didn't say anything – perhaps because they fancied a bit of controversy.

"Nobody could ever seriously accuse Florence of being a racist. Anyone who knew that situation would know that mud was never going to stick and not much harm was going to be done. But yes, maybe they did think 'Let's get it viewed more, talked about a bit more.' Storm in a teacup, really. I wouldn't even qualify that as a scandal but that's certainly the closest she's come to one. She's managed to come a very long way in a very short time without really pissing anybody off, which is unusual."

Naturally, in her fans' eyes, Florence could do no wrong, but they were vehement in defence of their heroine not least because they knew how much she respected black artists. "I don't think Florence is racist," wrote a fan under the name of 'Getaway Girl' on the blogging site Tumblr. "She is a woman who loves soul, respects black artists, regularly cites them amongst her hugest influences."

Amazingly, it wasn't just the 'black/white' issue that was getting online commentators hot under the collar – the use of religious iconography fuelled feverish speculation that Florence was either heavily into the occult or was a member of the mysterious Illuminati, a highly exclusive secret religious society who are, apparently, intent on creating a New World Order. Florence thought the fact her video to 'No Light, No Light' had led to accusations that she was an Illuminati member was rather funny – and somehow complimentary. After all, she would be in excellent showbiz company.

"Really?" she spluttered on hearing the rumour. "I heard Jay-Z and Beyoncé were [members] so I don't know how I feel about it, because I think Jay-Z and Beyoncé are the most incredible artists ever, so in a weird way, it's slightly complimentary. But also completely ridiculous. I'm definitely not. It's just not true." Sorry, conspiracy theorists.

But not everything surrounding 'No Light, No Light' was ominous. A "luxurious special edition", as Island Records/the Vinyl Factory put it, was coming out on January 16, 2012, and it would showcase Florence Welch's creative collaboration with Karl Lagerfeld.

The cover, which encased a white heavyweight 12" record, was screen-printed, silver-foiled and hand-numbered, and featured a series of photographic portraits of Florence taken by Lagerfeld himself, exclusively for this. Florence looked truly elegant, and the images were almost Tamara de Lempicka-like in their structure and feel.

This lavish edition was in fact the only physical release of the single, and included a remix by TV On The Radio's Dave Sitek. Quite a treasure for Florence collectors.

In real life, however, Florence was looking understandably tired and pale, with dark shadows under her eyes. The lack of sleep was taking its toll and the sense of sadness was still palpable as she emerged to be interviewed in January about the upcoming Brit Awards, where Florence would give a typically spectacular performance.

Florence admitted that life had been draining, and that while the rewards of life as a performer were incredible, the work was tough and she diplomatically hinted at the knock-on effect this had had in her own life: "The highs and the lows come with the same package – touring and travelling and being away from home."

Florence was never one to complain without backing up her statement with one of gratitude and appreciation, insisting as she did that "I'm doing my absolute dream job and I wouldn't want to do anything else," almost as if she was afraid of jinxing it. But anyone could see that here was a woman who needed some time out. She'd done her growing up on the road and in the music industry, and now she was 25, with two hit albums to her name that had moved millions of people (and shifted millions of units). It was time to take stock, if she could only grab the chance, as the merry-go-round showed no sign of slowing.

Thankfully there was comfort on hand from a young man who had been special to Florence for some months – James Nesbitt; no, not the actor from Coleraine, but a toothsome 29-year-old event organiser and former model from Hull. Nesbitt, who had previously dated Paloma Faith and Fearne Cotton, had started his own company, named the Velvet Project, which saw him organising charity balls and star-studded parties for huge stars. He had apparently met Florence working on the 'Shake It Out' shoot.

"James was working on her shoot and offered to pass something up to her while she was sitting in a tree. It was quite high up but he's a fit lad," his mother Anne said proudly. "They got chatting up the tree and things went from there. When she came back from Australia, she even bought him a book called *Tree Houses In Great Britain*." Nice touch.

Initially, the pair started seeing each other in secret – not least because there had evidently been chemistry at quite an early stage in their friendship, and if the maths is correct (Nesbitt's mother claims they'd been together since May 2011, while other reports state Florence had split from Stuart Hammond in October 2011) then it does indicate some blurring of the edges, not that it's particularly the business of anyone other than the parties involved. Romance is rarely cut and dried, especially when one's life is as complex as someone battling to retain some kind of a private life while in the public eye.

Their cover was finally blown at the end of January when they were spotted by paparazzi on holiday in Rio. Pictures showed the couple looking suitably in love, and Florence looked ravishing in a vintage turban and swimming costume (skin as lily-white as ever). It was good to see Florence looking happy and relaxed, not to mention enjoying a well-earned break. After three years with the man who had inspired so much of the heartrending material on both *Lungs* and *Ceremonials*, Florence was moving on.

Once the news broke, the media became extremely interested in this "posh boy from Hull", as they tagged him. The *Hull Daily Mail* went straight to Nesbitt's mother. "She rang our land line a few times while

James was here over Christmas and I spoke to her," she told the paper. "She then took him to Suffolk to stay with her uncle, the journalist Craig Brown. They went to Rio on January 15.

"She always wants him with her, but sadly he's often got work commitments. It must be quite lonely for her sometimes. He said she's always on the phone when she's away and they are joined at the hip when they're together."

Once again, Florence was understandably feeling the urge to nest, an instinct which was still in conflict with her lifestyle for the time being. This time it wasn't a castle she had her heart set on. Just a house in Camberwell, on the patch where she grew up.

"I know what I want – a Victorian property, maybe something with a bit of gothic flair to it. I think some people expect me to flit off to America, but I just feel engrained in these streets," she said. "I've lived in the same street my whole life. That's quite archaic, a bit village-like for a Londoner, for a modern London girl. But I like it that way."

Camberwell held so many memories for Florence. It was as if there was a cord that still attached her to this area of South London, so no matter how far she roamed, there was a part of her that always longed for it, and for her family. And similarly, Evelyn was rarely happier than when Florence was at home where she could keep an eye on her.

"My mum worries about the strain on me," said Florence. "I think she realises that perhaps this is not a phase. She worries whether I am eating and sleeping. No matter the time of day, as soon as I walk in the house she tells me to eat something and go to bed."

Perhaps Florence will be keeping on that old bedroom of hers at her mum's house for a little while yet. Nothing could be more comforting after a heavy stint on the road than being taken care of at home.

Florence + The Machine had work to do – yes, *Ceremonials* was out, but Florence already was anxious to get back in the studio; her head was full of ideas that she was desperate to express musically. Fortunately there had been a stimulating project for her to get her teeth into before she started plunging into the making of album number three: she and Isabella had been commissioned to create a track for the movie *Snow White And The Huntsman*, starring Kristen Stewart as Snow White and

Charlize Theron as the Evil Queen Ravenna. It was fun for Florence to get involved in something a little different, and the concept of the film was exactly the sort of thing she loved. Romance, beauty, death, a villainous queen… how could she not be inspired?

"The Queen is just this incredible character; so hungry for life but so dead inside," Florence gushed. "She's sort of eternal, but inside there's nothing. She's kind of like charcoal or something…"

One scene that especially stood out to Florence, as well it might, was where the Queen starts to pick the hearts out of birds and eats them in a vain bid to protect her youthful looks.

"[She has] this thirst for youth and for life, but for what kind of life? This darkness, but she's so beautiful, so it's this kind of juxtaposition between beauty and, ultimately, death." Is it any wonder that Florence + The Machine were approached to compose for the soundtrack? This is pure Flo territory.

After falling head over heels with the film and its magical characters, Florence and the band headed back to the confines of Abbey Road where they would record the song they had written, 'Breath Of Life', with a full choir. Florence spent the day feeling highly emotional; hearing an audience sing her songs back at her was truly a thrill, but listening to a choir interpret her and Isabella's new song was a positively celestial experience. Manager Mairead Nash had to keep an eye on her, not least because she didn't want Florence to insist on having a choir from now on. Someone had to look after the purse-strings…

"It was one of the best days of my life," said Florence. "I love choirs and I love choral music, and there was a 60-piece choir singing the vocal parts that I had written. When the baritones came in, I nearly wept."

"My manager was looking at me going, 'Do not get used to this. We cannot afford this 60-piece choir!' It was just wonderful. Me and Isa were in there, these young women who made music for love, but with not much money or much reason." You've come a long way, baby.

A run of 16 US dates was already in the diary for the spring, which Florence was feeling excited about – not least because she would be joined by her old friend Dev Hynes (currently recording as Blood Orange), who was confirmed as the support act. The pair had a lot of history and affection for each other, so it would be a hoot for them to tour together after all this time.

"It's going to be so fun, I can't wait," trilled Florence. "I used to be his backing singer in Lightspeed Champion, he took me on tour with him for one date, in Manchester. He was one of the first members of Florence + The Machine."

A change of pace was required for the stage show, Florence and her team had decided. After the quirky ostentation of the *Lungs* tour, it was time to let the songs speak for themselves. As Florence always maintained, the sound on *Ceremonials* was bigger, therefore the sets didn't have to be quite so imposing. They chose a minimal but high-lustre art deco look for the shows.

"It's not going to be too big a production; we've done a lot of quite extravagant stuff, and that's been amazing, but for this tour, it's definitely going to be about showcasing the music."

Costumes were being sewn, designs were drawn up and itineraries planned, but first, award season loomed. Yes, it was February and Florence was up for two Brit Awards: Best Album and Best Female. She admitted she wouldn't mind an extra couple of Brits on the kitchen dresser to keep the rest of her accolades company, but as always, insisted that it wasn't about the winning.

"I mean, it would be nice to win. But I'm not gonna put pressure on myself to win; that would spoil it for me. I'm just really looking forward to going, enjoying being there, seeing everyone, and getting a bit drunk. Anyway, I've got two. I don't want to be greedy."

Florence was also concentrating rather more on the performance of 'No Light, No Light' she would be giving at the ceremony, as it would feel like something of a homecoming.

"It's going to be a celebration of this album, and of coming back to the Brits with a record that I'm really, really proud of. We haven't really done any big UK TV stuff for this record, so this will be the first time we get to create something around [it]."

Florence stormed it in rehearsals, looking regal yet a little wild in a pale embroidered dress with chiffon sleeves and skirt created by Sarah Burton, the Alexander McQueen designer who was behind Kate

Middleton, Duchess of Cambridge's wedding dress. Burton and Welch had met several times at various events and had hit it off; as Florence admitted, "We always end up giggling at the back like schoolgirls." This would be Burton's first design after that Grace Kelly-inspired bridal gown that took the world's breath away the previous April.

But as the evening drew near, and it was time to brave the stage, all Florence felt was "pure white fear. I find myself thinking 'What do I do again?'" she laughed. "But once you're in it, you can't stop it. It's like, 'Oh, it's happening now. I can't actually stop the whole thing...'" Florence admitted she often had to fight mischievous impulses when performing on live television, and this night was no different.

"[It's] like when you are standing too close to the edge of the tube, anything could happen. Having that sort of power, like, 'I could do something really weird on live telly!' But I never do. Why doesn't it happen more? Like, people just wigging out. [Playing] the hurdy-gurdy or something." She warned, jokingly, that she might suddenly start doing star jumps in the middle of her Brits performance.

Well, there were no star jumps, although there were plenty of tumbling dancers in flowing robes and Florence once again stole the show, even if she was beaten by Adele in both of the categories she was nominated in. It was, incidentally, that fateful Brits year that Adele raised her middle finger to "the suits" that had communicated – via host James Corden – that her acceptance speech had to be curtailed

Florence could at last relax – and legitimately do as many star jumps as she wished – once the awards were safely over and the after-parties had begun. Alongside Rizzle Kicks' Jordan Stephens and the Black Eyed Peas' Will.i.am, she took to the decks at the Universal bash at the imposing Tate Modern, getting "really drunk" and standing on the speakers "dancing around in Rihanna's confetti".

The no doubt monstrous hangover had barely lifted before Florence + The Machine were off to another awards ceremony on February 29 – this one being the *NME* Awards at London's Brixton Academy. Florence had been announced as one of the live acts at the awards show, during which she would sing with the Horrors (their track 'Still Life') in a highly anticipated merging of dark, doomy British talent.

Florence was up for a 'Hottest Female' award, Best Track (for 'Shake It Out') and the coveted Best Solo Artist gong, alongside Adele, Noel Gallagher, Frank Turner, Miles and Laura Marling – although this nomination confused Florence and made her uncomfortable: while Florence + The Machine was a project she had indubitably started herself, it was a collaboration, not a solo effort. Critics were surprised also to see that *Ceremonials* was not up for an award in the Best Album category, in which Best British Band-nominees the Horrors were represented (*Skying*).

It had always been a dream of Florence's to win an *NME* Award, not least because the magazine had always been so supportive of her, and this year she would be honoured with Best Track and Best Solo Artist, which she made a point of insisting was as much her band's achievement as her own.

"I'm grateful to win solo awards but it's strange because I've never been sure how the solo act came out of the band idea," she said. "I've worked with so many amazing musicians and it's such a collaborative thing. The solo award is for them and I dedicate it to everyone I've worked with."

Again, another after-party beckoned, this one organised by uber-party planner Fran Cutler, and sporting a distinctive flowery suit, Florence made her way to the glamorous W London Leicester Square hotel in the city centre to cut loose, dance whilst draped in fairy lights, and drink raspberry cocktails with Kasabian, Kate Moss and the TV presenter Alexa Chung, with whom she often shared the front row at catwalk shows. As she threw shapes on the dancefloor to the strains of 'Brown Sugar' by the Rolling Stones, it became clear that, with a clutch of awards, and a loving boyfriend by her side, maybe Perez Hilton *was* right with his New Year proclamation for Florence – the dog days really did seem to be over.

# CHAPTER SIXTEEN

*'I will be the most mad old lady...'*

March 2012, and the London weather was suitably apocalyptic (fitting perfectly with *Ceremonials*) but, happily, this didn't reflect Florence's own life. Not now. After recovering from a triumphant gig at Alexandra Palace in North London, during which Florence performed the dramatic and sinister 'Seven Devils' (which features in the trailer for the hit TV series *Game Of Thrones*), well, Adele might have been the queen of the Brits, but Florence would be crowned the 'greatest woman who rocks of all time' by listeners of alternative music station XFM. This dizzying accolade meant that she came out above her own more seasoned rock heroines Siouxsie Sioux, PJ Harvey, Debbie Harry and Courtney Love to name a few.

This led, fairly understandably, to some critics wondering whether those that voted had any sense of history. No disrespect to Florence, but "of all time"? At number two was the Kills' Alison Mosshart. Björk, the Pixies' Kim Deal and Patti Smith didn't even make the top 10.

It must have been hard to get her head around it, but Florence seemed to take it in her stride, thanking XFM listeners profusely and declaring that being a "woman in rock" was about "doing something unexpected for someone who is perhaps more feminine. Perverting the idea of femininity – managing to be vulnerable and powerful at the same time – is a big thing in performance."

Away from the showbiz side of her life, Florence was enjoying her romance with James Nesbitt (although, as we know, he was fairly showbiz himself), but she wasn't the only one to be loved-up and starry-eyed...

In April, the band performed at the California festival Coachella on the prestigious main stage between At The Drive-In and Snoop Dogg. Florence had a Swarovski crystal-covered stage cat-suit and cape prepared, custom-designed by Hannah Marshall ("I think people were probably awake for days sewing on these crystals," Florence told *Vogue*) and it was clear that it was going to be a special night. But it would be special for Rob Ackroyd for a different reason, and it didn't matter how many crystals were dazzling and shining away on Florence's sexy cat-suit, he only had eyes for one girl: Katy Perry.

Florence and Katy had, of course, been friends for a while, and Florence loved the down-to-earth, heart-led pop star, so their circles were not dissimilar. Katy was also good friends with *Twilight* heart-throb Robert Pattinson, who apparently brought the pair together. It had been some months since Katy had split up with Russell Brand (although their divorce wasn't final until that July) and there was clearly a spark between herself and Ackroyd. Mere flirting soon turned into something that looked rather more official.

The pair first set tongues wagging when they were spotted wandering through the festival site hand-in-hand. Then they were snapped hugging each other during Rihanna's set with Calvin Harris. The tabloids were already going crazy when they then heard that, in the Artist Lounge backstage, she had turned down an invitation to watch Dr Dre because she was "waiting to watch her boyfriend perform..."

Both of them looked blissfully happy in each other's company, and it didn't go unnoticed that, after Florence + The Machine's set, the blue-haired, big-eyed party girl bounded up to the stage from the wings straight into Rob's arms. Soon they were dining together at the legendary Hollywood hedonists' paradise, the Chateau Marmont, where Katy introduced him to some of her friends, including her stylist Johnny Wujek, actress Shannon Woodward, and jewellery designer Markus Molinari. Sounds serious... (Ackroyd's former girlfriend Molly Rigg, who apparently thought they were "on a temporary split", wasn't best pleased when she saw the pictures.)

News of their romance immediately prompted Ackroyd's friends to tease him on his Facebook and Twitter pages, leaving enquired: "Did you kiss a girl and like it? The taste of her cherry chapstick?" quoting the notorious lyric to Perry's hit song 'I Kissed A Girl'. Another jovial fellow wrote: "I'm guessing there is probably f★★k all chance of you getting an autograph off Russell Brand now?" Sounds about right. Brand had seen the photos and, although he too had been dating other people, reportedly now wanted to reconsider the divorce.

Days later the band were off to Houston's Bayou Music Center. Florence admitted that, while she had never played Texas's Bayou City before, it had a place in her heart, not least because her mother, Evelyn's, side of the family has its roots in Galveston. She was keen to explore the area and visit the Rothko Chapel, a spiritual sanctuary set up in 1971 by philanthropists John and Dominique de Menil.

But the Florence + The Machine magic that would hit Houston that night would be a spiritual experience in itself for many of the audience present – local press commented on the mesmerised crowd who were "eating out of Florence's hand", and responded rapturously when the pop priestess before them declared she wished to "get to know Houston a little better" and asked fans to "sacrifice" themselves to the music.

Girls were held aloft by their boyfriends during 'Rabbit Heart (Raise It Up)', and the spell was only broken when Florence found that one adoring fan had thrown a bra at her – something normally saved for male heart-throbs. This prompted a fit of the giggles from Welch who admitted that for the first time in her life, she now felt like a member of a boy band.

New York City's Radio City Music Hall would also be graced with Florence + The Machine's presence the night after a hard-partying session at the Met Gala on May 8 – described by *The Guardian* as "like the Oscars but with a dash of crazy'… This particular Met event, which celebrated the designers Schiaparelli and Prada, would be especially crazy: at the after-party at Manhattan's Standard Hotel, the glamorous throng was suddenly thrown into panic when the DJ's decks burst into flames. Who saved the day? Florence, that's who. Her Alexander McQueen tiered white gown might have not been the critics' favourite outfit of the night, according to the 'Worst Dressed' polls that would emerge the following day, but Florence is all about the music, and had she not whipped out her iPod and started DJ-ing herself, there would have been nothing for Met guests to boogie to. Her playlist even kicked off a 'dance battle' between Beyoncé Knowles and Gwyneth Paltrow. The whole thing reads like one of Perez Hilton's wet dreams…

"Whenever I come to New York, I never seem to get any sleep!" Florence confessed to her audience the following night before whirling through the *Ceremonials* set like "an excited child playing tag", as *Spinner* put it. As always, the black-clad 'Machine' melted visually into the background, letting Florence take the limelight as only she could. Katy Perry, naturally, was in the audience, gazing up at her rock 'n' roll beau.

The *Ceremonials* tour would continue into the autumn of 2012 – with the Maccabees in support – taking in NY's Nikon at Jones Beach Theater and the Hollywood Bowl. No chance of slowing down for Florence yet: those dreams of studying in Italy, or moving to the country, would have to go on hold for a little while yet.

Florence continues to evolve artistically and personally, and fans can only stand by and wait for her to weave her next spell over them, as the music of Florence + The Machine evidently has the power to lift people up, soothe them in times of darkness and reflect and articulate emotions in ways that have helped admirers of the group to find themselves when lost, lonely or simply navigating the turbulence of adolescence.

As Rachael Scarsbrook, one of the founders of the huge and ever-growing (and Flo-acknowledged) Florence + The Machine Army, puts it, one of the things that Florence's loyal fans know for sure is that, while Florence is always progressing, there are some elements that will always stay gratifyingly constant. "It is natural for artists to progress the further into their career they get and whilst Florence has done exactly that, she has held onto her own stage diving, cat-suit sporting and whimsical self," she says.

"In an industry of perfectly media-trained faceless starlets, it's refreshing to hear Florence talking about still living at home or getting lost while she rides her bike around Central London. There's no denying that the stakes are getting higher, but Florence keeps upping her game with an effortless poise.

"Nothing is ever certain in the music industry, but I can guarantee that wherever Florence + The Machine land, we – the fans – will always be there as a constant source of love and support. Florence has brought us all together in a way that none of us could have ever imagined."

And Florence's goals for the future? Well, they're fairly cut and dried: 1) Play the Pyramid Stage at Glastonbury Festival. 2) Go to India. And 3) You guessed it – leave her childhood home at last.

The one thing she truly wished for was to live a normal life. It reads like a cliché, but for Florence, this was something that had burned away inside of her for years. Even though her music represents freedom and escapism to so many people, can Florence find her own escape route when she needs it? Maybe her dream of living in the country "where everyone has bare feet and love is everywhere" is at least on the horizon after all. The pastoral, romantic sounds she's been creating ever since she entered adult life certainly seem to have forged a strong sonic link to that very vision of the future – even if her inner defence mechanisms still try to convince her that it might not even be a life that's meant for her.

"I'd like maybe one day to have a child, maybe plural," said Florence. "A house and a family… it sounds so nice, doesn't it? But perhaps I'd regret it. Maybe I need that chaos. Maybe I'd miss the road. Maybe I'm not cut out for domestic life, I'm just meant to be onstage singing. Maybe that's worth any other sacrifice…

"But I have to move out of mum's house. If I die and I'm still in my mum's house I'll be really cross."

# DISCOGRAPHY/VIDEOGRAPHY

**ALBUMS**

*Lungs*
Released: 6 July 2009
Label: Island

*Ceremonials*
Released: 28 October 2011
Label: Island

**LIVE ALBUMS**

*Live at the Wiltern*
Released: 28 June 2011
Label: Island

*MTV Unplugged*
Released: 9 April 2012
Label: Island

**EXTENDED PLAYS**
*A Lot of Love. A Lot of Blood*
Released: 28 April 2009
Label: IAMSOUND

*iTunes Festival: London 2010*
Released: 21 July 2010
Label: Island

*iTunes Live from SoHo*
Released: 16 November 2010
Label: Island

**SINGLES**

2008
'Kiss With A Fist'

'Dog Days Are Over'

2009
'Rabbit Heart (Raise It Up)'

'Drumming Song'

'You Got The Love'

2010
'Cosmic Love'

'Heavy In Your Arms'

2011
'What The Water Gave Me'

'Shake It Out'

2012

'No Light, No Light'

'Never Let Me Go'

'Breath Of Life'

**MUSIC VIDEOS**

2008

'Kiss With A Fist'
Director: James Price

'Dog Days Are Over'
Tom Beard + Tabitha Denholm

2009

'Rabbit Heart (Raise It Up)'
Tom Beard + Tabitha Denholm

'Drumming Song'
Dawn Shadforth

'You Got The Love'
Tom Beard + Tabitha Denholm

2010

'Dog Days Are Over'
Georgie Greville + Geremy Jasper

'Cosmic Love'
'Heavy In Your Arms'
Tom Beard + Tabitha Denholm

2011

'What The Water Gave Me'
Paul Epworth

'Shake It Out'
Dawn Shadforth

'No Light, No Light'
Arni & Kinski

2012
'Never Let Me Go'
Tabitha Denholm

# ACKNOWLEDGEMENTS

The author would like to give special thanks and appreciation by the truck-load to Rachael, Atlanta and Kristian and the Florence + The Machine Army – hope you all enjoy this book! Also to the brilliant Dylan Howe, Mike Walsh at XFM, Bruno Wizard, Ellie Emptage, Naomi Bristow, Ev Sekkides, Marzipan 'Hovis' Howe for encouragement to take screen breaks, Debra Fear, Toby Woby, Julian Marszalek, Adam Cotton, Piney Gir, Mat Priest and everyone who tried to help with this project! I really appreciate it. Love to all of my family and friends who are always so supportive. And last but not least, thanks must go to David Barraclough, Chris Charlesworth, Helen Donlon, Jacqui Black, Richard Hudson and all at Omnibus Press.

# SOURCE MATERIAL

*The Guardian, New Band Of The Day*, October 10, 2007, Paul Lester

*Run Riot, Interview: Florence + The Machine*, August 15, 2008, Interview with Patrick Hussey

*The Guardian, Go With The Flo*, November 22, 2008, Florence Welch interview with Sylvia Patterson

*Sound On Sound – Paul Epworth, Producing Almost Everyone*, January 2009, Paul Epworth interview with Sam Inglis

*Absolute Radio*, February 4, 2009, Florence Welch interview with Geoff Lloyd

*This Is Fake DIY, The Weird, Wonderful, Wacky World Of Florence Welch*, May 18, 2009, Interview with Alexia Kapranos

*Daily Telegraph, Florence + The Machine Interview: Sound and Vision*, June 4, 2009, Interview by Francesca Ryan

*The Independent, Florence And The Machine: Meet The Sound Of The Summer*, June 27, 2009, Florence Welch interview with Tim Walker

*Absolute Radio*, July 6, 2009, Florence Welch interview with Sarah Champion

*BBC Radio 4, 'Woman's Hour'*, July 7, 2009, Florence Welch interview with Jane Garvey

*The Daily Mail*, 'She's the achingly fashionable singer from Florence + The Machine. To me she's just the Daffy Diva… but I am her dad.' July 25, 2009, Nick Welch writes

*The Daily Mail*, 'The only time my dad worried about me was when Pete Doherty proposed', Florence Welch interview with Louise Gannon

*The Fly.com, Go With The Flo, July 27, 2009*, Florence Welch interview with Harriet Gibsone

*Clash Magazine, Step Forward: Florence + The Machine*, August 2009, Florence Welch interview with Laura Foster

*Dummy Magazine, 'I'm Definitely Still In The Woods'*, August 23, 2009, Florence Welch interview with Rowan Woods

*NME, The Bands Blog: Florence Welch 'Why I Love Billie Holiday'*, October 7, 2009

*The Quietus, Florence Welch*, October 21, 2009, Florence Welch interview with Laura Snapes

*Faster, Louder – Florence And The Machine*, October 30, 2009, Interview with Keely K

*TaraOWeb.com, My Interview With Florence (Best In British Music Show)* November 2, 2009, FW interview with Tara O

*Under The Radar Magazine, Ready To Raise It Up*, December 1, 2009, Florence Welch interview with Chris Tinkham

*The List, Florence Welch Interview*, December 2, 2009, Interview with Jonny Ensall

*Citylife*, December 4, 2009, Florence Welch interview with Sarah Walters

*Hearty Magazine*, December 14, 2009, Florence Welch interview with Hana May

*Drowned In Sound, Gang Gang Dance Ask Florence For Royalties*, February 23, 2010

*The New York Post, Florence Is Obsessed With Lady Gaga*, March 31, 2010

*Music Producers' Guild (MPG.org)*, April 4, 2010, Paul Epworth interview with Dave Robinson

*Venus Zine, Interview: Florence Welch*, May 20, 2010

*Why Music Matters, Florence Welch On Janis Joplin*, July 1, 2010

*Lucky Magazine, Florence Welch Interview*, July 29, 2010

*Music Tech Magazine, Interview – Paul Epworth*, Issue 95

*MSN.JuiceOnline.Com*

*Artist Direct, Interview: Florence + The Machine*, September 7, 2010, Florence Welch interview with Rick Florino

*Autostraddle, Florence + The Machine*, September 9, 2010, Interview with Corey

*The New York Post, 'Florence Welch Talks New Music, VMA Performance & Eat, Pray Love'*, September 16, 2010, Florence Welch interview with Jarrett Wieselman

*China Shop Magazine, Florence Discusses Haunted Dresses And Living With Her Parents*, September 30, 2010, Florence Welch interview with Nicole Pajer

*CNN*, 2010

*Mint Magazine, Ivan Ink 'N' Isa Inteview*, January 2011, Interview with Isabella Summers

*Roland.co.uk, Isabella Summers – Florence + The Machine*, January 24, 2011

*Culture Compass*, January 26, 2011, Isabella Summers/Oli Briggs interview with Sophie Eggleton

*The Sun, 'I was on the floor with the worst hangover of my life when I learned album was number one'*, 2011

*USA Today, Five Champion Faves For Best Album Grammy*, February 9, 2011

*The New York Times, The Bohemian Fashion Muse*, February 11, 2011, Florence Welch interview with Bee-Shyuan Chang

*Gibson.com – The Gibson Interview: Rob Ackroyd of Florence + The Machine*, February 17, 2011, Rob Ackroyd interview with Bryan Wawzenek

*The Daily Mail, 'I was awkward, intense and ridiculously self-conscious...'* April 30, 2011, Florence Welch interview with Jane Gordon

*Nylon Magazine*, cover feature, May 23, 2011

*Clash Magazine, Inner Visions – Florence + The Machine*, October 2011, Florence Welch interview with Laura Foster

*Planet Notion, Luv Luv Luv Records' Launch Party*, October 3, 2011, Words by Thomas Morse

*East Anglia Daily Times, Ex-Suffolk Schoolboy At Heart Of Florence + The Machine*, October 11, 2011, Tom Monger interview with Steven Russell

*Interview Magazine*, October 2011, Florence Welch interview with Baz Luhrmann

*Dazed And Confused, Gucci Turns 90!* October 2011, Kin Woo interviews Frida Giannini

*USA Today, Quirky Mind Behind Machine*, 30, October 2011, Florence Welch interview with Marco R Della Cava

*The Guardian, 'I Was Almost Out Of Control'*, October 30, 2011, Florence Welch interview with Tom Lamont

*Look Magazine*, October 2011

*Oh No They Didn't*, October 2011

*Digital Spy, 'I don't want more fame'*, October 31, 2011, Florence Welch interview with Robert Copsey

*The Vine TV, Florence + The Machine interview*, 2011

*ES Magazine, 'Success of Lungs left me gasping for breath'*, November 1, 2011

*AnOther Magazine, Florence Welch On Karl Lagerfeld*, November 2, 2011

*Time Out Chicago, Florence Welch of Florence + The Machine*, November 9, 2011, Interview by Brent DiCrescenzo

*BMRB interview with Florence Welch*, November 10, 2011, Interview with James Merritt

*RTE.ie, Machine Head*, November 14, 2011, Florence Welch interview with Alan Corr

*Spin Magazine, Florence On Her Fear Of Treadmills, Lady Gaga and Ceremonials*, November 21, 2011, Florence Welch interview with John Sellers

*BBC 6 Music – Vinyl Revival*, December 2011, Florence Welch interview with Pete Paphides

Q magazine issue Q308, January 2012, Florence Welch interview with Ted Kessler

*British Vogue*, cover feature, January 2012

*The Hull Daily Mail, The 'posh boy' from Hull who wooed pop star Florence'*, January 28, 2012, Anne Nesbitt interview with Katy Forrester

*Metro, Florence Welch: Angel & Demon*, February 8, 2012, Interview with Kenya Hunt

*The Independent, Dress For Excess: Florence Welch reveals how she'll be rocking the Brit Awards,* February 19, 2012, Florence Welch interview with Craig McLean

*Daily Record, Award-winning singer Florence Welch admits she's keen to move to Rome and learn Italian,* March 4, 2012, Florence Welch interview with John Dingwall

*Daily Mirror, Pop Star Florence Welch Says Her Mum Won't Let Her Move Out! (3am)* March 11, 2012

*Company Magazine,* Cover feature, April 2012, Florence Welch interview with Catherine Bennion-Pedley

*Daily Telegraph, Why Florence Is A Star, Not A Machine,* May 12, 2012, Florence Welch interview with Linda Simalis

*NME.com*

*MTV.com*

*BBC Radio 1*

*Rolling Stone* magazine

*Radio Alice*

*XFM*

*Florenceandthemachine.net*

*Gigwise.com*